European elections and British politics

David Butler
and
David Marquand

Longman
London and New York

Longman Group Limited
Longman House
Burnt Mill, Harlow, Essex, UK

*Published in the United States of America
by Longman Inc., New York*

© David Butler and David Marquand 1981

First published 1981

British Library Cataloguing in Publication Data

Butler, David, *1924*
   European elections and British policy.
   1. European Parliament – Elections, 1979
   2. Elections – Great Britain – History – 20th century
   I. Title   II. Marquand, David
   324'.21   JN36   80–41086

   ISBN 0–582–29528–9
   ISBN 0–582–29529–7 Pbk

Set in 10/12 pt Linoterm Bembo by
Parkway Group, London and Abingdon
Printed and bound in Great Britain by
William Clowes (Beccles) Limited, Beccles and London

Contents

Acknowledgements

We are most grateful to Nuffield College and Salford University for giving us the time and facilities to prepare this book and to the Social Science Research Council for covering most of our direct costs.

We have to thank many people in the political parties and in the European institutions for great numbers of hours spent in talking with us and in filling in questionnaires: they gave us much uncovenanted help.

Among the many who read parts of our manuscript or proofs we would like in particular to acknowledge the help of François Camenen, Bill Emmott, Paul Jowett, Dennis Kavanagh, Paul McKee and Anthony Teasdale.

Among those who worked more directly with us we must thank Hazel Batchelor, Pat Bellotti, Brian Gosschalk, Clive Payne, Audrey Skeats and, last but not least, our wives and our children.

DAVID BUTLER
DAVID MARQUAND
May 1980

CHAPTER ONE
Introduction

The elections to the European Parliament, held in June 1979, involved the largest body of electors (outside India) ever to vote at one time and constituted the first simultaneous multinational popular election. In every one of the nine countries that took part they affected the domestic political situation. For the United Kingdom the implications of the event were far larger than most people realised.

The British campaign had been lack-lustre; the media had shown little interest; and the turnout was barely half the European average. Yet an examination of the way in which the contest was prepared for and conducted, as well as of what happened after it was over, shows that it had repercussions throughout the political system.

This book does not offer an analysis of the kind exemplified by the successive Nuffield Studies of general elections. It is rather a political essay. We describe the role of the European Parliament before direct elections and the part played in it by its British members; the way in which direct elections came about; the varied responses of Government, Parliament and the political parties to the decision to hold them; the way in which they were fought in this country; and the response of the newly-elected British MEPs[1] to the unfamiliar problems which they had to face after they were elected. Our focus throughout is on the impact of the elections – first the impact of the decision to hold them, then of the campaign itself and finally of the new Parliament which they brought into being – on the established political processes of the United Kingdom. The Euro-election was like a stone thrown into the pool of

[1] In advance of the election there was some discussion of the proper designation for those elected to the European Parliament (or Assembly, as some would still style it). Whatever the semantic niceties British members have come to be known as 'members of the European Parliament' or MEPs.

British politics from outside; the ripples might seem small, but they would long continue, spreading to its furthest corners. Their future course cannot be charted in advance, but it is possible to map the course they have taken so far and, in doing so, to lay the groundwork for a discussion of their likely speed and direction. That is what we have tried to do in what follows.

The European Community had a major effect on the British political system long before direct elections came to the forefront. The surrender of sovereignty implicit in the Treaty of Accession had altered significantly the powers of Government, Parliament and the Courts over the wide range of matters covered by the Rome Treaty and subsequent amending Treaties. Since 1973, Community laws have taken precedence over British law, and the Community Court over British courts. The continuing controversy over British membership had led in 1975 to the holding of the first nationwide Referendum, with all that implied for the supremacy of Parliament. But these developments had left little obvious mark on the everyday working of Parliament or the political parties. Direct elections penetrated further and more obviously into the working of the system. The legislation which made them possible provided the first occasion on which a British Government advocated a nationwide system of proportional representation. It saw collective Cabinet responsibility being waived, on a major issue of policy, as it had been only twice before (in 1932 and 1975). It played an important role in the Lib–Lab pact which kept a minority Labour Government in office for 18 months. The campaign itself and, still more perhaps, the preparations for it confronted the British parties with a host of new problems, political, administrative, ideological and personal.

The elections had a less obvious significance as well. The founding fathers of the Community had assumed that, as economic integration developed, political union would follow. But, although economic integration proceeded rapidly in the early years, progress was much slower by the end of the 1960s; and by the late 1970s its impetus seemed to have been dissipated in a *Europe des Patries,* each more anxious to defend its own people against the impact of a world recession than to collaborate with its Community partners. The European Commission in Brussels had not provided the driving force to restart the movement to a united Europe. Still less had the Council of Ministers. If change was to come at all, the elected Parliament, commanding the energies of 410 members, mostly full-time, and enjoying the enhanced legitimacy which its election had conferred upon it, might be the instrument. Such at least was the hope of many enthusiasts for European integration (who, naturally enough, were disproportionately represented among the MEPs). Even a few opponents saw in the elected Parliament an instrument to control what they regarded as a bureaucratic juggernaut. It may take years to tell whether these hopes will be borne out. As we show in Chapter 2, what is clear is that even the old, nominated Parliament had acquired more influence over the development of the Community than was generally appreciated in this country; and that its British members – not least, the anti-Marketeers in the Labour delegation – helped considerably to add to its status and authority.

It is clear, too, that the British contingent in the new, directly-elected Parliament has had its own special impact. The fact that the British electoral system had given the Conservatives a three to one majority of the UK seats had a decisive effect on the balance between right and left in the Parliament as a whole. The fact that the British MEPs came from single member constituencies meant that they brought a special set of interests (and a special oratorical style) to the debates. But although they came from the one country (apart from Denmark) in which Community membership was not fully accepted as a permanent fact of life, and from the country with the greatest grievance against the Community's financial arrangements, there is no evidence that they acted as a brake on the development of the institution to which they now belonged. As we show in Chapter 10, both the Conservative and Labour delegations joined happily with their continental colleagues in the December 1979 vote rejecting the Community Budget – a striking assertion of Parliament's power and of its appetite for more power in future. They did this, not out of adherence to some 'communautaire' ideology, but because they believed that they were helping to rectify the agricultural over-spending which lay at the heart of Britain's budgetary grievance. The fact remains that their votes seemed likely to enhance Parliament's visibility, credibility and authority.

As well as discussing the impact of the British on the European Parliament we have tried to discuss the impact of the European Parliament on the British. Direct elections have opened up a new career ladder in British politics. The 81 British MEPs included a few eminent businessmen, a few Eurocrats, and a few local government figures who would never have sought election to Westminster, as well as some who had failed to get chosen for winnable Westminster seats and now found an outlet for their frustrated political talents. They came from diverse backgrounds to an unfamiliar task which was likely to shape them as much as they shaped it. As we show in Chapter 2 most of the British members of the nominated Parliament found their membership of it satisfying and worthwhile; some played prominent parts in its work and enjoyed more influence in it than they exercised at Westminster.

Inevitably, their perceptions of it became more favourable as time went on. It seemed probable that similar changes of attitude would occur among the elected members. Some Conservative enthusiasts for the Community might become more sceptical; many Labour anti-Marketeers found themselves participating enthusiastically in the Parliament's work. The education forced upon them was likely to be echoed back to the domestic political scene as they reported to their constituents, and as they rubbed shoulders with party colleagues at Westminster and in their party organisations.

Two European political phenomena in particular seemed likely to have repercussions on British politics. The procedures of the European Parliament, and in particular the committee arrangements, owe far more to the French and German models than to the British. In so far as they have advantages, these may in due course become appreciated and perhaps copied in Britain, as increasing numbers of people in direct contact with British politics gain experience of them. But the way in which growing awareness of the European example, buttressed by direct initiatives from the European Parliament, is most likely to challenge established British ways, is by strengthening existing pressures to change the electoral system. Britain alone among Community countries uses first-past-the-post voting (except in Northern Ireland). Article 138 of the Rome Treaty lays down that the European Parliament should be elected by a common system, and in 1976 it was agreed that, while diversity was inevitable for the first elections, the Community should move to a common system by 1984. Any common system acceptable to the Nine would have to be largely proportional. It is true, of course, that the United Kingdom cannot be compelled to accept a proportional system, even for European elections, against her will: the Treaty explicitly provides that the Council of Ministers must decide this by unanimous vote, and the British Government could therefore always veto a proposal with which it disagreed. All the same, arguments on the electoral system which had had a new life in British domestic politics since 1974 seemed likely to receive further stimulus from the debates at Strasbourg and Luxembourg.

In one crucial respect, the position of the directly-elected MEPs differs fundamentally from that of their nominated predecessors. The nominated members all belonged to the Westminster Parliament; their positions in British political life derived from that fact. Only five of the directly-elected members have dual mandates; there are also four peers but the other 72 are members only of the European Parliament. Such roles as they play on the domestic political scene are Strasbourg roles, not Westminster ones. Within a few weeks of their election, the parties had to absorb them into their structure, national and local. The ways in which apparently minor problems of staffing and accommodation were solved might have implications for the general working of politics: the money and other assistance available to MEPs was not inconsiderable in relation to normal party funds.

It proved equally difficult to decide what status MEPs should enjoy. A year went by before they were given passes to enter parts of the Palace of Westminster closed to the general public and there was great opposition among MPs, particularly on the Labour side, to the suggestion that they should attend party committees. Whitehall was more welcoming. Departments treated MEPs' letters as though they had come from Westminster MPs and they also supplied particular briefs on request.

Some MEPs met problems in working out a *modus vivendi* with the Westminster MPs with whom they shared constituents. Most of the MEPs had been elected by more votes and represented more people than anybody before in British history; they had an obvious incentive to assume a public role as regional 'Mr Barsetshires'. They had also to work out to whom, and by what methods, they were to be accountable. Was there any party committee to whom they could report back? How were they to keep in touch with their electorate? If there was to be a drastic change in the electoral system how did the sanction of seeking re-election operate on them?

The directly-elected Parliament seemed likely to differ from its nominated predecessor in another respect as well. Until 1979 interest groups in Britain had mostly worked through Whitehall when they wanted to affect the proposals put forward by the European Commission; few had made even cursory contact with Luxembourg or Strasbourg. One or two bodies had set up offices in Brussels; trade unions' and employers' representatives sat on the advisory, but moderately influential, Economic and Social Committee; the unions were represented, along with their counterparts in other Community countries, in the more influential European TUC. But the coming of full-time elected MEPs made it conceivable that bodies like the TUC, the Confederation of British Industry and the National Farmers Union, and perhaps more important, local authorities and industrial interests in areas entitled to regional aid, might try to use MEPs to press their special cases, bypassing Whitehall even more completely than the Economic and Social Committee and the European TUC had already done.

All this raised a further question. What impact would an elected Parliament have on British public opinion? For 20 years, attitudes to Community membership had been remarkably volatile. There was no reason to believe that European elections had stabilised them. But the existence of 81 MEPs whose raison d'être was membership of a European Parliament, whose salaries were paid by the Parliament, and who could gain publicity for their views, might affect public attitudes. Attitudes might also be affected by the collective actions of the Parliament, particularly if, in its eagerness to justify itself and expand its powers, it challenged the Commission or the Council of Ministers. And the impact would of course depend on the attitude of the media to the elected Parliament; would the various gatekeepers of the news regard the activities of the new body worth covering?

To all these themes we shall return at the end of the book. But first we must try to tell the story of how the situation came about – how the European Assembly evolved, how direct elections were decided upon, and how each of the British parties reacted to the prospect – and we must look at the British campaign and its sequel. Then we can offer some analysis of the implications of this whole venture for the conduct of British politics.

CHAPTER TWO
The European Parliament

The first British members of the European Parliament took their seats on 15 January 1973. It was a moving occasion. Tom Normanton remembered later that there had been two great moments in his life – the first when as a young member of Montgomery's staff during the Second World War, he had ridden in with the tanks at the liberation of Brussels; the second when he took his seat in the hemicycle in the old European Parliament building in Strasbourg in 1973. He and his colleagues felt, he said later, as though 'we were gladiators back from Gaul'. But the euphoria soon passed. The British members who arrived in Strasbourg in January 1973 in fact represented only part of the British political nation. During the battles over Community entry in 1971 and 1972, Harold Wilson had managed to paper over the divisions between Labour pro-Marketeers and anti-Marketeers with a commitment to 're-negotiate' the terms of entry agreed to by the Conservatives. In the eyes of the predominantly anti-Market majority of the Labour movement, 're-negotiation' implied that it should refuse to play any part in the working of the Community until the Conservatives' terms had, in fact, been re-negotiated. Thus, the TUC refused to send delegates to the Economic and Social Committee or to play any part in the European TUC. Following a vote at the Labour Party Conference in October 1972, the Parliamentary Labour Party decided by 140 to 55 at a stormy meeting on 13 December 1972 that no Labour MPs should attend the European Parliament.

The logic of non-participation, it should be noted, was less apparent to Labour's sister parties on the Continent than to the anti-Market majority within the Labour Party. The German Social Democrats, in particular, probably the most 'European' of the continental Socialist parties, and, as such, particularly well aware of the fact that British

Labour participation would make the Socialist Group the largest in the Parliament, were particularly pained by Labour's decision – a fact which was to have some significance for the Labour members concerned when the party eventually decided to participate in the work of the Parliament, following the 1975 Referendum. For the moment, however, Labour was not present. The first British delegation consisted of 18 Conservatives and two Liberals (two cross-benchers were later added).

The Conservative team had been chosen with some care in terms of geographic and political balance. The leader of the delegation was Peter Kirk, a Junior Minister in the Defence Department. He was an experienced Euro-politician, having been Chairman of the General Affairs Committee of the Western European Union Assembly before the Conservatives won the 1970 election. He was an excellent linguist and knew the Continent well, having spent some time as a Diplomatic Correspondent before entering politics. He was not particularly enthusiastic about his new assignment, regarding it as, at best, a 'sideways move', and believing that it would harm rather than help his career in British politics to be obliged to spend most of his working life away from the House of Commons. Despite his hesitations, however, Peter Kirk proved an excellent choice. He ran the Conservative delegation rather like a cabinet. Each member was allocated a special subject of his own, and was also asked to look after a particular Community country. During the sessions they met every day: and they also met regularly in the United Kingdom. Sometimes Kirk would summon a special, *ad hoc* meeting on a particular issue.

The Conservative Group's impact on the European Parliament is hard to assess, partly because of an odd paradox at the heart of the Conservative Party's position in European politics. Since the early 1960s, it has been much more 'pro-European' than the Labour Party, but it fits much less well into the pattern of continental European politics. The Labour Party is recognisably part of the family of European democratic socialist parties. There is no family of European Conservatives. Most of the continental right-wing parties belonged either to the Liberal Group in the European Parliament or to the Christian Democratic Group (now the EPP). There are great differences between Christian Democracy and British Conservatism; although the German Christian Democrats are, for the most part, fairly close to the British Conservatives, the Belgian and Italian Christian Democratic Parties fight very shy of a 'Conservative' label. Equally, the British Conservatives fight shy of a 'Liberal' or Christian label. Though the ideological differences between the British Conservatives and the Dutch or Italian Liberals are small, the Conservative Party could never contemplate joining the Liberal Group in the European Parliament. Thus, the Conservatives, when they arrived at Strasbourg, had no transnational home to go to. They were obliged to form themselves into a group with the Danish Conservative Party, which sent two members; a further Dane, from the Centre Democratic Party, joined in 1974. It had been hoped that this Anglo-Scandinavian Group would also be joined by the Norwegian Conservatives, but the result of the Norwegian Referendum put paid to that. Though one vice-chairman was Danish, the Group was overwhelmingly British in composition. In practice, its chairman was always appointed by the leader of the Westminister Conservative Party; though the Group soon adopted rules of procedure stating that the chairman was elected by the group, the reality remained unchanged.

In some ways, no doubt, this gave the Conservatives an easier life than they would have had in a transnational group. But the disadvantages outweighed the advantages. The European Parliament revolved around the political groups; inevitably, the bigger groups had more influence than the smaller ones. Though the Conservatives held slightly more than half the British seats, theirs was a small group in Strasbourg terms. Their share of debating time, committee chairmanships and rapporteurships was the same as it would have been had they been members of one of the large transnational groups. But as a big constituent section of a large group they would almost certainly have had more influence on the attitudes and thinking of their continental colleagues, and therefore on the development of parliamentary opinion, than they could have as a small group of their own. On a rather different, more nebulous, level, moreover, the fact that they were isolated in a separate, virtually all-British group emphasised their 'un-Europeanness' and, to some extent, at any rate, the 'un-Europeanness' of their country. Despite these disadvantages, however, some members of the Conservative Group made significant individual contributions to the Parliament's work. Michael Shaw and Rafton Pounder played leading parts, in particular on the Budget Committee, while Peter Kirk was described later by one observer as having 'dominated' the Political Affairs Committee.

Perhaps because his interests in any case lay in that direction, perhaps because he believed that an important way to influence continental opinion was to confirm the widespread continental belief that the British possessed particular parliamentary skills and a special dedication to parliamentary government, Kirk concentrated his efforts on the development of Parliament as an institution. In an eloquent speech at the first plenary session after British entry – a speech expressing

---

The development of the European Parliament (see also p. 35)

5 May 1949	Council of Europe established at Strasbourg
3 Jun. 1950	Britain declines participation in Schuman Plan
25 Jul. 1952	European Coal and Steel Community established by Treaty of Paris
10 Sep. 1952	European Coal and Steel Community Assembly meets
2 May 1955	Conference on European Co-operation meets at Messina (Britain does not participate)
25 Mar. 1957	Treaty of Rome signed by Six
19 Mar. 1958	First meeting of European Assembly
17 May 1960	Dehousse Report on direct elections
30 May 1962	European Assembly decides to call itself European Parliament
14 Jan. 1963	President de Gaulle vetoes Britain's first application to join Community
29 Jan. 1966	Hallstein Plan/Luxembourg Compromise
27 Nov. 1967	President de Gaulle vetoes Britain's second application to join Six
30 Jun. 1970	Britain re-opens negotiations to join Community
22 Jun. 1972	Britain signs Treaty of Rome
4 Oct. 1972	Labour Conference votes not to participate in European Parliament (decision confirmed by Parliamentary Labour Party 13 Dec.)
16 Jan. 1973	British delegation, led by Peter Kirk, enters European Parliament
1 Apr. 1974	British Government opens 're-negotiation'
25 Oct. 1974	Patijn Report on direct elections
10 Dec. 1974	Paris Summit agrees to direct elections in 1978
11 Mar. 1975	'Re-negotiation' completed at Dublin
5 Jun. 1975	Britain votes 67.2 per cent to 32.8 per cent to stay in EEC
18 Jun. 1975	Parliamentary Labour Party votes to send Labour delegation to European Parliament

---

Group policy and not merely his personal predilections – he urged Parliament to seize initiatives where the Treaty did not preclude it from doing so, and called for the establishment of a new committee to examine its working and its relationship with the other Community Institutions. Without a strong Parliament, the Community was in danger of strangling in bureaucracy or drowning in apathy; accordingly, the Conservatives' policy was

a simple one – power to the Parliament. Our rules must be shaped with that and that alone in mind. There must be power over the Commission first because that is implied in the Treaty. But we must examine our relations with the Council as well . . . By this means the Parliament will live and the peoples will clamour to be directly represented in it.

In stressing the theme of power and representation, Peter Kirk was representative of a long tradition. The European Parliament in which he and his fellow Conservatives had just taken their seats was descended

22 Jun. 1975	Council of Ministers allows European Parliament power to reject Budget
1 Dec. 1975	British Government accepts principle of direct elections
7 Jan. 1976	Tindemans Report on Community reform
17 Feb. 1976	British Green Paper on direct elections
20 Sep. 1976	Council of Ministers signs European Assembly Elections Act at Brussels
6 Dec. 1976	John Prescott elected to succeed Michael Stewart as leader of Labour delegation
16 Apr. 1977	Sir Peter Kirk dies. (G. Rippon appointed to lead Con. delegation 3 May 1977.)

The most useful sources on Britain and the European Parliament include: *Agence Europe Presse;* D. Butler and U. Kitzinger, *The 1975 Referendum* (London 1976); F. Camenen, 'The Labour Party and the European Parliament', unpublished Oxford thesis; M. Camps, *European Unification in the Sixties* (Oxford 1967); Sir B. Cocks, *The European Parliament;* J. Fitzmaurice, *The European Parliament* (Farnborough 1978); G. Hand, J. Georgel and C. Sasse, *European Electoral Systems Handbook* (London 1979); W. O. Henderson, *The Genesis of the Common Market* (London 1962); S. Henig and G. Pridham, eds, *Political Parties in the European Community* (London 1978); V. Herman and M. Hagger, *The Legislation of Direct Elections to the European Parliament* (Farnborough 1980); V. Herman and J. Lodge, *The European Parliament and the European Community* (London 1978); V. Herman and R. Van Schendelen, *The European Parliament and the National Parliaments* (Farnborough 1979); see especially K. Featherstone's chapter on 'Labour in Europe'; R. Jackson and J. Fitzmaurice, *The European Parliament* (London 1979); U. Kitzinger, *Diplomacy and Persuasion* (London 1973); D. Marquand, *Parliament for Europe* (London 1979); R. Pryce, *The Political Future of the European Community* (London 1962); *The Times Guide to the European Parliament* (London 1980); W. Wallace, ed., *Britain in Europe* (London 1980).

from the Common Assembly of the Coal and Steel Community set up by the 1951 Treaty of Paris. This had provided for a parliamentary Assembly, to consist of 78 members, appointed by the Member Governments from the national Parliaments of the Member States. The Assembly's role was limited; Roy Pryce aptly described it as being 'much more akin to an assembly of shareholders than a normal parliamentary body'. It was to meet once a year to debate the annual report of the High Authority. The High Authority was not obliged to consult it, though the Assembly had the power to dismiss the High Authority by a vote of censure, carried by an absolute majority of its members and by a two-thirds majority of those voting. It also had the right to table questions to the High Authority and to make proposals concerning its own budget and to establish an independent secretariat.

Despite its limited power, however, the fact that the Assembly existed was more significant than might appear at first sight. In the

1940s, the movement for European unification had been divided between so-called 'federalists' and so-called 'functionalists'. The federalists had looked forward to the creation of a United States of Europe on the model of the USA. They had imagined that this would come into being through the election of a European Constituent Assembly. The functionalists, while accepting the ultimate goal of European union, had believed it could come only through the gradual intermeshing of governmental functions in different policy areas, and had seen no role for a parliamentary body.

The ECSC was overwhelmingly functionalist in inspiration and in character. Yet, by including a parliamentary Assembly, however weak, among its institutions the founding fathers had made at least an implicit obeisance in the direction of the older, 'federalist' conception. If the Assembly was to have a worthwhile role at all, that role would necessarily be political: if it was to have a political role, unification would have a political dimension after all.

The Common Assembly soon set about acquiring a more significant status than the Treaty had alloted to it. The annual session was split into several sessions; from time to time extraordinary sessions were held; a series of committees was set up to enable the Assembly to scrutinise the High Authority; and the High Authority took care to consult it about its policies and proposals, even though it was not obliged to do so. The High Authority did so because it saw the Assembly as a source of political support; the fact that it saw the Assembly in this way – rightly because the Assembly was itself overwhelmingly in favour of integration – has considerable significance for the history of the Community in general, and of the Common Assembly and European Parliament in particular. Early in the history of the European Community, there grew up a tacit alliance between the 'executive' and the 'legislature', directed, at any rate implicitly, against the Member Governments. Indeed, the terminology of 'executive' and 'legislature' – with its echoes of Westminster or Capitol Hill – is misleading. The High Authority was not an 'executive' and the Common Assembly was not a 'legislature'. In an important sense, both bodies were, among other things, institutionalised pressure groups for further and faster integration. And the same was true, at any rate in the early days of the Community, of their successors, the Commission and the European Parliament – a fact which was to play an important part in the opposition to direct elections, both in Britain and in France.

The European Parliament whose powers Sir Peter Kirk wished to increase was built on the foundations laid by the Common Assembly.

In general, the Rome Treaty, setting up the Economic Community, was less 'supranational' than the Paris Treaty. The Commission – the Economic Community's equivalent of the Coal and Steel Community's High Authority – was less powerful than the High Authority. The Council of Ministers was more powerful in the Economic Community than in the Coal and Steel Community. This whittling away of supra-nationality did not, however, apply to the parliamentary element in the structure. Whereas the Common Assembly had been consulted by the High Authority only as a matter of courtesy and for reasons of political expediency, the Assembly set up by the Rome Treaty enjoyed a legal right to be consulted on most Community matters by the decision-making authorities. The Commission made proposals, which were then put to the Council for decision; before taking its decision, however, the Council was obliged to consult the Assembly. To be sure, the Council had only to consult the Assembly; it was not obliged to do what the Assembly wanted. Nevertheless, such powers as the Assembly gradually acquired over the years were derived from this original right to be consulted.

There was another important difference between the Rome and Paris Treaties. The Paris Treaty had contained a provision that, at some unspecified stage in the future, the Assembly might be directly elected by a procedure to be determined by the Member Governments. But there was no suggestion that the Member Governments were obliged to agree on any such procedure; nor was anyone obliged to prepare a scheme for direct elections. The Rome Treaty went much further. As the text below shows, it stated specifically and unambiguously that the Assembly 'shall draw up proposals for elections by direct universal suffrage in accordance with a uniform procedure in all Member States'. The Assembly was remarkably quick to discharge the obligation laid upon it by Article 138. In October 1958, only a few months after its first meeting, its Political Affairs Committee set up a working party to prepare proposals for direct elections, under the chairmanship of the Belgian Socialist, M. Fernand Dehousse. The Dehousse Committee completed its labours in less than two years, and in May 1960 the Assembly passed a draft convention, which was then submitted to the Council.

By now, however, President de Gaulle was in power in France. He was firmly opposed to direct elections, on the grounds that they would erode national sovereignty; and thanks to French opposition, the Council took no action on the draft convention. Despite this setback, however, the Assembly returned to the question repeatedly during the

---

TREATY OF ROME, ARTICLES 137 TO 144

The Assembly

Article 137
The Assembly, which shall consist of representatives of the peoples of the States brought together in the Community, shall exercise the advisory and supervisory powers which are conferred upon it by this treaty.

Article 138
Bracketed paragraphs have been replaced by the Act of 20 September 1976 (see p. 31).
[The Assembly shall consist of delegates who shall be designated by the respective Parliaments from among their members in accordance with the procedure laid down by each Member State.]
The representatives in the Assembly of the peoples of the States brought together in the Community shall be elected by direct universal suffrage.
[The number of these delegates shall be as follows: . . .]
The number of representatives elected in each Member States be as follows . . .
The Assembly shall draw up proposals for elections by direct universal suffrage in accordance with a uniform procedure in all Member States.
The Council shall, acting unanimously, lay down the appropriate provisions, which it shall recommend to Member States for adoption in accordance with their respective constitutional requirements.

Article 139
The Assembly shall hold an annual session. It shall meet, without requiring to be convened, on the second Tuesday in March.
The Assembly may meet in extraordinary session at the request of a majority of its members or at the request of the Council or of the Commission.

---

next decade and a half. In 1961 it passed a resolution on political co-operation, insisting on the importance of direct elections. In December the same year, a further resolution was tabled, calling for elections within three years. In 1968, a group of members, led by the German Christian Democrat, Herr Deringer, tabled a motion threatening the Council that, unless it took action, Parliament would bring an action before the Court of Justice, under Article 175 of the Treaty. In the final communiqué issued after the Hague Summit conference in December 1969, the Heads of Government declared *inter alia:* 'the question of direct elections shall be given further consideration by the Council'.

In fact, however, no further consideration was given to it for the next three years. The Pompidou Government in France made it plain that it shared its predecessor's position on the matter; and it was therefore clear that little purpose would be served by bringing more pressure on the Council. Moreover, President de Gaulle's departure from office had left the way open for Britain's accession to the Community; and in

Article 140

The Assembly shall elect its President and its officers from among its members.

Members of the Commission may attend all meetings and shall, at their request, be heard on behalf of the Commission.

The Commission shall reply orally or in writing to questions put to it by the Assembly or by its members.

The Council shall be heard by the Assembly in accordance with the conditions laid down by the Council in its rule of procedure.

Article 141

Save as otherwise provided in this Treaty, the Assembly shall act by an absolute majority of the votes cast.

The rules of procedure shall determine the quorum.

Article 142

The Assembly shall adopt its rules of procedure, acting by a majority of its members.

The proceedings of the Assembly shall be published in the manner laid down in its rules of procedure.

Article 143

The Assembly shall discuss in open session the annual general report submitted to it by the Commission.

Article 144

If a motion of censure on the activities of the Commission is tabled before it, the Assembly shall not vote thereon until at least three days after the motion has been tabled and only by open vote.

If the motion of censure is carried by a two-thirds majority of the votes cast representing a majority of the members of the Assembly, the members of the Commission shall resign as a body. They shall continue to deal with current business until they are replaced in accordance with Article 158.

the summer of 1970 negotiations with Britain, Ireland, Denmark and Norway began. Until they were completed, direct elections were clearly out of the question. Once enlargement was an accomplished fact, however, Parliament returned rapidly to the issue. In June 1973 (only six months after Britain and the two other new Member States had entered the Community) Parliament instructed its Political Affairs Committee to draw up a new report on the matter. In September, the Dutch Socialist, Schelto Patijn, was appointed rapporteur. The Patijn Report was ready in a little more than a year; in January 1975, the European Parliament passed a draft convention, based on the Patijn Report, which was then submitted to the Council.

By this time, Pompidou was dead; and Giscard d'Estaing was President. The new President's attitude was favourable, and at the Summit conference in December 1974 the Community's Heads of Government had agreed that direct elections should take place in 1978. As this implies, it would clearly be a mistake to suggest that direct elections came about because of the efforts of the European Parliament.

The European Parliament had been pressing for direct elections for 15 years before the Summit acted; the reason the Summit acted in the end was not that the Heads of Government suddenly came to the conclusion that the European Parliament's pressure could no longer be resisted, but that French policy had changed. On the other hand, it is equally important not to underestimate Parliament's role. As was to become clear when the enabling legislation for direct elections came before the French National Assembly, powerful forces in France were still strongly opposed to the whole notion of a directly-elected European Parliament. If there had been no countervailing pressure from Strasbourg and Luxembourg, it is quite conceivable that Giscard d'Estaing would not have changed French policy in the way that he did.

Meanwhile the Assembly had also managed to extend the powers accorded to it by the Treaty. As we have seen, the Treaty had conferred upon it the modest powers which had been enjoyed in practice by the Assembly of the ECSC. The Council of Ministers was obliged to consult it on most (though not on all) Commission proposals; it could dismiss the whole Commission (though not individual Commissioners) by a vote of censure; like the Common Assembly of the ECSC, it had the right to put questions to the Commission and to debate the Commission's annual report. Though these powers were limited, however, the founding fathers of the Economic Community almost certainly expected them to expand fairly rapidly. After a transitional stage, most Council decisions were to be taken by a complicated system of weighted majority voting. Since Commission proposals could be amended by the Council only if the Council were unanimous, this would enhance the Commission's influence and authority and, *a fortiori,* the influence and authority of the Assembly, to which it was account-able. At the same time majority voting would change the whole character of the Council of Ministers. It would cease to be a kind of standing international conference, and become something much more akin to a legislative body – to an embryo 'Upper House' or 'Chamber of States', in Dr Hallstein's phrase, on the model of the early United States Senate or present German Bundesrat. Direct elections, meanwhile, would turn the Assembly into an embryo Lower House or House of Representatives. The Commission would be the embryo Government, accountable to its directly elected Parliament as real Governments are accountable to their Parliaments.

At first, it looked as though this evolution would proceed fairly quickly. One small symbol, it may be, was the decision of the Assembly in 1962 to call itself the European Parliament. In 1965, however, the process was brought to an end, at any rate for the time being. The

Commission put forward an ambitious proposal to link the coming into force of the arrangements for financing the Common Agricultural Policy with a change in the Community Budget, designed to make the Community financially independent of the Member Governments, and to increase the powers of the European Parliament. Perhaps because he thought this step towards a supranational Community particularly dangerous, perhaps because he had in any case decided that it was necessary to call a halt to developments of a supranational kind, President de Gaulle reacted by plunging the Community into the most serious crisis in its history. For six months, France boycotted all Council activities designed to produce new decisions. At the same time, de Gaulle made it clear that he was not prepared to accept any further movement along the supranational road set out in the Treaty; and, in particular, that he was not prepared to implement the Treaty provisions on majority voting. The crisis was ended in January 1966, by the so-called 'Luxembourg Compromise', in which France and the other five Member States agreed to disagree about the French demand that Member States should be allowed to insist on unanimity when they considered that matters of vital national importance were being decided. But the 'Compromise' was a compromise only in name. On the crucial issue of majority voting, it was a victory for France. In effect, the French had announced that, no matter what the Treaty might say, they would veto proposals with which they did not agree when it suited them to do so; the other Member States had acknowledged that they could not compel France to abide by the Treaty if she did not wish to do so. Because the French got what they wanted, moreover, the other Member States also got what the French wanted. After the Compromise, any Member State could insist on unanimity whenever it wished to do so. Though many Council decisions have, in practice, been taken by a majority, most Council decision-making is conducted in the shadow of a possible veto.

The effect was three-fold. Not only were the Treaty provisions on majority voting not implemented; the Commission failed to gain the extra influence and authority which full implementation of those provisions would have given it. The increase in Parliament's powers for which the Commission had asked did not take place. Parliament was adversely affected by the shift in the balance of institutional power between the Commission and the Council of Ministers. The Treaty gave Parliament power only over the Commission. If the Commission had evolved gradually into a European Government, these powers might have had considerable significance. In destroying such hopes, the Luxembourg Compromise also rendered Parliament's powers over the

Commission less valuable. From 1966 onwards, the Commission played the role of 'motor of integration', assigned to it by Community theology, only fitfully and without much success. In practice, even if not in theory, the 'motor of integration' became the European Council, or Summit meeting of the Heads of Government. The centre of decision-making remained the Council of Ministers, and the Commission was much more subservient to the Council than it was in the early days, or than the Treaty envisaged it as being. Increasingly, moreover, decisions were made, in practice, on the margins of Council Meetings, or even outside the formal Council structure altogether. But Parliament, as we have seen, had no sanctions over the Council of Ministers. In weakening the Commission, the Compromise had therefore weakened Parliament as well. By the same token Parliament's road to a more effective say in Community decision-making would henceforth lie, not through attempts to increase its powers over the Commission, but through the acquisition of influence over the Council.

As with direct elections, no further steps took place until President de Gaulle's departure from office. As with direct elections, however, the road opened up after the Hague Summit of 1969. This paved the way for the Treaty of Luxembourg of 1970, in which some of the aims the Commission had tried unsuccessfully to achieve in 1965 were finally realised. Instead of depending, as hitherto, on contributions from Member Governments, the Community would itself own the resources required to finance Community expenditure as from 1975. These resources would be derived from the agricultural levies, the customs duties, and from 1 per cent of the Member Governments' VAT revenues. In making the Community financially independent of the Member Governments, however, the Luxembourg Treaty also made it independent of the national Parliaments. Henceforth, parliamentary control over the Community Budget would have to be exercised at the Community level, if there were to be any parliamentary control at all.

Accordingly, the European Parliament was given certain powers over the Community Budget for the first time. The system laid down by the Luxembourg Treaty and an amending Treaty of 1975 was a complicated one, but the essential principles were simple enough. Community expenditure was divided into two categories – 'obligatory' expenditure, and 'non-obligatory' expenditure. 'Obligatory' expenditure was defined as expenditure necessarily resulting from the Treaties establishing the Community, or from acts adopted in accordance with them. 'Non-obligatory' expenditure was expenditure on the administrative running costs of the Community and on policy areas not covered by the Treaties. Parliament's powers were to vary according to whether the expenditure was 'obligatory' or 'non-obligatory'. First, the Commission would prepare a draft Budget, to be sent to the Council. The Council could amend the Commission draft by a weighted majority: and the draft as revised by the Council then be sent to Parliament. Parliament could propose modifications in the 'obligatory' sector of the Budget only by an absolute majority of its total membership, but it could pass amendments in the 'non-obligatory' sector by a simple majority of the members present. After Parliament had considered the draft, it would be sent back to the Council, which would consider any amendments put down by the Parliament. In the obligatory sector, Parliament's modifications were treated differently depending on whether they increased expenditure or not. Modifications that increased expenditure could get through the Council only if a weighted majority voted in favour: modifications that did not increase expenditure would get through unless a weighted majority voted against. In the 'non-obligatory' sector, Parliament had more power. Here, even amendments increasing expenditure would pass unless a weighted majority voted against. Finally, Parliament would reconsider the Council's amendments to its amendments. In the 'obligatory' sector it could make no further changes. In the 'non-obligatory' sector, however, it could amend the Council's amendments by a majority of its total membership and a three-fifths majority of the votes cast. In this sector, it was to have the last word. In addition to all this, Parliament was to have the power to reject the Budget altogether.

There was a good deal of debate in Community circles as to the real significance of these provisions and in particular of Parliament's right to reject the Budget *in toto*. It is therefore of some significance that one of the directly-elected Parliament's first acts was precisely to reject the Budget *in toto;* and, as we shall see (p. 150 ff.), one of the chief motives for rejection was that Parliament wanted to gain power over areas of Community policy which it had hitherto been unable to influence. Secondly, the role given to the European Parliament in the 'non-obligatory' sector of Community expenditure, though of small significance when the Luxembourg Treaty was signed, has grown in importance over the years. When the Luxembourg Treaty was signed only 3 per cent of Community spending was 'non-obligatory'; to-day the figure is 30 per cent. Since expenditure arising from policies adopted since the Treaties were signed falls into the 'non-obligatory' sector, it is clear that the adoption of new Community policies in future, and any expansion in the size of the Community Budget necessitated by such new policies, must automatically enhance Parliament's role in Community decision-making. Thirdly, and perhaps most importantly, the

Luxembourg Treaty gave Parliament the chance to engage in a direct dialogue with the Council of Ministers for the first time. Hitherto, Parliament had been, at most, a listener, (albeit on occasion an obstreperous listener) to the basic Community dialogue between the Council and the Commission. Now it could force national ministers to engage in a direct discussion with it.

The same was true of the second significant increase in Parliament's role – the establishment of the so-called 'conciliation procedure' in 1975. This procedure followed logically from the decision to give Parliament budgetary powers. The Community Budget is, in a sense, the end product of Community legislation: the object of the 'conciliation procedure' was to give Parliament some say in that legislation. Wherever there is a conflict between Parliament and the Commission on one side, and the Council on the other, concerning a Commission proposal of general application but with 'appreciable financial consequences', the procedure can be activated by either side. A conciliation committee is established, consisting of nine ministers from the appropriate specialist Council and a delegation of nine members of the Parliament, including the relevant committee chairman and rapporteur. A maximum of three months is set in which to reach agreement. In effect, therefore, the procedure gives Parliament a 'suspensive veto' for a period of three months. If agreement is reached between the two sides during the three-month period, its substance is included in a new report from the relevant committee of the Parliament, which is then adopted as a resolution by Parliament as a whole. Parliament's new opinion is then accepted by the Council. If no agreement is reached, the Council's original decision takes effect.

Of course, the Council still has the last word. Parliament's 'suspensive veto' lasts for only three months, a short period in a Community whose decision-making process is so slow-moving and cumbersome that a delay of that length seldom matters. None the less, the establishment of the 'conciliation procedure' marked a significant step forward for Parliament. As was recognised in the 1972 Vedel Report, Parliament's best route to a voice in Community decision-making clearly lies through the acquisition of powers of co-decision with the Council. The 'conciliation procedure' was a tiny, but important, step towards just that.

The British impact on the nominated Parliament must be assessed against this background. In October 1974 Kirk was appointed rapporteur of the Political Affairs Committee study of the role of the European Parliament. In 1975, he produced a draft report on the 'powers of the European Parliament' incorporating the results of his work. It contained two proposals for strengthening Parliament's legislative role. In the first place, Kirk suggested that Parliament could be given a power of initiative, analogous to the right of a British Member of Parliament to bring in a private member's bill. A parliamentary committee would draft legislation: if the Bureau of the Parliament approved it, the draft would be voted on in plenary sessions. If approved there, it would be sent to the Commission. The Commission would then submit it to the Council in the usual way: and after that it would follow the normal course of Community legislation. Secondly, Kirk suggested that the so-called, 'conciliation procedure' should be extended to all Community legislation. When the Commission had made up its mind to make a legislative proposal, it would send the text to Parliament. Parliament would then debate the Commission's proposal – before it had been sent to the Council and before the Member Governments started to entrench their positions. The Commission would then send its proposal to the Council together with any amendments passed by Parliament. The Council would then make a decision on the Commission's proposal, and also on Parliament's amendments: and it would do so in public, not in secret. If the Council differed at all from Parliament, the latter would hold a second debate. If, within a specified time limit, the Council refused to change its decision so as to agree with Parliament or *vice versa,* the 'conciliation procedure' would automatically come into operation.

How effective were these pressures? One of the Conservative delegation's first acts was to table a memorandum amplifying the themes of Peter Kirk's initial speech in January 1973. From this stemmed the establishment of the so-called 'Control' sub-committee of the Budget Committee. Peter Kirk's original idea had been to create a European equivalent of the British Public Accounts Committee. This had aroused fierce opposition from the Chairman of the Budgets Committee, the German Social Democrat, Erwin Lange. Lange was bitterly opposed to the establishment of a new committee, on such lines because he saw it as a threat to the Budget Committee. He was, however, equally opposed to the establishment of a sub-committee of the Budget Committee, to do the same work as the Public Accounts Committee does in the British House of Commons, because he was opposed on principle to sub-committees, and thought that the establishment of sub-committees would detract from the work of the main Committee. Despite Lange, however, the Control sub-committee was eventually set up with Labour backing; and there is little doubt that this was largely a British achievement. Another innovation for which Kirk had pressed was the holding of public hearings by committees of the

European Parliament. That, too, was achieved – though only in part.

The fate of the 1975 Kirk Report was less happy. By the time it appeared, the Summit decision in favour of direct elections in 1978 had already been taken; the Patijn Report was almost ready for acceptance by the Parliament. By a curious, though understandable, paradox, the approach of direct elections made the Parliament more hesitant about pressing for an extension in its powers, and had a similar effect on the Commission. In Britain and France, opposition to direct elections focused on the alleged danger that a directly-elected Parliament would increase its powers at the expense of national sovereignty. Correctly, or incorrectly, the British and French Governments believed that, if they were to get the legislation for direct elections through their respective parliaments, they had to bend over backwards to assure the opponents of direct elections that there was no question of the European Parliament gaining any more power if direct elections were held; and in both countries, the legislation eventually contained a provision making it illegal for the Government to agree to increases in the European Parliament's powers unless the national Parliament agreed. In this climate, the Kirk Report was almost an embarrassment to friends of the Parliament and of direct elections. The Commission carefully refrained from taking any action on it: the Political Affairs Committee did little about it either. Sir Peter Kirk's death in the spring of 1977 left it, for all practical purposes, in a state of limbo: though Lord Reay, another British Conservative, was appointed rapporteur in his place, little more was heard of it.

The second phase of British participation began in July 1975, following the Referendum on British membership of the Community. Once the British people had voted in favour of continued membership, non-participation could no longer be justified; and the Labour Party accordingly decided to join in the work of the European Parliament after all.[1] It was not an easy decision to implement. The Referendum on Community membership had originally been an 'anti-Market' demand: until a few months before it was held, the anti-Marketeers had reason to think that they would win it. Their crushing defeat left them bruised and apprehensive. Moreover, they still comprised half the parliamentary party – indeed more than half of the back-benchers who on 9 April 1975 just before the Referendum, voted 92 for and 107 against the re-negotiated terms. To complicate matters still further, many of the strongest critics of Wilson's leadership were to be found among the

---

[1] On many points in what follows, as well as in Chapter 4, we are indebted to François Camenen and his unpublished thesis. 'The Labour Party and the European Parliament'.

ranks of the strongest pro-Marketeers. For all these reasons, the leadership and the party managers were determined that the first Labour delegation to the European Parliament should be 'balanced' as between pro-Marketeers and anti-Marketeers and that it should not contain the strongest, most vociferous or, in party terms, the most 'divisive' members of either camp. They wanted, above all, to heal the wounds inside the party. A Strasbourg delegation dominated by pro-Marketeers would pour salt into the defeated anti-Marketeers' wounds, while a delegation composed of the most articulate and passionate proponents of either point of view would be likely to find itself in a state of endemic civil war, and would therefore make it more difficult to call a halt to the civil war at home. What the leadership wanted was an unprovocative delegation: that meant a balanced delegation, and it also meant an inconspicuous delegation.

To make sure of this, the leadership wanted to appoint the delegation itself; and a proposal to this effect was put to a meeting of the PLP on 18 June 1975. It was greeted with considerable hostility on both pro- and anti-wings of the parliamentary party: and William Hamilton proposed an amendment calling for the 'direct election of the Labour delegation by the members of the Parliamentary Party in their respective houses'. His amendment was defeated by 68 votes to 28; but, as a sop to the supporters of an elected Strasbourg delegation, it was also decided, on 26 June, that the nominated delegation should hold office for only a year, and that after a year the method of choosing the delegation should be reviewed.

Much complicated politicking then ensued. Under the terms of the liaison committee's proposal, the Strasbourg delegation was to be chosen by the liaison committee from among those members of the PLP who submitted their names to it. In practice, however, the whips made strong efforts to persuade certain members of the PLP to put their names forward, so as to ensure that the delegation would be balanced in the way the leadership wanted. In the end, it consisted of 18 members of the House of Commons. It was carefully balanced regionally, and also carefully balanced between pros and antis. Seven of the 18 had voted in favour of British entry into the Community in 1971, against a three-line whip. Six had voted against acceptance of the 're-negotiated' terms in 1975, and could be assumed to have voted NO in the Referendum. Of the five remaining members, two (Lady Fisher and Betty Boothroyd) had not been in Parliament in 1971, but were members of the Labour Committee for Europe, and could be counted in the pro column. One (Gwyneth Dunwoody) could be counted as an anti, having voted against the Labour Government's application in 1967, against a three-line whip, and against continued membership in 1975. One (Richard Mitchell) was a convert from the anti to the pro camp, having voted with the majority against entry in 1971, but having voted for acceptance of the 're-negotiated' terms in 1975. The last, William Hamilton, was a law unto himself. A strong pro of many years standing, he was also a strong party loyalist. In 1971 he had abstained on the motion approving the Conservative Government's terms of entry; in 1975, he had voted in favour of continued membership. Thus, if those who supported continued membership of the Community in 1975 were to count as pros, the pros were in a majority of 11 to 7; if the term is to be confined to those who both had an opportunity to vote in 1971, and voted in favour of British entry, the pros were in a minority of seven to eight. More significantly still, none of the most prominent and embattled figures on either side of the argument – apart, perhaps, from Hamilton – were included in the delegation. On the anti-side, John Prescott was the only prominent opponent of British membership: Eric Heffer, Nigel Spearing and Bryan Gould, all of whom had played prominent parts in the argument on the anti-side, were conspicuous by their absence. Among the pros, it was significant that no place was found for John Roper, John Mackintosh or Dickson Mabon, leading lights of the pro campaign of many years standing.

The choice of leader of the Labour delegation provoked a good deal of acrimony as well. Tam Dalyell, then the chairman of the back-bench Foreign Affairs Group, appears to have been the Foreign Secretary's candidate for the post, but Mr Dalyell was a bitter and outspoken critic of Harold Wilson's leadership, and it seems clear that Wilson vetoed Jim Callaghan's suggestion that Dalyell should lead the delegation. Another candidate for the leadership was Sir Geoffrey de Freitas, a former president of the Council of Europe Assembly, and a long-standing 'European', who had been among other things chairman of the Labour Committee for Europe. In the end, however, the leadership went to Michael Stewart, Foreign Secretary from 1965 to 1966 and from 1968 to 1970, and one of the Party's most respected elder statesmen, who had voted both for British entry in 1971 and for continued membership in 1975.

The party meeting which had voted in favour of the liaison committee's proposal that the delegation should be nominated rather than elected had also carried an amendment, moved by the pro-Marketeer, Michael Thomas, laying it down that the members of the delegation should seek to become members of the Socialist Group. The Thomas amendment had been carried on a show of hands, but the number of hands raised against the amendment reflected a deep suspicion on the part of the antis, and more particularly of the left-wing antis of entanglement with continental social democracy, which was believed to be insufficiently 'socialist'. However, there appears to have been no opposition from within the delegation to carrying out the Thomas amendment and the British Labour delegation accordingly applied for membership of the Socialist Group as soon as it arrived in the Parliament. From the start, therefore, there was a crucial difference between the experience of the Labour members and that of their Conservative counterparts. The Conservatives belonged to a small group, slightly isolated from the mainstream of continental politics. The Labour members belonged to the largest, most multinational and perhaps most influential group in the entire Parliament. They could influence the Parliament not only by direct action in committees and plenary sessions, but indirectly through the influence they could bring to bear on the policy of the wider Socialist Group; and of these two forums – the Group and the Parliament itself – the former was almost certainly the more important.

Labour's arrival was warmly welcomed by the rest of the Socialist Group – partly because it symbolised the fact that British membership of the Community had been legitimised by the Referendum a few weeks before, and partly for the more mundane, but perhaps more important, reason that it made the Socialist Group the largest group in the Parliament. In the early days, however, there was a good deal of suspicion, particularly on the part of the German Social Democrats, of the Labour antis. In part, this was a legacy of the resentment which Labour's non-participation policy had produced in the SPD during the previous two-and-a-half years; in part, it reflected a widespread SPD belief that once the Referendum had decided that Britain should remain in the Community, it was undemocratic for British members of the European Parliament to stick to a line which conflicted with the Referendum result. These tensions sometimes led to real acrimony at Group meetings: on one occasion, Lord Castle was fiercely interrupted in the middle of a contribution attacking the working of the Common Agricultural Policy by Erwin Lange, who shouted out angrily: 'Why have you come?'

As time went on, however, the Labour delegation as a whole – and, by a curious paradox, its anti members in particular – gradually acquired much more influence on their continental colleagues than they had expected to do at the beginning. One reason for this was simply that the activity rate of the Labour members was significantly higher than that of the general run of members of the Parliament: and that the anti Labour members were even more active than the pros. Another reason was that the arrival of the Labour members had a marked effect on the balance of national power within the Group. Before 1975, the Socialist Group had been dominated by the German SPD. The smaller parties – although the French Socialists came from a big country, they were a small party, while the Dutch, though coming from a big national party in Holland, came only from a small country – resented SPD domination, but could do little about it. Labour's arrival weakened the Germans' domination. The German President of the Group could now retain office only if the British supported him. There can be little doubt that this change was welcomed by the smaller parties. Furthermore, the Labour delegation's general political stance, apart from its position on the rights and wrongs of Community membership as such, was probably closer to that of the non-German element in the Socialist Group than was the attitude of the monolithic and rather right-wing German delegation.

A revealing illustration of this point occurred quite early on in the history of the Labour delegation. The newly-arrived Labour members discovered that a Conservative member, Tom Normanton, had carried through the relevant parliamentary committee a report on competition policy, which, in their view, was totally unacceptable to any socialist, because it extolled the virtues of free competition and implicitly criticised nationalisation and state intervention on straight laisser-faire grounds. However, the Socialist member of the relevant committee had accepted the report without consulting the Group, and the Labour members were told that it was now too late to object. They insisted on doing so, however, and in the debate which they forced on the issue it turned out that the Danes, French and Dutch Socialists present shared their disapproval of the line taken by the German Socialist member of Tom Normanton's committee; and at the end of the debate the vote went in favour of the Labour view. Though it would be wrong to make too much of this, it is worth noting that more than one Labour member of the old, nominated Parliament believed that one of the main achievements of the Labour delegation had been to raise the 'ideological temperature' of the Group, and, in doing so, of the Parliament as a whole. The Labour delegation could also claim that it was through initiatives taken by Labour chairmen that the Parliament's committees first held hearings in public.

It is, however, difficult to make firm generalisations about Labour's policy. One of the first decisions taken by the new Labour delegation when it arrived in Luxembourg was that it should not adopt an agreed, binding line before meetings of the wider Socialist Group. The proposal that it should refrain from adopting policy positions before Socialist Group meetings was put by the pro members of the delegation, and was opposed by some of the antis. The pros won; and thereafter the Labour delegation acted within the wider Socialist Group as individuals, unbound by any prior decision among themselves. This means that – in striking contrast to their Conservative opposite numbers – it is, almost by definition, impossible to examine the success or failure of the Labour members in carrying a coherent Labour policy through. The Labour members did not work as a group, but as individual freelances; their impact has therefore to be assessed on an individual, rather than on a group, basis. That said, the most striking single fact about Labour's participation in the nominated Parliament is that a number of Labour members did achieve prominence, and make a considerable impact, within the Parliament – and that the members who did so were almost all antis, or former antis. Chief among them was probably Mark Hughes, MP for Durham, who became a rapporteur on the Agriculture Committee, and who played a major role in shifting the Parliament's Agricultural Policy against high prices and in favour of the low-price policy of the Commission. Lord Bruce, an accountant by profession, proved a highly effective member of the Budget Committee and also served as a rapporteur. John Evans, the first anti to become a Committee Chairman, managed to hold back action on lorry tachographs. John Prescott, MP for Hull East, played a major part in formulating the Socialist Group's policy on fisheries and carried a report condemning the violation of human rights in Argentina through the Political Affairs Committee. Among the pros, only Michael Stewart and Tam Dalyell made an equivalent impact.

The European Parliament affected the British Members at least as powerfully as they affected it. As we have seen, the Conservatives arrived in Strasbourg as strongly committed pro-Europeans. There is no evidence that their membership of the European Parliament changed their attitudes. Though Sir Derek Walker-Smith, who had been a leading anti during the passage of the legislation as well as on the question of principle in 1971, now took the view that the right thing to do was to make the decision to enter work, there do not appear to have been any big changes of heart, or even any significant changes of emphasis, among the Conservatives after they arrived. What is noticeable, however, is that the Conservatives who belonged to the European Parliament in 1978 and 1979, when direct elections were approaching, nearly all sought nomination as members of the elected Parliament; and that most of them found membership of the European Parliament more satisfying and worthwhile than membership of the House of Commons. In part, this was a function of the Strasbourg structure, with its emphasis on committee work as opposed to gladiatorial combat on the floor of the House; in part, it reflected the relative openness of the Community bureaucracy as compared to Whitehall, and the fact that, as a result, MEPs can influence the 'pre-legislative' stage of Community decision-making much more easily than MPs can influence the 'pre-legislative' stage at Westminster. In some cases, it also reflected the Community's growing weight in world affairs and the increasing attention paid to the Community in the outside world. At Westminster, one Conservative MEP insisted a few months before the Euro-elections, he had no influence whatever: the whips' sole concern was to make sure that he appeared in the right lobby at the right time. His membership of the European Parliament, by contrast, gave him access to influential politicians all over the world, and gave him far more influence over the development of the Community than he had on the development of his own country.

About the impact of the European Parliament on the Labour delegation there is more to be said. Partly, because they did have more impact than they had originally expected, many of the antis slowly began to shift their perceptions of the European Parliament, and to some extent even of the Community as such. None changed his position on the original issue which had divided pros from antis – whether Britain should have joined the Community at all in 1971. All maintained that they had been right to oppose British entry then, and that they had also been right to oppose continued membership in 1975. Equally, the antis were more prone than the pros to take a reticent line on direct elections in 1976 and 1977, and to risk the wrath of their continental colleagues by doing so. Another issue on which old anti positions could be detected was that of the Kirk Report and the related question of the powers of the European Parliament. Here, it seems clear that one of the reasons why the Political Affairs Committee took no action on the Kirk Report after Peter Kirk's death was that, thanks to the influence of the Labour antis in the Socialist Group, the Socialists helped to prevent it from doing so.

On less highly charged issues, however, the differences between pros and antis gradually became blurred, and the attitudes of the antis gradually mellowed. Like their Conservative compatriots, most Labour MEPs found their Luxembourg and Strasbourg roles more satisfying than their Westminster ones at least for a spell. Had the Labour Party's rules permitted them to do so, several would have sought nomination for the directly-elected Parliament, and a few might even have been prepared to give up their Westminster careers in order to sit in it. The fact that they could, and frequently did, influence the behaviour of the largest and most influential political group could hardly fail to make the antis less suspicious of the Parliament in general, and of their continental comrades in particular, than they had been when they first arrived. The fact that they were, after all, members of the Parliament, that they shared in its life and that their ability to influence events was in part a function of its influence, gave them a sence of solidarity with their colleagues from other countries, and even from other parties, which often proved stronger, in practice, than their doctrinal objections to the assumptions on which the Parliament was based, though most antis remained firmly opposed to direct elections. The fact that pros and antis shared the same strange (and to Westminster eyes slightly suspect) Euro-life, finding themselves waiting for planes in the same desolate airport bars, staying in the same hotels and spending much of their working lives together on the Continent, created a similar sense of solidarity within the Labour delegation itself. At first, the old antagonisms were marked; they could be detected beneath the surface throughout. As time went on, some new antagonisms appeared. But by the end of the nominated Parliament's life, the division between pros and antis no longer had much significance so far as the day-to-day work of the Labour delegation was concerned.

Perhaps the most significant example of this was the election of John Prescott as leader of the delegation. The Labour delegation had, in effect, three official positions – its own leadership and deputy leadership, and a place on the Bureau of the Socialist Group which it held by virtue of the fact that it also held a vice-presidency of the Parliament itself. At first, the pros took all three. Michael Stewart was leader, and with Sir Geoffrey de Freitas, who became the Labour vice-president of the Parliament, was *ex officio* on the Bureau of the Socialist Group; Tam Dalyell was chosen as the delegation's third member of the Bureau. Not surprisingly the antis objected to this monopoly; and in March 1976 Tam Dalyell was replaced by John Prescott. In the autumn of 1976, Michael Stewart resigned from the delegation, partly because he had found it a strain to reconcile the differences between its pro- and anti-wings, and partly because the Prime Minister had asked him to chair the Privileges Committee of the House of Commons in a pending enquiry. After some complicated manoeuvring, two candidates emerged – Richard Mitchell for the pros, and John Prescott for the antis. John Prescott was strongly supported by Lord Ardwick and Lord Walston and by Lady Fisher – all staunch pros of many years standing – and was elected in the end by 11 votes to 6. It was a tribute to his personal qualities. In some ways, it was an even more striking tribute to the absorptive powers of the European Parliament.

CHAPTER THREE
Legislation

The Treaty of Rome clearly committed the signatories to direct elections. But the provisions of Article 138 and the likelihood of a relatively early attempt to implement its provisions were scarcely discussed during British attempts to join the Community or even during the 1975 Referendum. It has been said that direct elections crept up unawares on all the countries of the Nine; the initiative came from a determined and long-standing majority in the Parliament and at the December 1974 Summit a decision in principle to proceed to direct elections was nodded through. Thus in 1976 the Governments found themselves in a position where they could not evade the issue. They put it off at the Luxembourg Summit in April but in Brussels in September they agreed they would try to pass the necessary legislation for elections to take place, if possible, in the spring of 1978. However, Britain, together with Denmark, expressed reservations about completing preparations in time, although promising 'our best endeavours' to do so.

The Queen's Speech of 24 November 1976 contained a promise to introduce legislation but it became more and more plain that there was no serious drive to meet the 1978 deadline. The Government's difficulties were political rather than practical. The Cabinet was divided and lacked a parliamentary majority; it was committed to two complicated and controversial devolution Bills, and it was reluctant to cause new problems for itself, either by deciding how direct elections were to be conducted or by forcing the necessary legislation through Parliament. A third of the Cabinet (and the majority of Labour's National Executive) were opposed to direct elections and too vigorous a pursuit of European commitments might have split the Cabinet. Michael Foot, a leading opponent of Community membership, played a critical part in the Government by virtue of his left-wing past. His willingness to stay in office was seen in some circles as an index of its socialist faith; rightly or wrongly, some of his right-wing colleagues believed that he was more likely to resign over Europe than over any other issue. Since they believed his resignation would destroy the Government, this explains some of the compromises and delays over the legislation. In addition, many ministers feared that European elections would damage and divide the party and believed that they must not be allowed to take place before the general election was out of the way. Labour was bound to fare badly in a European contest; the outcome might demoralise the party before the real battle for Westminster – and it would inevitably bring more into the open the party's conflicts between pros and antis, between right and left, and between Government and NEC. There was no public pressure to hasten on direct elections, even though from mid-1976 onwards, the Community's opinion poll, the Eurobarometer, showed a rather unstable three to one majority in their favour in the UK.[1]

But approval for direct elections did not mean approval for the EEC itself. Throughout this period the Common Market was becoming more unpopular. The EEC Eurobarometer poll regularly asked the question 'Generally speaking do you think Britain's membership of the European Common Market is a good thing, a bad thing, or neither good nor bad?' The trend was from positive to negative throughout the discussion of the direct elections legislation.[2]

Table 1. Difference between percentages saying 'good thing' and 'bad thing'.

Nov. 1975	+ 23%
Nov. 1976	+ 5%
Nov. 1977	− 2%
May 1978	− 9%
Nov. 1978	+ 8%
May 1979	− 1%

News about the Common Market tended to focus on butter mountains and wine lakes and on seemingly absurd harmonisation directives about lawn-mowers and whisky prices. It is important to remember, the British contribution to the Community Budget which was to become so great an issue in the autumn of 1979 was very little heard

[1] See Chapter 4 for a fuller discussion of Labour Party attitudes.
[2] See D. Butler, 'Public Opinion and Community Membership', *Political Quarterly* (April 1979), pp. 151–6.

ACT OF COUNCIL OF MINISTERS   20 September 1976

Article 1

The representatives in the Assembly of the peoples of the States brought together in the Community shall be elected by direct universal suffrage.

Article 2

The number of representatives elected in each Member State shall be as follows:

Belgium	24	France	81	Luxembourg	6
Denmark	16	Ireland	15	Netherlands	25
Germany	81	Italy	81	United Kingdom	81

Article 3

1. Representatives shall be elected for a term of five years.
2. This five-year period shall begin at the opening of the first session following each election.

It may be extended or curtailed pursuant to the second subparagraph of Article 10 (2).

3. The term of office of each representative shall begin and end at the same time as the period referred to in paragraph 2.

Article 4

1. Representatives shall vote on an individual and personal basis. They shall not be bound by any instructions and shall not receive a binding mandate.
2. (Privileges and immunities of representatives)

Article 5

The office of representative in the Assembly shall be compatible with membership of the Parliament of a Member State.

Article 6

1. The office of representative in the Assembly shall be incompatible with that of:
   – member of the Government of a Member State,
   – member of the Commission of the European Communities,
   – active official or servant of the institutions of the European Communities or of the specialised bodies attached to them.
2. In addition, each Member State may, in the circumstances provided for in Article 7 (2), lay down rules at national level relating to incompatibility.
3. Representatives in the Assembly to whom paragraphs 1 and 2 become applicable in the course of the five-year period referred to in Article 3 shall be replaced in accordance with Article 12.

Article 7

1. . . ., the Assembly shall draw up a proposal for a uniform electoral procedure.
2. Pending the entry into force of a uniform electoral procedure and subject to the other provisions of this Act, the electoral procedure shall be governed in each Member State by its national provisions.

Article 8

No one may vote more than once in any election of representatives to the Assembly.

Article 9

1. Elections to the Assembly shall be held on the date fixed by each Member State; for all Member States this date shall fall within the same period starting

on a Thursday morning and ending on the following Sunday.

2. The counting of votes may not begin until after the close of polling in the Member State whose electors are the last to vote within the period referred to in paragraph 1.

3. If a Member State adopts a double ballot system for elections to the Assembly, the first ballot must take place during the period referred in paragraph 1.

Article 10

1. The Council, acting unanimously after consulting the Assembly, shall determine the period referred to in Article 9 (1) for the first elections.

2. Subsequent elections shall take place in the corresponding period in the last year of the five-year period referred to in Article 3.

Should it prove impossible to hold the elections in the Community during that period, the Council acting unanimously shall, after consulting the Assembly, determine another period which shall be not more than one month before or one month after the period fixed pursuant to the preceding subparagraph.

3. . . . The Assembly shall meet, without requiring to be convened, on the first Tuesday after expiry of an interval of one month from the end of the period referred to in Article 9 (1).

4. The powers of the outgoing Assembly shall cease upon the opening of the first sitting of the new Assembly.

Article 11   (Credentials)

Article 12

1. Pending the entry into force of the uniform electoral procedure referred to in Article 7 (1) and subject to the other provisions of this Act, each Member State shall lay down appropriate procedures for filling any seat which falls vacant during the five-year term of office referred to in Article 3 for the remainder of that period.

2. Where a seat falls vacant pursuant to national provisions in force in a Member State, the latter shall inform the Assembly, which shall take note of that fact.

In all other cases, the Assembly shall establish that there is a vacancy and inform the Member State thereof.

Article 13   (Implementation of Act)

Article 14   (Amendments to Treaty)

Article 15   (Texts of Act)
Annexes I to III shall form an integral part of this Act.

Article 16   (Coming into force of Act)

Annex I
The Danish authorities may decide on the dates on which the election of members of the Assembly shall take place in Greenland.

Annex II
The United Kingdom will apply the provisions of this Act only in respect of the United Kingdom.

Annex III   . . . .

Declaration by the Government of the Federal Republic of Germany. . . .
   (on position of Berlin)

about at this period. (The cushion of the five-year transitional arrangements was not removed till 1978 and the vast deficit only developed with developments in the Common Agricultural Policy and the sharp rise of the pound in international exchanges in 1979.)

In so far as the moves towards direct elections were given prominence in the media it was largely in terms of the Labour Party's internal difficulties. But another theme was the vast salaries that MEPs would receive: the assumption was that they would have to be paid at a common level which could hardly be much less than the Bundestag member's £30,000. In Westminster and outside this caused much resentment at a time when MPs were paid £6,270. It was not until the Summit of December 1978 that it was decided that the payment of MEPs should be determined by national Goverments; the Cabinet decided that British MEPs were to be paid the same as MPs (but without any of their fringe allowances; it was left to the European Parliament to provide for expenses, which it did on a generous scale).

The Government had made some early preparations. In February 1976 it published a Green Paper *Direct Elections to the European Assembly* (Cmnd. 6399). In setting out the matters to be decided by the Community and by Westminster before elections could take place, the Green Paper stressed Britain's commitment to direct elections but expressed doubts about the practicability of holding then as early as June 1978. It envisaged an Assembly of 355 (with 67 British members and an optional dual mandate system) and it spoke of the necessity of Parliament legislating to provide for elections organised much along the lines of Westminster elections. It conspicuously refrained from discussing alternative electoral systems, though it stressed the difficulty of meeting the provision of Article 138 (3) of the Rome Treaty providing for uniform Community-wide arrangements.

On 29–30 March 1976 the House of Commons held its first full debate on direct elections. It was on an adjournment motion and there was no vote but only 10 of the 18 Labour MPs who were called proved to be supporters. The speeches divided 29 to 13 in favour of direct elections but Labour speakers only divided 10 to 8 in favour. Varied points were made, most notably on dual mandates and on voting rights, but the main argument focused on the extent to which the mere fact of direct elections would increase the powers of the Parliament. As so often on European issues, the anti case was most eloquently put by Enoch Powell,

It will not be very long before we shall be told . . . 'What is the point of this House (of Commons) reviewing regulations . . . (which have) already received

---

The coming of direct elections

10 Dec. 1974	Summit agrees to direct elections (see p. 11 for earlier chronology of European Parliament)
17 Feb. 1976	Green Paper on direct elections (Cmnd. 6339)
29–30 Mar. 1976	Debate on Green Paper
12 May 1976	Commons Select Committee established (1st Report, 15 June, H.C.445, 489; 2nd Report, 3 Aug., H.C.515; 3rd Report, 9 Nov., H.C. 715)
12 Jul. 1976	Summit settles on 410 seat Assembly with elections in May or June 1978
20 Sep. 1976	Brussels signing by Foreign Ministers of European Direct Elections Act
22 Mar. 1977	Lib-Lab Pact agreed
1 Apr. 1977	White Paper on Direct Elections (Cmnd. 6768)
20, 25 Apr. 1977	Debate on White Paper
14 Jun. 1977	Prime Minister announces free vote on direct elections and on voting system
7 Jul. 1977	Second Reading of European Assembly Elections Bill carried by 394 to 147
24 Nov. 1977	Second Reading of new European Assembly Elections Bill carried by 381 to 98
13 Dec. 1977	Proportional representation rejected by 319 to 222
17 Jan. 1978	Brussels Summit agrees that 1978 is not possible
26 Jan. 1978	Commons approve guillotine on Elections Bill by 314 to 137
13 Apr. 1978	Lords reject PR by 123 to 68 and 85 to 61
5 May 1978	Royal Assent to European Assembly Elections Bill
21ff May 1978	Boundary Commissions publish draft proposals for Euro-boundaries
4 Dec. 1978	Final Boundary Commission proposals approved by Commons by 112 to 23
24 Jan. 1979	Labour NEC approves manifesto
Jan.–Mar. 1979	Selection of major party Euro-candidates
13 Feb. 1979	Launch of EEC British Euro-publicity
28 Mar. 1979	Government defeat 311–310 leads to general election
3 May 1979	Labour defeated in British general election
7 Jun. 1979	Britain votes in Euro-election
10–11 Jun. 1979	Results announced
17 Jul. 1979	First elected Parliament meets at Strasbourg

---

detailed scrutiny . . . by a directly elected Assembly?' The very fact of direct elections brings about an immense and decisive shift of power and of control . . . from this House . . . to the European Parliament . . . .

As . . . our discussions on direct elections go by, every Member . . . will once again be taking the crucial decision that involves the future political independence of this country and the political power of this House. (H.C. Deb.908 c.1147, 1150)

Sir Peter Kirk on the other side said that while he was a dedicated federalist, he was also a realist – a federal Europe would not come in this generation. The two front-benches were agreed in their restrained support for direct elections. As Mr Callaghan stressed, in his last speech before becoming Prime Minister, no move towards federalism was involved and no new powers were being conferred on the Assembly.

Following this debate, a House of Commons Select Committee was appointed under Sidney Irving to discuss the subject. Between May and November 1976 the committee met 22 times. It received about 100 submissions and it heard 44 witnesses. In its first report on 15 June (H.C. 489, 1975–6) it asked for the Assembly to contain between 350 and 425 members allocated primarily by population and it favoured an election date in May or June 1978. This report was debated on 12 July on the very day when these issues were being settled in Brussels by the Heads of Government and the debate was more concerned with the impropriety of the Government's timing and its alleged contempt for the House than with the actual points at stake. A second report from the Select Committee on 3 August (H.C. 515, 1975–6) considered electoral systems and (with only Jeremy Thorpe dissenting) came down in favour of the traditional first-past-the-post arrangements.

The main arguments in favour of proportional representation have been presented to the Committee as follows:
(i) It could be introduced without undue administrative difficulty, and it avoids the disadvantages inherent in the first past the post system used for United Kingdom Parliamentary elections, which tends to exaggerate the effects of comparatively minor swings in the relative popularity of the two main parties and to lead to under-representation of minority parties.
(ii) It would ensure that the British membership of the European Assembly reflected more nearly the overall pattern of political opinion, both regionally and nationally.
(iii) It would be particularly suitable for a multi-national Assembly, from the membership of which no executive body has to be formed.
(iv) Most other Member States of the EEC use a form of proportional representation. The Community is committed to choosing eventually, perhaps before the second European Assembly elections, an electoral system which will be the same for all Member States. This will almost certainly be a system using some kind of proportional representation. The United Kingdom would stand a better chance of influencing the choice of system for future elections if it was already using a proportional representation system and had some experience of its operation.

Equally strongly held arguments have been adduced by those in favour of the existing first past the post system. The main arguments used are:
(i) If the United Kingdom were to change the electoral system for the first round of elections for the European Assembly, the electoral system would have to be changed twice within a comparatively short period.

(ii) It would not in practical terms be easy on this issue to reach agreement on a particular new system in the time-scale envisaged.

(iii) The first past the post system is familiar to the electors and to the returning officers' staffs. It could be implemented in the time available with little difficulty and there would be no risk that the electorate would become confused by having not only a new tier of elections, but also a new electoral system different from that used for national elections.

(iv) It would be easier for the existing constituency organisations of the political parties to operate.

(v) Voters would identify more easily with their existing Parliamentary constituency.

The Committee are of the opinion that it would not be appropriate to bring in what is for most of the United Kingdom an entirely new method of voting at this stage. Elections for the European Assembly are themselves novel enough and the Committee are much impressed by the argument that a later change will in any event be necessary. The Committee therefore recommend that the first past the post system at present in use for Parliamentary elections should be used in the United Kingdom for the first round of elections for the European Assembly.

In its final report (H.C. 789, 1975–6) the Select Committee summarised its recommendations and, on almost all administrative points, argued that normal Westminster procedures should be followed.

Mark Hagger, in a detailed study of the Euro-elections legislation, noted

As an example of detailed pre-legislative investigation, strongly advocated by some critics of Westminster, the experience of the Select Committee is hardly to be commended.[3]

Only its first reports were debated and that too late to affect the decisions with which it dealt. But, in any case, he concluded

The Committee was characterised by a narrow vision, a failure to search out and investigate real alternatives and an over-whelming concern to meet the June 1978 'indicative target date'.

The Government was slow in responding to the Committee and was much reproached for its delays (particularly in a critical adjournment debate on 25 March 1977) before Merlyn Rees, the Home Secretary, finally embodied the Government's proposals in a White Paper 'with green edges' published on 1 April 1977 (Cmnd. 6768). This concen-

---

[3] V. Herman and M. Hagger, *The Legislation of Direct Elections to the European Parliament* (London 1980) p. 218. Mark Hagger provides a full critique of the preparation and passage of the Act.

trated mainly on electoral systems and left completely open the choice between a Regional List approach, the single transferable vote, and first-past-the-post. But in fact the Cabinet two weeks earlier, on a proposal by David Owen, who had just joined the Cabinet as Foreign Secretary, had decided to support the Regional List system.[4]

The political situation was in flux. On 23 March, after the Cabinet decision but before the White Paper's publication, the Government had staved off defeat in Parliament by agreeing to the Lib-Lab pact with David Steel. One of the Liberals' conditions for supporting the Labour Government for the rest of the session was that legislation for direct elections should be put to Parliament during the summer, with a free vote on proportional representation.

The Government's promise to its European partners to use its 'best endeavours' to get the necessary laws passed speedily was a much less powerful commitment than Mr Callaghan's deal with Mr Steel.

But the legislation was to make little progress that summer. It passed a Second Reading on 7 July by 394 to 147 but got no farther. It had to be reintroduced for another Second Reading in the new session which it received in November by 381 to 98, and spent the winter lumbering through Parliament to the Royal Assent in May 1978.

Considerations of tactics and the European timetable coloured the whole history of the legislation. Some supporters of it, like Douglas Hurd, were willing to accept a majoritarian system because they thought that otherwise the whole project might be jeopardised and because the system was for the first round of elections only; some, like Merlyn Rees, promoted the Regional List system of PR because it would cut out the delays of boundary drawing; some, like John Roper, were ready to offer an arbitrary set of boundaries as an amendment to the Bill in order to get it through in the summer of 1977 in time for June 1978 elections.

On the other hand opponents of direct elections were eager to invoke every possible delaying tactic in order to postpone or frustrate an unwelcome innovation. Eight hundred amendments were tabled and 50 were actually discussed. Nigel Spearing, Peter Shore, Enoch Powell, Neil Marten and many others were persistent and ingenious objectors at every step of the way, with objections of procedure and objections of principle. Many hours were taken up with points of order and essen-

---

[4] He had undoubtedly heard the arguments developed by the Labour Committee for Europe; its leaders had concluded that under a Regional List system selection would have to be devolved to the regions where pro-Marketeers would have a far better chance. They were worried about the possibility of a National List system in which the NEC might dominate the situation and bar all pro-Marketeers.

tially wrecking amendments before Parliament passed a guillotine resolution on 26 January.[5]

The passage of the direct elections legislation was remarkable for several features. Although the Bill had only nine substantial clauses, it received 98 hours of debate on the floor of the House of Commons and it required a guillotine resolution to get it through – and the guillotine was carried by 314 to 137 with opposition support (the only occasion since the war when the bulk of the opposition has actually voted for a guillotine). It was introduced, as we shall see, containing two flatly contradictory sets of clauses, providing for two opposite systems of voting, so that the House could choose. It was carried through with an odd mixture of whipping and free voting, and with a Government agreement to differ that had only the limited precedents of 1975 and 1932 (six members of the Cabinet voted against the Second Reading of the Bill).

The Government advocated proportional representation not only as a sop to the Liberals. The Regional List system was sold to a majority of the Cabinet because it would make the result in seats less disastrous for Labour and because it could be implemented at once, without the delays involved in a Boundary Commission. The Government does not seem to have spent any time discussing alternatives: the single transferable vote, the additional member system and a National List system were dismissed out of hand. But the Regional List system, based on a Finnish model and persuasively advocated by the Liberal psephologist Michael Steed, attracted few convinced supporters. Under it, seats were allocated to the existing standard regions of the country. Each voter cast only one vote, but the votes for all on a party list were to be totalled up and seats were to be divided proportionately between them. It was simple for the voters and it would involve no delay, but it would be dangerously divisive within the parties. The number of seats each party would get in a region would seldom be in much doubt and the real battles would be internal. Labour candidates would be tempted to direct their campaigns much more to differentiating themselves from their colleagues than to crushing the Conservatives. Some at least of the opposition to proportional representation on both sides of the House came from MPs more worried about the party consequences of the specific Regional List proposals than about the principle of PR.[6]

---

[5] The *Tribune* group of Labour MPs recommended voting against the guillotine but the NEC refrained from doing so by 20–7 vote, on the ground that they should not interfere with the PLP. One minister, Tony Benn, voted with the minority.

[6] See p. 184 for an analysis of what might have happened if the Regional list system had been adopted.

The key day in Committee was 13 December 1977 when by 319 to 222 the House voted for first-past-the-post elections in preference to the Regional List system. It was a free vote but the Government mustered great efforts to get a majority of Labour votes in the same lobby as the Liberals, to honour the Lib–Lab pact.

Table 2. Vote on Regional List system, 12 December 1977.

	For	Against	Not voting
Labour	147	115	49
Conservative	61	198	24
Liberals	13	–	–
SNP	–	–	11
Plaid Cymru	2	–	1
Ulster Unionists	–	8	2
Others	1	–	3
	224	321	90

Mr Heath, Mr Pym, Mr Prior, Mr Walker, Mr Younger and Sir Ian Gilmour were among the Opposition figures who voted for PR. Conservative advocates of electoral reform regretted that the issue had been tested on the Regional List system and not on the more acceptable alternative the additional member system. An amendment advocating the additional member system was not called in the Commons and was defeated in the House of Lords on 13 April 1978, by 85 to 61, primarily because its acceptance might delay the passage of the Bill and the calling of direct elections. The Liberals had to be satisfied with Mr Callaghan getting a majority of Labour MPs voting (though not a majority of Labour MPs) to support PR as evidence of the 'best efforts' promised in the Lib–Lab pact. Looking back, David Steel believed that if the Liberals had played their hand more ruthlessly they might have secured proportional representation – its rejection led to the calling of a special Liberal Conference at Blackpool on 21 January 1978 at which a quarter of the representatives voted to end the pact.

Apart from the rejection of the Regional List system the only significant change to the Bill in the course of its passage was the addition on 8 February of a declaratory clause stating that there could be no increase in the powers of the European Assembly unless it had been approved by Act of Parliament. This sop to the anti-Marketeers had been promised at an early stage. It was reflected in Mr Callaghan's October 1977 letter to Ron Hayward (see p. 49 n.) which promised a firm stand against an increased role for the Community. When the clause came to the vote it was approved by 101 to 7.

In the passage of the Bill some other issues had been important. A Nationalist move to adopt the Alternative Vote in single member constituencies was crushed on 12 January 1978 by 226 to 22, and another Nationalist move to increase the representation of Scotland and Wales failed by 132 to 47 on 2 February. A Unionist move to prevent the use of the single transferable vote in Northern Ireland elections went down on 2 February by 241 to 150.[7] A Conservative move to secure voting rights for British citizens resident in Europe was defeated on 8 February by only 160 to 149 (because the Conservative members of the European Parliament session did not return to Westminster for the vote). But the central debate was always on the two major issues. There was the question of principle: should Britain be involved in this election to an international assembly and sacrifice to it some of the unique legitimacy of the Parliament at Westminster? And there was the question of the electoral system: would the adoption of a proportional system for European contests be the thin end of the wedge for its adoption in Westminster elections?

These were great issues but it could hardly be said that the two Houses rose to their challenge. The debates were not of a very high standard. The European Assembly Election Act received the Royal Assent on 5 May 1978 and it was left to the Boundary Commissioners and the Home Office to implement its provisions and to the political parties to find candidates and prepare for the campaign.

In drawing up the 78 European constituencies, the Boundary Commissioners had a far simpler task than in devising boundaries for Westminster seats.[8] They had the Westminster seats, clearly defined, as their building blocks and they had to group them into constituencies

---

[7] The Government, needing the support of the two MPs from the Northern Ireland minority Community and anxious to keep a fair balance in the Province, had from the first insisted on some form of PR for the area; only with PR was there any chance of a Catholic getting one of the three seats allotted to Northern Ireland. For the actual working out of the single transferable vote in Northern Ireland see pp. 137 and 178–80.

[8] One irony of the European Assembly Elections Act that promised to affect the British domestic politics was the provision that the next Westminster redistribution proposals due by 1984 and expected by 1982 should not be presented to the House of Commons for approval until the consequential Euro-constituency changes had also gone through the process of provisional publication and consideration of objection. This provision could delay the coming into force of a Westminster redistribution by a year or so and in some circumstances could mean that an election would have to take place on the old boundaries – or that the uncertainty over whether new boundaries would be in force would cause grave delay and confusion over candidate selection and local party reorganisation.

that would each contain about 500,000 voters. The Government had resisted suggestions that the Boundary Commissioners should be asked to get on with the job while the legislation was still under consideration, but it was plain that they had not been idle. On 21 May 1978, only two weeks after the European Elections Act had become law, they produced draft proposals for England and Wales. Their constituencies in England were all within 11 per cent of the English quota. The Welsh seats were each within 7 per cent of the Welsh quota. In Scotland, the Highlands and Islands constituency was 37 per cent below the quota, but the other Scottish seats were within 17 per cent of it. There was a one month period for objections and 878 were received within the time limit. The Commissions were not empowered to hold any public enquiries, but in the light of the objections they made modifications, affecting ten Euro-constituencies and involving the transfer of 16 Westminster constituencies. In the event none of the changes could have affected the outcome. Their revised recommendations were ready by September but because of a strike at the Stationery Office they could not be released until 23 November 1978. In most areas the parties went ahead, assuming that the provisional recommendations of May would stand but the delay did cause some uncertainty and provided a few who were idle or malcontent with an excuse for inaction.

As the Appendix (p. 182) shows the boundaries could hardly have been any fairer than they were as between the main parties. There was no way in which boundaries could have been drawn to produce a Liberal or a Plaid Cymru seat. An alternative set of boundaries, drawn up independently and published in *The Economist* (30 October 1976) long before the Boundary Commissioners' proposals, would have produced almost identical results.

In drawing up of detailed regulations for the conduct of the election, the Home Office followed the policy implicit in the Act. The draft regulations (Cmnd. 7323) published for discussion in August 1978, sought to make the European elections as similar to Westminster elections as possible. The deposit was to be £500 not £150. Ballots were to be verified and bundled face down locally (on 8 June) before being counted centrally within each Euro-constituency on 10 or 11 June. There were some differences in timing because a local election rather than a parliamentary timetable was followed. Nominations had to be made 27 days (not ten) before the vote. Postal voting lists closed 20 days (not 12) before 7 June.

The draft regulations did not excite much comment and the final regulations that were approved by the House of Commons by 124 to

73 on 14 March 1979 showed only small modifications. The candidate's deposit was raised from £500 to £600 and the number of nominators was cut from 50 to 30 while the expense limit was altered to £5,000 per candidate *plus* 2p per elector (i.e., about £16,000). The regulations, except in relation to the verification of ballot papers and the timetable of nominations, conformed very closely to practice in Westminster elections.

As with Westminster elections a lot of discretion was left to the Returning Officers. In Devon ballots were verified at the level of local government districts while everywhere else they were verified at the level of Westminster constituencies. And the attempt to get the vote counted, as it was throughout most of the rest of Europe (Holland and Ireland excepted) on Sunday night, only succeeded in 49 out of the 78 British constituencies, despite the Home Office provision of extra money for overtime and the encouragement of the broadcasting authorities.

One important but quite accidental by-product of the impending European elections was that it prepared the way for the simultaneous general and local elections on 3 May. Conventional wisdom at the Home Office and among Returning Officers had long ruled out simultaneous elections as legally and administratively impossible. But after Mr Callaghan had decided against an election in October 1978 it seemed increasingly likely that he might want to call one on 7 June to coincide with the already immutable date for the European contest. In Transport House the shortage of money for fighting Euro-elections and the likelihood of a low turnout made simultaneous elections seem increasingly attractive. The Home Office started to explore how to get round the administrative difficulties – the need for special legislation on using the same polling station for two contests, the possibilities of different coloured ballot papers, and, above all, the provision of twice as many ballot boxes as were normally required.

In the early months of 1979 it became clear that the problems were less insuperable than had been supposed, and when the Government was defeated on 29 March, five weeks before the statutory date for local elections (except in London and Scotland), no one seriously argued that simultaneous elections on 3 May would be impossible (as they certainly would have done a year earlier).

The logistics of the election were to proceed smoothly enough. But the enabling Act, though more thoroughly debated in terms of hours per line than most British legislation, hardly reflected the British Parliament at its best. The Government had decided that, to make them

43

more acceptable, European elections should be as like Westminster elections as possible. Nothing in the law, or in the discussion of it, suggested that different rules might be appropriate to contests involving constituencies of half a million electors from those involving 60,000, or that an election which did not determine the complexion of a Government might be different from one that did.

CHAPTER FOUR
Labour

The factors which delayed the passage of the enabling legislation, and which led the Government to frame rules as close as possible to the Westminster rules, had an even bigger impact on the Labour Party outside Parliament than on the Government and parliamentary party. The balance of forces in the party changed a great deal between the Referendum in 1975 and the Second Reading of the European Assembly Election Bill in 1977. For a while, the Referendum had demoralised the anti-Marketeers and encouraged the pro-Marketeers. As time went on, however, it became plain that the magnitude of the pro-Marketeers' victory had weakened their position in their own party. Most activists were strongly opposed to entry into the Community in the early 1970s, and only slightly less strongly opposed to continued membership of the Community in 1975. They had been humiliated by the Referendum result in which, by a narrow majority, Labour supporters had actually voted YES; as victims of humiliation often do, they sought a scapegoat. It was easy enough to find one. The pro-Market campaign had been dominated by the all-party Britain in Europe organisation, headed by Roy Jenkins. Britain in Europe had been lavishly financed by big business; that and the fact that it was an all-party organisation, made it easy for the defeated anti-Marketeers to imply that their defeat had somehow been illegitimate or even unreal. They could indeed point to the way in which the dice had been loaded against them by the Government's stance, by the overwhelmingly one-sided attitude of the press and by the funds provided by big business. Above all, Labour anti-Marketeers resented the 'disloyalty' of the Labour pro campaigners who had colluded with Liberals and Conservatives against the authentic Labour movement. As a delegate told the 1976 Labour Conference,

If ever there was a cooked referendum, that was it. (Applause). . . In that referendum there was ten times as much money spent on putting the case for us as on putting the case against.

Within a year or so of the Referendum, moreover, the Government's economic difficulties gave a further boost to anti-Market feeling in the Labour movement. The left of the party favoured an 'alternative strategy', involving, among other things, the imposition of import controls. Since import controls could produce the required results only if imports from the rest of the Community were controlled along with imports from third countries, this strategy was clearly incompatible with Community membership. Thus, the left were able to argue that Community membership had become a constraint on the adoption of 'socialist policies' by a Labour Government. The sterling crisis in the autumn of 1976 and the deflationary measures made necessary as conditions for the IMF loan which the Government secured to tackle the crisis, made their argument even more attractive than it would have been in any case. So did the electoral and party unpopularity of the deflationary package which the loan entailed. 'Europe' became a scapegoat for domestic economic failure, and for the hardships which failure brought in its train.

The revival of anti-Market feeling was apparent in the Parliamentary Labour Party as early as the beginning of the 1976–7 session; it was partly responsible for the Government's unwillingness to push the legislation for direct elections through Parliament in time to meet the 1978 deadline. It was still more apparent in the party outside Parliament. Anti-Europeanism as such, moreover, was buttressed by more specific objections to direct elections. Anti-Marketeers – in this, at any rate, sharing the attitudes of continental federalists rather than of pragmatic pro-Marketeers in the British Government – sensed that a directly-elected European Parliament would be bound to acquire more power, and to push the Community in a federalist direction. They also believed that direct elections would make it more difficult to reverse the decision taken in the 1975 Referendum at some future date. Some of them may also have feared that if direct elections took place, a separate, 'European' group of elected Labour people would come into existence, with their own funds and their own separate machine. These would belong to a European-wide grouping, and would be independent, or virtually independent, of Transport House, at any rate in the long run. They might be able to fight elections with their own finance, and eventually they might do so under their own separate banner. Ever since 1931, fears of a breakaway have played a potent part of the Labour politics; such fears helped to make some party members even more apprehensive of the whole idea of a directly-elected Parliament than they would have been in any event.

Most, though not all, pro-Marketeers were in favour of direct elections in principle. Few of them had devoted much time to the issue during the Referendum campaign. Nearly all, however, supported the propositions that the European Parliament should be directly elected by the people of the Community and that a structure which most democratic Socialists, on the Continent as well as in Britain, thought excessively bureaucratic and publicly unaccountable should be put under more democratic control. Quite apart from these reasons of principle, moreover, the pros had strong tactical reasons for wanting direct elections. They believed that a directly-elected Parliament would help to 'legitimise' EEC membership, both among the general public and, more particularly, among the rank and file of the Labour Party. They also believed – probably correctly – that direct elections were more popular, or at any rate less unpopular, both with the public at large and with Labour Party activists in particular, than any other aspect of Community membership, and that on this issue it might therefore be possible for them to put the antis on the defensive. But, within the mass party, the pro-Marketeers' case for direct elections carried much less weight than the scepticism of the antis.

The attitudes of the party leadership must be considered against this background. Throughout 1975 to 1977 the Government was carrying through an economic policy which was bitterly unpopular with a large minority of its parliamentary followers, with most of the National Executive of the party and with a substantial majority of party activists in the constituencies as well. Particularly after Mr Jenkins's departure from the Government in September 1976, to prepare for his future post as President of the European Commission, the position of the strongly-committed pro-Marketeers in the Cabinet was very weak. Though supporters of a YES vote in the Referendum outnumbered opponents by two to one, very few of them were deeply committed to direct elections as a matter of principle. The Prime Minister and the Foreign Secretary were both pragmatists on Europe. They were in favour of continued British membership of the Community, but they saw the Community as an association of sovereign states, not as an emerging supranational entity which would one day transcend the classical nation state. For them, direct elections have few attractions in themselves. They were prepared, without enthusiasm, to agree with their Community partners that the European Parliament should be directly elected but they did so only as a concession to what seemed to them an unnecessary, perhaps even undesirable, piece of sentimentality.

Overwhelmingly the most important political priority for Cabinet ministers was to keep the party united behind their economic policy. As we have seen, support for direct elections became a condition of their continued existence in office after the Lib-Lab pact; because of that, and because, other things being equal, they did not want to cause unnecessary offence to their Community partners, they eventually introduced legislation and pushed it through Parliament. But they were not prepared to force the pace, even in the House of Commons, where the pro-Marketeers in the Labour Party were strongest. Still less were they prepared to engage in avoidable conflicts with the substantial anti-Market majority on the party's National Executive. On other issues, the parliamentary leadership fought hard against National Executive opposition. On the direct elections it treated discretion as the better part of valour. It had offended the NEC by the mere fact of bringing in legislation; it did not wish to compound its offence by bringing pressure to bear on the National Executive over the question of how the Labour Party should prepare for the election campaign when it came.

Hence, the National Executive was to play a much more central role in determining the Labour Party's actions in the run-up to the election in June 1979, and, for that matter, during the campaign itself, than is normally the case in domestic general elections. It is clear that the General Secretary, Ron Hayward, and the National Agent, Reg Underhill, believed that it would be folly for the party to stand aloof from direct elections if they took place, and that they also believed that once the Government had introduced legislation in the summer of 1977, direct elections were sooner or later inevitable. Mr Hayward, indeed, warned the party on several occasions, while the legislation was going through Parliament, that the party would have to take part in the campaign eventually. On 28 May 1977 he told the Welsh Regional Council that if the Labour Party boycotted the election,

people would contest the election under some form of Labour banner, with their own well-funded organisation throughout the United Kindom. . . . (Then) we would face the most serious split the party has ever known.

At the July meeting of the National Executive two months later, he repeated the warning; and, after a joint meeting between the National Executive and the Cabinet at the end of November, he said it yet again. If Labour did not fight, he declared,

there would be a rag-bag of politicians who would fight. Some would be former members of the party who would have organisations to support them financially, with people to work for them. We would be on the side-lines and this Party would find itself split between European Independent Labour and the Labour party as you and I know it.

Mr Hayward was not alone in this attitude. On 8 June 1977, John Prescott, now the leader of the Labour delegation in the European Parliament, published an article in *Labour Weekly* arguing that the Labour Party should take part in direct elections when they came, on the grounds that a boycott would inevitably produce a situation in which independent candidates, claiming to represent the Labour movement, would stand in any event, and would benefit from financial support from Community Institutions; this, Mr Prescott added, would create an embryo alternative Labour Party, which would ultimately fight domestic elections as well. He also made the point that the Parliamentary Party had committed itself to direct elections when it approved the terms of the Lib–Lab pact. Even the Labour Safeguards Committee, in its broadsheet published after the 1977 Party Conference, while regretting that direct elections were likely to take place at all, added that: 'We can take the opportunity to have a public debate about the Common Market, and get support for the changes needed to bring power back to national government.'

As the tone of this statement itself suggests, however, the National Executive of the Labour Party took a different line. The 1976 Party Conference voted by 4,016,000 to 2,264,000 that:

This Conference opposes the introduction to Britain of direct elections to the European Economic Community Assembly for which no mandate was given by the electorate at the time of the referendum. Direct elections are intended as a major step towards the merging of this Country in a new superstate which would further weaken the British peoples' democratic control over their own affairs and in which the possibility of carrying out the British Labour Party's basic programmes would be increasingly remote.

The resolution did not receive the two–thirds majority which would have put it into the party programme and made it binding on the leadership. By the autumn of 1977, moreover, it was clear that the Government would not be deterred from introducing legislation by the Party Conference and that, since there was a majority for direct elections in the House of Commons, the Government's legislation would sooner or later reach the statute book.[1] As early as 1976, the Organisation Sub-Committee of the National Executive was instructed to consider the 'mechanics' for Euro–elections if they should come; and Reg Underhill, the National Agent, was authorised to give oral evidence on the Labour

[1] In an unusual move Mr Callaghan on 1 October 1977 during the Party Conference, published a letter to the party's General Secretary, outlining the Government's position. While stressing the commitment to continuing membership and to direct elections, he also emphasised the need to reform the Common Market and to prevent any extension of its role.

Party's views on these to the House of Commons Select Committee. At the same time, however, the National Executive refused to decide whether, in principle, the party should fight the elections if they were held or what policy it should adopt if it did fight.

In November 1977 two motions were put before the NEC. One advocated boycotting the elections. The other reaffirmed the Executive's opposition to the principle, but went on to say that, if the House of Commons passed the legislation then being debated, the National Executive would 'not wish to let the mounting feeling of dissatisfaction with the EEC go unrepresented', and concluded that the Labour Party should contest the elections. The Executive agreed that consideration of these two motions should be postponed until its next meeting in December. On 13 December, it once again decided to postpone consideration of the question until January. In January 1978, it decided that, since it was now clear that elections would not be held in 1978, it should postpone consideration of the matter yet again. It was not until its meeting on 26 April – nearly two weeks after the European Council had decided that the elections would take place in June 1979 – that the Executive finally passed the motion reaffirming its opposition to the principle but saying that, if the House of Commons passed the legislation, the Labour Party should participate. An amendment moved by the pro-Marketeers, deleting the reference to the 'mounting feeling of dissatisfaction with the EEC', was defeated. The Executive then passed the resolution by 17 votes to 0, with the five pro-Marketeers abstaining. It was not until July 1978 that the National Executive instructed the National Agent, Reg Underhill, to go ahead with preparations for Labour's campaign. As late as 11 September, the Home Policy Sub-Committee of the NEC made a further attempt to delay the elections on the grounds that the Labour Party could not afford to contest them in 1979. Mr Benn was asked to convey this view to the Prime Minister, who rejected it.

Meanwhile, however, Reg Underhill, and the Assistant National Agent, Walter Brown, had gone ahead with drawing up plans for a procedure for candidate selection. These were laid before a group of senior Regional Organisers in October 1978. They were designed to keep the procedure as close as possible to Westminster procedure. Each ward branch or affiliated organisation could nominate candidates to the Westminster constituency general management committees. The Westminster GMC could then forward up to three names to the 'European Selection Committee', which would consist of 20 nominees from each Westminster constituency. The European Selection Committee would approve a short list of candidates who would be interviewed and voted upon by its full membership (ranging from 120 to 200 depending on the number of Westminster seats involved), using the same exhaustive balloting system as a GMC choosing a Westminster candidate. The Regional Organiser or his Deputy would supervise the proceedings and guarantee that due procedure had been observed.

There was to be no vetting of candidates. Anyone whose name was approved by his constituency party could have his biographical particulars circulated on an advisory official list of potential Euro-candidates, and 148 did so. But in fact the list carried little weight. Only 20 of the 78 who were chosen, and only three of the 17 actually elected, appeared on this list. As in the Westminster procedure, anyone accepting nomination had to sign a form guaranteeing that he would abide by the party manifesto and on 12 March 1979, the NEC also decided that candidates must promise that any research money coming to the group as a whole should be put under Labour Party control.

There was some argument over this form being more elaborate than the usual Westminster one. There was also some consciousness that the guarantee to abide by the manifesto had a rather different significance when the text of the manifesto was already available than in Westminster elections, in which candidates normally sign the guarantee long before the publication of the manifesto. Moreover, there was an inherent conflict with the European Parliament's rule that no MEP should be subject to a binding mandate. The research money promise was inoperative from the start since European research money would not in any event be distributed in that way.

In November the NEC approved the Underhill plan without much argument and, without waiting for the final promulgation of the constituency boundaries, the constituency organisations were set up. The National Agent proposed a timetable by which nominations would be completed by the end of January and selections by the end of February. There were, inevitably, complaints about the rush, but in general the timetable was adhered to. The greatest cause of delay was the initial refusal by a few anti-market constituency parties to take any part in the process. Walsall North, Lincoln, Ilkeston and Derbyshire North-East were among those which stood out, but in the end virtually all played some part in the selection process (see p. 60 ff.).

The selection process provoked surprisingly little acrimony in the party. The production of a manifesto on which to fight the election was a different matter. For reasons discussed elsewhere (pp. 8–9), there was a paradox in Labour's European position. In policy, it was the least 'European' British party; at the same time it was more deeply enmeshed in a trans-European structure than any of its rivals. In April 1974, the

Community Socialist Parties set up a revised 'Confederation of the Socialist Parties of the European Community'. Labour was entitled to membership of this body, but as part of its policy of boycotting all European institutions until a future Labour Government should have renegotiated the Conservative's terms of membership, it refused to join. As with its participation in the European Parliament, however, it lifted its boycott after the 1975 Referendum. In November 1975, the International Sub-Committee of the NEC decided that the International Secretary, Jenny Little, should attend Confederation meetings as an observer. In March 1976, the Executive accepted a recommendation made by the International Committee that Labour should join the Confederation altogether.

The implications of Confederation membership turned out to be more far-reaching than most of the still largely anti-Market National Executive could have appreciated when it decided to join. The Confederation set up four working parties to prepare a draft of a possible Confederation manifesto for the direct elections when they came. The Labour Party refused to participate in these working parties, although Ian Mikardo and Jenny Little were now regularly attending confederation meetings together with John Prescott, who came as a member of the Bureau of the Socialist Group.[2] On 7 June 1977, the Confederation's Bureau Meeting in London adopted a draft manifesto prepared by the working parties. The Labour Party was not fully represented at the Bureau meeting – it was a Bank Holiday in Britain. Partly because of the absence of the British, the Confederation draft manifesto was a strongly 'integrationist' document. It began with a chapter on the Community's institutions, asserting roundly that:

there is . . . not enough democratic control over those areas which cease to fall within the sphere of competence of the National Parliaments when they become the responsibility of the Community. Social and employment policy, agricultural and regional policy, external trade and development aid, and environmental and consumer protection are of great importance to the well-being of the European citizen. These policies are now determined partly at European level but are not subject to the Parliamentary decision-making process.

It followed, the draft went on, that powers 'lost by the National Parliaments' should be 'transferred to the European Parliament'; and, *a fortiori,* that the European Parliament should gain certain powers. More specifically, the draft urged that Parliament should 'exercise a legislative

---

[2] Even before the NEC agreed to take part in direct elections, John Prescott had negotiated for an increased allocation to the Labour party of the Socialist Group's subsidy for 'information' activity.

function', that Commissioners should be appointed with the assent of Parliament and that 'as a first step towards making the Community more democratic, the Council should undertake to consider initiatives and opinions of the European Parliament and report to it within a certain period on action taken'. Later sections came out in favour of European monetary union, called for a 'forward-looking structural policy for the various industrial sectors' and demanded the extension of the European Regional Fund.

This went much too far for the Labour Party; on 6 December 1977, the International Sub-Committee of the NEC rejected it without discussion. But the Labour Party was not the only Community party which found the draft difficult to accept. The French and Danish Socialist Parties were equally critical of it; even the Dutch were far from enthusiastic. Originally, it had been intended to submit the draft to national parties for consideration, and to hold a conference in February 1978 to adopt a final draft. By the end of 1977 it was clear that too few constituent parties would accept even the broad outlines of the draft for this to be possible. In January 1978 the Bureau of the Confederation met in the European Parliament building in Luxembourg to consider the comments of the national parties. Ron Hayward and Reg Underhill attended the meeting on behalf of the Labour Party – the first time they had visited the European Parliament. At this meeting Mr Hayward reported that the Labour Party National Executive had not properly discussed the draft as yet, since it had not yet officially decided even to participate in the elections. The National Executive would be discussing the question of participation for the first time the following week. However, the International Committee had looked at the manifesto and had condemned it as 'federalist'. The clear conclusion was that it was impossible to produce a manifesto acceptable to all nine parties. Accordingly, it would be better to produce a short collection of 'guidelines', allowing each party to fight separately, but in some kind of loose association. In the end, it was agreed that there should be a meeting of the nine party leaders in April or May 1978 to decide, in principle, what form the Confederation's election document should take; that this would be followed by a congress representing all the member parties in the autumn; and that the party leaders would have to choose between two possible options – a short general statement of principle, and a more specific statement committing the Confederation to a clear position on at least some of the concrete questions facing the Community.

There then ensued a complicated series of comings and goings, in which four groups of actors took part. In the first place, there were the

British anti-Marketeers, who commanded a majority of the National Executive of the Labour Party. Secondly, there were the British pro-Marketeers – a small minority of the National Executive, but a minority of some significance, by virtue of their informal links with the 'integrationist' social-democratic parties on the Continent. Thirdly, there were the 'integrationist' social-democratic parties themselves – notably the Germans. Finally, there were the non-British, anti-integrationist parties – principally, the Danes and the French. The attitudes and objectives of each of these four groups need to be considered in turn. The British anti-Marketeers were coming reluctantly to accept that direct elections were inevitable, and that – largely for the reasons so frequently and so powerfully adduced by Ron Hayward – the Labour Party would have to fight them when they came. They were anxious to fight the elections on as strongly an anti-European platform as they could. On the other hand, they were reluctant to do so in complete isolation from the rest of the socialist camp – not least, because the Confederation had funds from the European Parliament to spend on a direct-election campaign, while the Labour Party would find it hard to raise money for an election in which its backers took little interest. They could not accept a manifesto of the 'integrationist' kind which had been produced by the Confederation working parties in the summer of 1977. They were, however, prepared to accept loose and non-committal 'guidelines' of the sort which Mr Hayward had mentioned in his statement to the Bureau meeting in Luxembourg in January 1978.

For its part, the British pro-Market minority was desparately anxious that the Labour Party should not fight the elections separately from the rest of the Confederation. They feared that if the Labour Party went its own way, it would fight on a virulently anti-European manifesto, and that it would be difficult, if not impossible, for pro-Marketeers to stand as Labour candidates if that happened. More generally, they also saw it would be an enormous advantage to their cause if Labour fought in association with the other Community socialist parties, because this would enable them to argue that the Community was not, as the antis claimed, irrevocably un-socialist, and that it was possible for British Labour, in association with other socialist and working-class parties, to change it from within. Left to themselves, the pro-Marketeers would have been happy to fight on the draft manifesto produced by the working parties of the Confederation in the summer. But they recognised that, the NEC being what it was, the Labour Party would never accept a manifesto of that kind. Hence, it was strongly in their interests that the Confederation should produce a much more general, less 'integrationist' and less 'committal' document, which the Labour Party could accept. That view, it can safely be assumed, was made clear to the 'integrationist' member parties of the Confederation.

The view of the 'integrationist' parties themselves was somewhat more complicated. In their countries 'Europe' was popular. They feared that their Liberal and Christian Democratic opponents would gain votes in the elections if they were able to present the Socialists as being, in some way or other, lukewarm about further integration. What the 'integrationist' Socialist parties wanted, therefore, was a manifesto making it clear to the electorate that they were as strongly committed to further European integration as were the parties of the right. On the other hand, the 'integrationist' parties were – almost by definition – particularly conscious of the dangers to themselves of a split in the Confederation. They saw that if the British Labour Party, in particular, refused to accept a Confederation manifesto at all, and fought the elections on a manifesto drawn up by itself, with no reference to the views and aspirations of its continental sister parties, the end result might be the election to the European Parliament of a block of Labour anti-Marketeers, who would be so anti-European in their orientation as to refuse to join the Socialist Group. It was worth paying a high price to avert that threat.

Meanwhile, the Danish and French parties – though not as 'anti-integrationist' as the British – were clearly unhappy about the draft manifesto produced by the Confederation working parties, and reluctant to commit themselves to anything as 'integrationist' as that. Thus, all four of the groups of actors mentioned above, albeit for different reasons, converged on what might be called the 'Hayward solution' – a general statement of aims, which would leave it open for each affiliated party to fight the elections on its own lines. Accordingly, nothing more was heard of the draft manifesto prepared by the Confederation working parties in 1977. It gradually became clear that a general statement of 'guidelines' was all that was at issue.

Yet even the apparently innocuous 'Hayward formula' contained more pitfalls for the British anti-Marketeers than they could have expected when they agreed to it. The conference of party leaders finally took place in Brussels at the end of June 1978. It was a star-studded gathering, including Willy Brandt from Germany, François Mitterrand from France, Bettino Craxi from Italy, Joop Den Uyl from Holland and Anker Jørgensen, the Prime Minister of Denmark. Present as observers were Mario Soares, the leader of the Portuguese party, and Felipe Gonzalez, the leader of the Spanish party. Alone among the participating parties, the British did not send their leader. Mr Callaghan had been invited, but although he had announced his intention of going, the British Labour Party was represented in the end by Ian Mikardo and Ron Hayward.

The assembled party leaders agreed to a draft declaration couched in fairly general terms, setting out a Socialist approach to the problems faced by the Community and its Member States and emphasising, in particular, the 'grave problem' of unemployment, the 'trend towards less equality and solidarity as seen in the ever-widening gulf between the rich and the poor throughout the world and within the European Community', and the danger that 'uncontrolled growth in production and consumption, especially in the wealthier regions of the world, is being achieved at the cost of exhausting and polluting the environment and of declining living and working conditions for millions of workers'. In a document of 31 clauses, virtually no mention was made of the Community as such, though there were a few references to 'Europe' and to 'European solidarity'. It was a platform for a series of national election campaigns – not for a co-ordinated European campaign. However, it did make one mention of the European Parliament; and that mention was more significant than might appear at first sight. It ran as follows:

The directly-elected European Parliament must initially develop within the framework of the existing treaties. We recognise that any further transfer of powers from national governments to the Community institutions or from national parliaments to the European Parliament can take place only with the clear and direct assent of the national governments and parliaments.

Clearly, this marked a big change from the 'integrationist' assertions of the original Confederation draft, and represented a significant concession by the 'integrationist' member parties. On the other hand, the text of the paragraph was by no means as 'anti-integrationist' as most British anti-Marketeers would have preferred. For although it made it clear that there could be no increase in the powers of the European Parliament without the agreement of national Governments and national Parliaments, it explicitly recognised that powers might be transferred from national Governments to Community Institutions, and did not commit the signatories to oppose any such transfer. In January 1979, the long-awaited conference of Confederation parties met in Brussels to adopt an 'appeal to the European electorate', based on the statement agreed to by the party leaders in June. It differed hardly at all in content from the June declaration, though it made more acknowledgement of the elections. The paragraph on the directly-elected Parliament, emphasising that its powers would have to develop within the framework of the existing treaties, but implying that there was nothing objectionable in such a development, remained in place, despite a last-minute demand by the chief British representative at the January conference, Tony Benn, who tried to delete it from the final text. Since the paragraph had originally been drafted by Ian Mikardo, this attempt was strongly resisted; and in the end, Mr Benn gave way. The appeal was agreed unanimously, the British Labour Party's agreement being made manifest by the signature of Mr Benn. It is doubtful if he foresaw how valuable his signature would be to the pro-Marketeers.

In the manoeuvring over the Confederation's appeal to the electorate, the anti-Market majority on the NEC had conceded more than it had gained; the net effect of the whole episode had been to tie the Labour Party more firmly into a transnational party structure and to give the pro-Marketeers some useful ammunition in internal party arguments. But, in the manoeuvring which took place in late 1978 and early 1979 over the Labour Party's own manifesto for the Euro-elections, the boot was on the other foot. Two questions had to be settled. Who was to produce the manifesto? What was it to contain? On both, the pro-Marketeers were thoroughly defeated.

According to Clause Five of the Labour Party constitution, Labour manifestos in general elections are discussed between the National Executive and parliamentary party. In practice this has meant that, when the election is fought by an incumbent Labour Government at any rate, the contents of the manifesto are determined primarily by the Prime Minister and Cabinet. But the party constitution says nothing about elections to a European Parliament; Clause Five therefore did not apply. Past precedent offered no guidance either. The role of the parliamentary leadership in general election manifesto-writing springs from the fact that the manifesto has to be implemented by the parliamentary leadership when the election is over, and that it is accountable to the House of Commons and the country for doing so. In the Euro-election, none of this was true. The parliamentary leadership was not standing in the Euro-election, and would have nothing to do with the way in which the manifesto was implemented. It could be argued that it therefore had no more status in the matter than a county Labour group would have in drawing up a national manifesto. If anyone could claim a position analogous to that of the Prime Minister and parliamentary party in a general election, it was presumably John Prescott and his colleagues in the outgoing Labour Group at Strasbourg. But even they were not standing for election to the new Parliament, and would have no say in deciding how the new Labour members would interpret their mandates. In these circumstances, it was difficult to contest the view that the Euro-manifesto would have to be produced by the NEC, and by the NEC alone.

That view would have had attractions for the NEC at any time. It was doubly attractive in the closing months of 1978 and the early months of 1979. In the Cabinet, the left was in a minority. In the NEC it had a majority. It was hardly surprising that the left-wing minority in the Cabinet should have wanted to call in the NEC to redress the Cabinet balance. The left knew that if the general election manifesto were drawn up by the Prime Minister and Cabinet, with only token consultation of the NEC, the 'socialist' commitments which they wanted to see would be watered down or omitted. Their only hope of obtaining a general election manifesto of the sort they wanted was to break the Prime Minister's monopoly of the manifesto-writing. For reasons quite unconnected with Europe, therefore, the left was anxious to establish a precedent for NEC control over the production of a manifesto, and would have wanted to assert the NEC's right to exclusive control over the Euro-manifesto even if they had not cared about its contents.

In fact, they did care about it contents. For there was a certain ambivalence in the left's approach to the Euro-election. They did not want a directly-elected European Parliament at all; if they were forced to have one, they did not, on one level, want to take part in it. Nor, however, did they want its Labour members to be pro-Marketeers. Once it had become clear that the elections would take place whether the Labour Party liked it or not, the anti-Marketeers on the NEC were torn between their desire to disparage the elections and undermine the legitimacy of the directly-elected Parliament that emerged from them, and their desire to make sure that Labour's representatives at Strasbourg were reliably anti-Market. In most cases, the latter impulse was stronger than the former; and from the anti-Marketeers' point of view it therefore became important to ensure that as few pros as possible were selected as Labour candidates. One way of doing this was to produce a Euro-manifesto so anti-European in tone that it would be difficult for pro-Marketeers to stand on it in the first place, or to behave in a pro-Market fashion once they had been elected. These 'European' considerations were buttressed by domestic considerations. By early 1979, in the depths of the 'winter of discontent', few Labour MPs believed that their party could win the general election when it came. Both factions in the party were manoeuvring for position in the post-election inquest which they secretly believed to be inevitable. The left almost certainly hoped to use Community membership as a stick with which to beat the right; it was good tactics from their point of view to prepare party opinion for the post-mortem which they expected to follow the election by fostering anti-Market opinion within the party, and by doing all they could to put the pros on the defensive. A vigorously anti-European Euro-manifesto would serve a useful purpose in that regard as well.

Had Mr Callaghan and his ministerial colleagues been determined to fight off the National Executive's attempt to control the production of the Euro-manifesto, they might have succeeded. But for the reasons given above, they were reluctant to engage in a serious struggle with the NEC majority on a European issue. The National Executive's attempt to determine the shape of the Euro-manifesto does not appear to have been contested at all. It was simply assumed by all concerned that the manifesto would be produced in Transport House, and that Mr Callaghan and his Cabinet would play no part in it. John Roper, the Chairman of the Labour Committee for Europe, tried informally to persuade the Prime Minister that, since Labour's objectives in the Community could not be achieved exclusively through the European Parliament, it followed that the parliamentary leadership should have some say in the production of a Euro-manifesto. Whether any notice was taken of this initiative is not clear. What is clear is that, in the end, the manifesto was drawn up exclusively by the NEC.

It was a remarkable document, hostile to the Community and all its works. It contained a strong implicit attack on the pro-Market attitudes of the parliamentary leadership. It set out a list of 'reforms' which were clearly incompatible with the principles on which the whole Community structure is based. Above all, it implied that the Labour Party might at some time in the future come out in favour of withdrawal. It declared in the opening section,

The promises and forecasts of the benefits that joining the EEC would bring have been shown to be false.

Unlike the Tories and Liberals who made these promises so freely, the Labour Party warned the British people in 1975 of the dangers of Common Market membership. Today we stand by everything we said.

The implication that Mr Callaghan and Sir Harold Wilson had been acting disloyally in advocating continued membership of the Community in the 1975 Referendum was not lost.

The manifesto then denounced the Common Agricultural Policy as 'an expensive farce'; declared that Community membership had 'gravely weakened' Britain's 'right to democratic self government'; promised that the Labour Party would 'vigorously oppose any moves' towards federalism; insisted that the European Parliament should not acquire more powers; and demanded the amendment of the 1972 European Communities Act 'so as to restore to the House of Commons the power to decide whether or not any European Economic Community regulation, directive or decision should be applicable to the United Kingdom'. Since the 1972 European Communities Act flowed directly from the Treaty of Accession, this was, of course, tantamount to a call for withdrawal. In the circumstances, it was almost redundant to include a penultimate paragraph declaring that

if the fundamental reforms contained in this manifesto are not achieved within a reasonable period of time, then the Labour Party would have to consider very seriously whether continued EEC membership was in the best interests of the British people.

When news of the National Executive's work percolated through to the pro-Market camp it caused a good deal of consternation. The pro-Marketeers knew that they had too few votes on the NEC to stop an anti-European manifesto from being produced. The Prime Minister and his Cabinet colleagues were preoccupied with the upsurge of industrial unrest which was to destroy Labour's chances of victory in the general election a few months later, and they were in any case disinclined to engage in a head-on battle with the NEC on this issue. It was too late to try to set up a separate, pro-Market Labour organisation to fight the elections independently of the official Labour Party; in any case it was doubtful if any Labour pro-Marketeers would be willing to risk expulsion from the Party by doing so. After much agonising, the pro-Marketeers in the Parliamentary Labour Party therefore decided that their only hope was to 'de-legitimise' the National Executive manifesto, and to do all they could to ensure it was not taken seriously in the party.

To this end, they organised an outcry in the PLP about the National Executive's failure to consult it, and managed to carry a motion instructing the PLP chairman, Cledwyn Hughes, to write a letter of protest to the NEC. But although the pro-Marketeers were well enough organised to pack the first of two PLP meetings on the issue in January, they omitted to pack the second. The end result of their manoeuvre was that the PLP passed a resolution moved by Eric Heffer, endorsing the NEC's Euro-manifesto, and calling on all Labour MPs to rally opinion behind it. Their second manoeuvre was more successful. This was to publicise within the party the Confederation of Socialist Parties' appeal to the electorate, and to publicise the fact that Mr Benn had agreed to it in the name of the party – thus implying that it had equal status with the Labour Party's own manifesto, and that Labour candidates in the Euro-election were standing on it as well as on the Labour Party's own manifesto.

The process of selecting candidates took place against this background.

For would-be candidates themselves, it was often a hectic and expensive affair. While many were content to take their chances only in their own localities, some rushed around the country, addressing ward parties and union branches, deciding in the light of railway timetables and personal enthusiasms, and of sometimes conflicting reports on the state of opinion in different parties, which invitations to pursue and which to abandon. It was an equally hectic process for the two organised Labour Party factions on the European question – the Safeguards Committee and the Labour Committee for Europe. Both played important roles in the choice of candidates. Neither played as important a role as it would have wished to play. Both displayed endearing mixtures of enthusiasm and inefficiency.

The Labour Safeguards Committee had produced an updated criticism of the consequences of Community membership on each anniversary of the 1975 Referendum; it had held well-attended fringe meetings at each Labour Party Conference; and it had sponsored the key anti-Market resolutions in 1976 and 1977. It had close links with the anti-Market forces on the NEC. Hilary Benn, one of its most active members, was in close touch with his father while the NEC was drawing up the manifesto. The Labour Safeguards Committee wrote to all candidates who had put their name on the official list, asking if they wanted to be recorded as being in support of the Committee's position; 50 or so did so. It made informal use of contacts around the country to support the prospects of friends and sympathisers. Ron Leighton, from 1962 a central figure in Labour opposition to the Market, attracted particular support. His name was pushed in every area of the country and he was put forward by 50 wards or branches in 16 constituencies. The fact that he was unsuccessful everywhere is an indication of the limits of the Labour Safeguards influence.[3]

There were other indications as well. Bryan Gould MP, one of the most articulate and effective members of the Labour Safeguards Committee, had put forward a series of questions which anti-Marketeers should ask at selection conferences. These were widely publicised in *Tribune,* which acted as a forum for the anti-Market forces. But they were almost certainly counter-productive. A leading Labour pro-Marketeer pointed out that he could honourably answer 'yes' to four of the seven questions; as for the rest, he had suitably well-prepared and pugnacious answers, and was ready to show up any

---

[3] However, a paradoxical by-product of his efforts was that in April 1979, when the European selections were over, he was chosen in the hasty election-eve choice of a Westminster candidate for Newham North East, which lay within the East London Euro-constituency where he had been particularly active.

interrogator as a mouthpiece of outsiders. At least one Labour Regional Organiser ruled the questions out of order, and they were in fact only used to a very limited extent. A more embarrassing tactic of anti-Marketeers at selection conferences was to ask would-be candidates if they had any reservations about the manifesto. The neatest answer was to ask 'Which manifesto? – The NEC document of January 1979, or the Euro-manifesto, which Tony Benn had also signed?' One standard and applauded line was 'I support the Socialist element in each manifesto'. The anti-Marketeers could protest that the NEC manifesto was the only one to which would-be candidates had committed themselves to subscribe, but the pro-Market candidates did not have much difficulty in obfuscating the issue.

The Labour Committee for Europe had a card-index of members and of supporters, largely compiled during the 1975 Referendum and, under the guidance of its secretary, Jim Cattermole, a former Labour Regional Organiser, information was exchanged and pro-Europeans were encouraged in promising directions. Leading members of the Labour Committee for Europe – Shirley Williams, Bill Rodgers, Dickson Mabon, Tom Bradley, John Roper and others – together with a large number of sympathetic MPs did what they could to put would-be candidates in touch with well-disposed local activists. But co-ordination was lacking. In some Westminster constituencies three anti-Marketeers were short-listed to the European Selection Committee only because no pro-Marketeer had been put forward. On the pro-Market as on the anti-Market side, the picture was one of well-meaning confusion, rather than machiavellian conspiratorial skill. There was no central body with the resources, the knowledge, the competence, or even the contacts, to see that gaps were filled.

On the whole, the selection process went more smoothly than many had feared. It was too diverse and too localised for central manipulation; even local manipulation was more difficult than in Westminster selection conferences, since the Euro-constituencies were so big that it was almost impossible for any single faction to deploy sufficient strength in the whole area. In a few cases there were procedural rows over the short-listing, notably in London South Inner, which led to meetings being held a second time and which delayed a final outcome. In some hopeless seats the shortage of candidates caused trouble. Three candidates were called to the Cotswolds selection on 25 February but only one turned up; he refused to be considered alone and a new meeting, with new candidates, was finally held on 8 April. In the Highlands and Islands (600 miles from end to end), where, as in all Scottish seats, selections were delayed until after the Referendum on 1 March, great doubts were expressed about fighting at all. The selection was finally decided by a postal ballot, which by a narrow margin, produced a majority in favour of fighting and a choice between the only two candidates on the short list.

In more promising seats, the fight was more serious. As in Labour selections for Westminster seats, the fiercest struggle often took place at the short-listing stage. Some rough politicking was alleged to be behind the exclusion of Sir Geoffrey de Freitas from the Birmingham North short list and of Peter Jackson from the Liverpool one. Gwyn Morgan, once Assistant General Secretary of the party, and subsequently George Thomson's Chef de Cabinet in Brussels, was excluded from the South Wales short list, in spite of having more local nominations than any other candidate. Efforts to pack the short list or to exclude particular people often backfired. However, in Greater Manchester West, when the selection conference refused to reinstate Barbara Castle and Ron Leighton to the short list, the Salford delegation stormed out, thus allowing a pro-Marketeer to be nominated.

Trade Unions played a smaller role than in Westminster selections. Many found that their rules would not allow sponsorship for an election other than a parliamentary or a local election. In the end the NUM partially sponsored Michael Gallagher in Nottingham as well as Stephen Bundred and Joe Holmes, both miners officials in the hopeless seats of London South East and Kent East. But the Cooperative Party was not restricted and it sponsored five candidates (two pros and three antis). Unions were not totally inactive, centrally or locally. On the pro-Market side there was some helpful co-ordination by APEX and the GMW; ASTMS and the TGW gave some help to the antis. It was agreed, however, that at selection conferences unions should not supply more than a third of each Westminster constituency's delegation. Partly because of this, and partly because of the size of the Euro-constituencies, no selections were dominated by union influences, though Michael Gallagher in Nottinghamshire may have owed his victory at the selection conference to the fact that he was a miner.

Given the general mood of ordinary party members, the pro-Marketeers fared better than had seemed probable at the start. In some places, where local constituency organisations were dominated by the left, pros stood no chance: this was true of most, though not all, of London, and it may have been true in one or two other big cities as well. In most places, however, it emerged that although most party members were instinctively suspicious of, and perhaps even hostile to, the Community, the issue was not very salient for them. Vehement antis, who gave the impression that they sought nomination only to wreck

the Community or to get Britain out, alienated moderates and pragmatic local councillors. In one branch selection conference in the
North-East, an anti who had just delivered an impassioned onslaught
on the Community was disconcerted to be told: 'Sending you to
Strasbourg would be like sending Guy Fawkes to Westminster.' Even
anti-Marketeers confessed that it was difficult to vote for a would-be
candidate who appeared to be seeking election to a body of whose
existence he disapproved. Calls for withdrawal rang particularly false;
who would take the trouble to get himself elected to a Parliament,
audiences tended to ask themselves, merely in order to leave it?
Moreover, selection conferences seemed to want candidates who
sounded as though they knew what they were talking about; vehement
antis were less likely to give that impression than pros or uncommitted
pragmatists.

If vehement antis were at a disadvantage, however, so were long-
standing and well-known pros. In striking contrast to what was
happening in the Conservative Party, Community officials and former
Community officials fared extremely badly. Several looked for a seat,
sometimes only informally, but none was selected. On a very rough
assessment just over 30 of the Labour candidates could be classed
as pro-Marketeers on the basis of past membership of the Labour
Committee for Europe or their own statements; at the time of the
election it seemed to us that the remainder divided evenly between
'hard' and 'soft' anti-Marketeers although the conduct of one or two of
the 'hard' ones at Strasbourg since the election suggests that we may
have overestimated their numbers.

Sitting Westminster MPs were inhibited from seeking nomination
by a decision of the NEC, requiring any candidate for the Westminster
Parliament to renounce his candidature before putting his name forward for a Strasbourg seat. In practice, this meant that a Westminster
MP had to abandon his Westminster career, not merely to stand for the
Strasbourg Parliament, but even to seek nomination for it. In the end,
only three Westminster MPs sought nomination for Strasbourg constituencies – Barbara Castle, Sir Geoffrey de Freitas and Colin Phipps.
Barbara Castle, a pugnacious anti-Marketeer, was selected for what
would in normal circumstances have been considered a safe Labour
seat. Sir Geoffrey de Freitas and Colin Phipps, both conspicuous pros,
failed to win selection. The same was true of former MPs. Several
sought nomination. But only two were selected and only one of them –
Peter Jackson, a long-standing anti, who had voted against the Wilson
Government's application to join the Community in 1967 – for
a winnable seat. Gwynoro Jones (Roy Jenkins' former PPS), Dick

Leonard, and Michael Barnes – all strong pro-Marketeers – sought
nomination without success. Among peers sitting in the nominated
European Parliament, it was the same story. Lord Kennet, Lady Fisher
and Lord Murray all had their names on the candidates' list. None was
selected. The only pro-Marketeer with anything approaching a substantial reputation selected to run for the Strasbourg Parliament was
Ernest Wistrich, Director of the European Movement, who was chosen
for Cleveland.

Table 3. Labour candidates

	42 Labour seats★	36 Con-servative seats†	All (78) Labour candidates	(Conservative comparison)
Occupation				
Businessman	4	1	5	(29)
Banker	1	–	1	(4)
Lecturer/teacher	15	14	29	(4)
Journalist	3	2	5	(8)
Lawyer	1	1	2	(9)
Politician	2	1	3	(4)
Professional technician	8	5	13	(5)
Eurocrat	1	–	1	(5)
Public Service	3	6	9	(3)
Farmer	–	–	–	(7)
Union official	3	3	6	(–)
Manual worker	1	3	4	(–)
Age				
Median	40	46	41	(43)
Oldest	67	60	67	(66)
Youngest	31	27	27	(27)
Other qualities				
Peer, VIP, ex-candidate for Commons	19	14	33	(41)
Councillor or ex-Councillor	24	17	41	(15)
Obvious Euro-connections	1	2	3	(31)
Already resident in Euro seat	25	21	46	(21)
Women	7	1	8	(10)
In *Who's Who 1979*	1	3	4	(28)

★ These seats are the 42 in which Labour candidates for Westminster in combination
got more votes than Conservatives in October 1974.

† These seats are the 36 in which Conservative candidates for Westminister in
combination got more votes than Labour in October 1974.

In part this reflected the anti-European attitudes which still pre-dominated in constituency Labour parties. In part it also reflected a revealing mixture of anti-metropolitanism and anti-elitism. The most salient characteristic of the selections was the emphasis on local notables as Table 3 shows. There were far fewer carpet-baggers among the Labour candidates than among the Conservatives. John Mills, in Greater Manchester South, a leading anti-Marketeer, and Ernest Wistrich were the only candidates fighting hundreds of miles from home. Barbara Castle, in Greater Manchester North, was the only Labour candidate actually elected who did not live in or near her constituency – and she had for 34 years been MP for Blackburn, only 30 miles away. Of the 17 Labour MEPs no fewer than 13 had been active figures in local govern-ment within their constituencies. Barbara Castle was the only person of any national reputation among the candidates. Selection conferences often focused far more on parish pump politics than on European issues and explanations of how delegates voted turned more frequently on local rivalries than on ideology. Among Labour candidates as a whole, teachers and lecturers predominated, supplying 29 of the 78. It was a very white-collar contingent, with 64 graduates, though the 10 union officials and manual workers were 10 more than the Conservatives could boast (see p. 78). But, as with the Conservatives, women fared slightly better than in Westminster selections. Very few had obvious European connections but 33 had stood for Parliament and at least 41 had served as councillors. 'They're not a very distinguished lot,' one commented when they at last assembled in Birmingham in May, 'but we do have solid local roots – and solid party roots.' It remained to be seen whether roots could be translated into votes.

CHAPTER FIVE
Conservatives

Direct elections to the European Parliament posed a threat to the Labour Party. For the Conservatives they offered an opportunity. Europe was a Conservative issue. Harold Macmillan had started to bring the party round to the idea of membership of the Community in 1961 and Edward Heath had completed the process in 1972–3. Indeed, entry into Europe was now looked back on as almost the only real achievement of Mr Heath's time as Prime Minister. The process of getting the European legislation through Parliament in 1972 had been accompanied by powerful educational efforts within the party and there were few significant figures left who were against European membership. Even those who had opposed entry were prone, like good Conservatives, to legitimise the *status quo*.

The Referendum of 1975 consolidated the party's commitment to Europe. Though the pro-Europe campaign was headed by Roy Jenkins the Conservatives provided most of the shock troops. As one official suggested, the party, which had just dispensed with its arch-European as leader, seemed eager to give Ted Heath a thumping endorsement for Europe as a going away present. Mrs Thatcher, though by no means as deeply committed a European, strove to keep the party united on the issue and to give Mr Heath and his friends in the party no cause for complaint on this score at least.

Observation of the anti-Europeans in the Labour Party, however, confirmed Conservatives in their pro-Europeanism. The more the Labour left made opposition to Community membership their special issue the more Conservatives were apt to make support for it a Conservative issue. Neil Marten was the only well-known Conservative consistently to oppose the moves towards a directly-elected European Parliament. The fact that he was joined in his efforts by that eminent former Conservative, Enoch Powell, did not make his task easier in loyal Conservative circles. Even the fact that Community membership had not yielded the benefits which had been foreseen at the time of entry produced no sign of hostility to the Market in the Conservative Party, at any rate before it took office again in 1979.

There were anxieties even in the Conservative Party. Europe was a Conservative issue, but it was not a popular issue. The great majority of would-be Conservative candidates for the European Parliament were likely to be enthusiastic pro-Europeans. Some feared that their enthusiasm might be embarrassing, perhaps even electorally damaging. Like their Labour opposite numbers, moreover, some Conservative officials feared that once the votes were counted, the Euro-members might be sucked into an alien structure, retaining only vestigial connections with the party at home and feeling little loyalty to it. Where Labour anxieties paralysed the party machine, however, Conservative anxieties stimulated it. Strenuous efforts were made to ensure that Conservative agents and party workers were made aware of the European Parliament and of the nature of the Euro-member's job; and over a considerable period before the election took place, parties of Conservatives were flown out to Strasbourg and Luxembourg for briefing sessions.

The same applied to the selection of candidates. For quite extraneous reasons, the Conservative Party addressed itself to this problem very early in the day. The National Union of Conservative Associations has always had an uncertain position in relation to the real centres of power in the Party. The leader and the leader's appointees run affairs, not the men from the constituencies. However, there was, in 1976, a particularly lively group of people who were seeking to find a role for the National Union. One of the issues on which the executive of the National Union expressed itself was the arrangements for European elections, should they come about. A vigorous Young Conservative leader, Clive Landa, in his capacity as Vice Chairman of the National Union, put forward a paper suggesting the procedure to be followed and this was eagerly taken up in January 1976 by Sir Charles Johnston, Lord Chelmer and other weighty figures in the executive of the National Union. Clive Landa's original paper was modified in the course of discussions during 1976 and early 1977 but its essentials were preserved.

Central Office was to arrange an approved list of 200 or so candidates. Constituency associations were to band together into European councils to choose their candidate by as democratic a process as possible. The essential principle was that nominations should not come from individual constituencies but from a Euro-Constituency Council executive which put up a short list to a wider body. Most Euro-constituencies would contain both strongly Conservative and strongly Labour areas and it was thought that the co-operation of people from these different backgrounds would foster new kinds of working together within the party.

As the procedures were discussed in the various levels of the National Union and in Central Office there was surprising harmony despite arguments on a few points of detail. However, there was some obstruction at Central Office to the appointment of a full-time European Officer and it was not until February 1978 that Roger Boaden took up the post. He then travelled around the country discussing the administrative arrangements; after the European Assembly Elections Act was passed in May 1978, he helped to set up Regional Conferences at which constituency activists could be briefed on how procedures were to operate. These conferences, held in every Conservative Area between September and November 1978 were well attended.[1] Most of those who came were constituency officers but it was apparent that among the rest there was a certain degree of self-selection by Euro-enthusiasts, eager to take part in Euro-Council activities. The process of setting up Euro-Councils was delayed because although the provisional boundaries had been announced in May there was no finality about the arrangements until late November. Some constituencies jumped the gun and set up their Euro-Councils by early November; all were in being by the middle of December 1978. These councils consisted of six representatives from each of the Westminster constituencies in the Euro-area. They mostly adopted the model rules which had been drawn up by a National Steering Committee under Roger Boaden's co-ordination, though in a few cases there were fractious arguments on detail.

The Conservative attitude to the legislation on European elections had been conditioned by the political situation of the time. They did not know when the Labour Government might fall – it had lacked a clear majority since early 1976. They were of course eager for an election of any sort as soon as possible in order to demonstrate the Government's unpopularity. They also feared that the Labour Government might try to evade its commitments to European elections. There was great unease about the unpopularity of Europe which further wrecking tactics by Labour might create. Conservative actions certainly were always designed to make it easy to hold elections in 1978 so long as that seemed possible. They did not wish to do anything that might give the

[1] From November 1977 onwards the European Conservative Group had also been organising Regional Conferences with the current MEPs talking to Conservative activists and to interest groups.

Government an excuse for backing down or delaying.

This explains Conservative tactics on the Regional List system. Mrs Thatcher was opposed to proportional representation in any circumstances; it could be the thin end of the wedge for proportional representation at Westminster. Even colleagues who favoured proportional representation were unwilling to go along with a scheme such as the Regional List which seemed to threaten Conservative interests. But the majority of the parliamentary party was critical anyway. When the 1922 Committee debated the Regional List on 3 April 1977 there were 21 speakers against to 7 for. Once it was plain that the Government would not get legislation through in time for June 1978 elections, there could be no argument against the single member seat on the grounds that Boundary Commission delays would frustrate an early election. Douglas Hurd, the Conservatives' front-bench spokesman on European matters (under John Davies, the Shadow Foreign Secretary) was himself basically in favour of proportional representation but he switched to the single member seat on the grounds that this would facilitate the legislation; moreover, he saw no point in having two different PR systems for successive elections, since he assumed that by 1984 there would be a common European system: the country did not want 'one innovation after another'. None the less 61 Conservatives did vote for the Regional List system and a number more indicated that they would have supported the additional member system that nearly got through the Lords, if the Government had put that forward.

The most remarkable feature of the Conservative tactics on the Bill was their support for the guillotine on 26 January 1978. Without this Conservative support, the Government might have had difficulty in getting the legislation through. The Conservatives had mixed feelings as they sacrificed some short-term parliamentary tactical advantage to the goal of getting European elections under way.

In the course of 1978 over 900 people sought to be approved as Conservative Euro–candidates. Most were interviewed by Marcus Fox, the party Vice Chairman in charge of candidate selection, and those whom he approved were then interviewed by a small committee, usually consisting of a senior member of the National Union and an MP sitting in the appointed European Parliament and another MP. Their assessments formed part of the evidence for a final decision made by the Standing Advisory Committee on European Candidates. In the end about 200 aspirants were approved. But some of these only made themselves available in their own locality and it was argued later that the number was too small to allow every constituency an adequate range of choice.

The idea of those engaged in selection was broadly to seek the same qualities as for Westminster candidates. However, although it is hard for anyone over 50 to get onto the approved list of Conservative candidates for Westminster, for Europe a wider age range was encouraged. Particular emphasis was placed in the interviews on the would-be candidates' knowledge of Europe and on their suitability to sustain the travelling life of an MEP. Considerable stress was placed on their knowledge of languages. Fears that unsuitable people might be attracted by the rumours of a huge tax free Euro-salary were on the whole not justified and, indeed, when in December 1978 it was announced that Euro-MPs would only be paid a Westminster salary only six candidates dropped out (and one of these soon applied to be reinstated on the list).

In the vetting process considerable stress was laid on party loyalty, although some new recruits to the party, particularly ex-public servants, were admitted. In at least one case a would-be candidate, suspected of being too pro-Heath, was asked to write a letter declaring loyalty to Mrs Thatcher.

Some quite well-established figures were refused places on the list and, in half a dozen cases, intervention from high places led to a decision being reconsidered. At least two of the ultimately successful MEPs failed to be approved and only got onto the candidates' list after representations from higher quarters.

In theory constituencies were not limited to candidates on the official list. Locally nominated candidates could be short-listed and put up for central vetting before the final selection conference. But only one of those eventually nominated (Spencer Batiste, in the unpromising seat of Sheffield) arrived by this path. In one or two other cases, a candidate was injected into the selection process at a late stage – most notably Paul Channon, unsuccessful in Essex North East, but also Lord Harmar-Nicholls, successful in Greater Manchester South.

One issue that caused considerable heartburning was the question of the dual mandate. An article by Ian Waller in the *Sunday Telegraph* of 21 May 1978 suggested that Mrs Thatcher was unequivocally against people being simultaneously MPs and MEPs. This was not exactly the case but for a long time the assumption was made that dual mandates were not in favour and indeed many constituency activists concluded independently that it was impossible for one person to do both jobs. However, almost all the 12 Conservative MPs at Strasbourg were keen to continue with a dual mandate and there were at least a dozen other MPs who aspired to go to Strasbourg without giving up their Westminster seats. In the end the Conservative leadership and the whips realised that it would certainly be desirable to have a few people with a dual mandate. The Chief Whip offered a letter to one MP seeking Euro-nomination which said:

I think that it would be right to say that the Leader's view, which I share, would be very much against many people having a seat both at Westminster and in the European Parliament. Having said that, I believe that there should be certain exceptions. . . .

There is certain to be a major problem in establishing a positive Conservative identity for this new Group. It will, after all, number approximately fifty members, and many of them will not have been involved in any party political activity prior to their election. As a Party, we are determined that this Group will give complete loyalty to both the Conservative Party and to its principles.

In practice two of the four MPs who succeeded in getting a dual mandate, cited to their selection committee a whip's letter of this sort, and two decided that it would be a mistake to do so.

The Conservatives established a European campaign committee under Douglas Hurd in March 1978. This was to bring together MPs, MEPs, the National Union, and Central Office to co-ordinate all preparations for the election and to put forward views on policy to a separate policy Committee. Douglas Hurd, who had been a key figure throughout the passage of the legislation, was now at the centre of election preparations.

Michael Fallon, under Sandy Walker, at the Conservative Research Department (aided by staff from the Conservative Group in Europe) set about preparing a manifesto at the same time as preparing the Conservative *Campaign Guide for Europe* published on 19 February 1979. John Davies, the Shadow Foreign Secretary, had chaired a Manifesto Policy Committee which had included Geoffrey Rippon and Douglas Hurd. But the manifesto was not made the subject of discussion with the existing Conservative European MPs or with those who were being selected to contest the election, nor indeed was it, in any formal way, made a matter of discussion with the secretariat of the Conservative European delegation, even though this had been recruited quite largely from the Research Department.

One of the thorniest problems facing the Conservatives was the leadership of the future Conservative delegation. Sir Peter Kirk had made a considerable impact in Europe as the first leader of the delegation. After his death in April 1977 Mrs Thatcher asked Geoffrey Rippon, a senior ex-Cabinet minister who had managed the entry negotiations in 1971–2, to lead the delegation. Geoffrey Rippon was keen to continue but faced difficulties with his Hexham constituency, which perhaps already felt a bit neglected by him and which was reluctant to support him for the dual mandate. Moreover, Geoffrey

Rippon had been scarred by his failures in 1964–6 when he lost his Westminster seat and was rejected by one or two constituencies before being chosen for Hexham. He was not willing to expose himself to similar rebuffs in pursuit of a Euro-seat, especially as declaring himself a Euro-candidate might lead to trouble in Hexham. On the other hand the Conservative managers found that it was impossible to get a Euro-constituency to forego its right to undertake a serious selection process and to nominate Geoffrey Rippon for the sake of the party. He did have clandestine meetings with safe Euro-seats in the south but they were not willing to consider him if he stayed on in Hexham. After some delays, while alternatives were explored, Geoffrey Rippon gave up the struggle. None of the leading contenders for Euro-nominations seemed an obvious leader for Strasbourg. Therefore, in an inept manoeuvre, a belated attempt was made to get a Euro-nomination in Essex North East for Paul Channon, the Conservative member for Southend West who had been a junior minister in the previous Conservative Government and who had served on the Council of Europe. But the candidates on the Essex North East short list were not prepared to withdraw and the whole plan backfired when David Curry defeated Paul Channon in the final selection conference.

In late February, Geoffrey Rippon abruptly resigned the leadership of the delegation. He had to be persuaded to withdraw his resignation and to carry on until the election in June and it was only near the end of the selection process that Jim Scott-Hopkins, at the time the deputy leader of the Conservative delegation, managed to secure nomination for Hereford and Worcester. He was finally nominated for the leadership by Mrs Thatcher on 28 March, plainly without much enthusiasm (since she had so blatantly passed him over in April 1977 on the death of Peter Kirk).

When the Conservative candidates first assembled together at the Penta Hotel in Kensington, 23–4 February 1979, some resentment was expressed about the party hierarchy's high-handedness both in relation to the leadership of the delegation and in relation to the manifesto.[2] The party authorities explained that in both cases they were only doing what was customary, and that it was necessary to keep the European delegation in harmony with the Westminster leadership. None the less, there was considerable uneasiness. In practice, however, it was recog-

---

[2] But as one insider commented 'But the candidates didn't seem terribly worried by this. This was partly because some of them, having tried to become parliamentary candidates for ages, were only too grateful to have succeeded and didn't want to make trouble and partly because they probably already sensed that it was not to be an election where manifestos mattered much anyway.'

nised that there was no obvious alternative to Mr Scott-Hopkins. The only other senior figures with experience of Europe and the European Parliament were Lady Elles and Basil de Ferranti and it was not felt that either was very appropriate. Neither would be as acceptable as Jim Scott-Hopkins.

The question of Euro-agents aroused continuing discussion. There were some who thought that the Euro-agent could be appointed by the area office and be a deputy central office agent operating both as a supervisor for six or eight Westminster constituencies and as Euro-agent. But this centralising suggestion, though it could have solved many Conservative administrative problems, found little support. In the end no great difficulty arose in getting one of the Westminster agents in each Euro-constituency to act as Euro-agent for the six months running up to the election for a limited fee. In one or two cases the Euro-Council had to make a choice between two aspirants and there were occasional problems when the agent's obligations to the Euro-Council seemed to conflict with his own Westminster constituency duties. Some Euro-agents were very much more active than others. After the election most Euro-agents were continued in office for another six months. In November 1979 more flexible arrangements were approved but there was no rush to adopt the alternative possibilities of part-time or shared Euro-agencies.

The European Conservatives received £270,000 in 1978 and £460,000 in 1979 from the European Parliament for educational purposes and almost all of this must have come to Britain. This was used partly on financing the area conferences which were held in the autumn of 1978 and partly on arranging trips to Brussels, Luxembourg and Strasbourg for candidates, agents and members of Euro-Councils. Six hundred Conservatives went on one-day trips to Luxembourg and 2,200 Conservatives went at some time on a trip to see some part of the European Community in action – and most of these served on a Euro-Council.

The Conservative Party claimed that they had been very scrupulous in their use of the European money. It had not at any point gone into campaigning and, although one or two Research Department activities and salaries were in effect Euro-financed, they had done none of the things that they suspected the Labour Party of doing with its allocation of Euro-money.

Looking back on the Conservative Party's attitude to European elections and their preparation between 1976 and 1979, it is striking how smoothly everything was conducted. Europe was not central to party activity. Domestic politics provided a far more important focus.

Few members of the Shadow Cabinet felt deeply involved in the European issue and it was not a source of controversy within the party. The interested enthusiasts were allowed to get on with the job. A few senior people, especially in the whip's office, developed their own worries about whether the European operation might threaten the stability and unity of the party. The leadership's belated changes of position on the question of who should lead the Conservative delegation, and on the question of the dual mandate, illustrate the potential for confusion that the neglect of the subject could cause. But in fact the party may have benefited from the problems Euro-elections caused. As one Area Agent remarked during the winter of 1978–9, 'Thank God for the Euro-elections. When Jim Callaghan didn't call the election in September, our people were more deflated than Labour's; since we were keyed up to a greater state of readiness. Selecting candidates for Europe gave our workers something to busy themselves with.'

For the candidates themselves the selection process was a remarkable affair. Their availability was not supposed to be known and active canvassing for nomination was firmly frowned upon. Some managed to be quite energetic in taking part in local party functions in areas where they had aspirations, but the real process of candidate selection did not get under way until the beginning of December because of the delay in settling constituency boundaries. Candidates on the approved list were asked to name not more than 15 seats in which they would like to be considered. Some seats attracted as many as 60 or 70 aspirants and some attracted none whatsoever. It was quickly seen that there could be major confusion in the selection process as candidates decided whether or not to wait for a good seat which was selecting later or to tackle a less propitious one selecting first. To some extent the Area Agents persuaded constituencies to arrange their timetable sensibly, so that the less hopeful seats would have a chance of picking up those who had just failed to be selected in the best seats. One or two constituencies that were moving slowly, abruptly revised their timetable when they found that all the most promising candidates were being picked off by seats which were operating more speedily. The first candidate selected was Sir Fred Catherwood who defeated Sir Henry Plumb for the Cambridgeshire nomination on 20 January 1978. John de Courcy Ling was chosen on 25 January for Midlands Central. Most of the better seats selected over the next two weeks but one or two had their proceedings delayed by bad weather, or the disappearance of their short-listed candidates elsewhere. The last selections were for Strathclyde East on 27 March and for Cleveland on 31 March.

The procedure was very similar in most seats. The Euro-Constituency

Council set up a selection committee which interviewed candidates, in some cases up to 30, over two or three days in January. The full Euro-Constituency Council then considered a short list of up to six and sent on two or three names for consideration by a much larger meeting, usually with 20 representatives from each Westminster constituency. In each constituency a local Conservative MP was added to the selection committee and, like the Area Agent who was also present, could monitor and report back on the proceedings. Some MPs were more tactful than others in the exercise of this role. The quality of the interviewing varied, although it was markedly higher in the safer Conservative seats. Shrewd questions were asked about the European Community, though it was noticeable that defence, not officially a subject for the EEC, was frequently raised. Candidates were usually given some opportunity to show their local knowledge and the relevance of EEC aid to specific constituency problems. Occasionally they were tested by a question in French, German or Italian. They were also given the opportunity to indicate how they thought the constituency ought to be fought. Almost always there were questions about how and where they planned to live when they were MEPs. The whole affair was conducted very privately and most Area Agents strove, usually successfully, to keep even the final short list out of the local press.

Pressure groups were less in evidence than many had expected. The most obvious one was the National Farmers Union and it was plain that in one or two constituencies their view was very important; although in a few places they were too energetic and their efforts may have been counter-productive since no constituency actually contains a farming majority. Sir Henry Plumb was alleged to have suffered from over-enthusiastic friends in Cambridgeshire and Devon before he was chosen for the Cotswolds. In Norfolk it was said that no one but a farmer had any chance. In some constituencies, a member of the NFU was co-opted on to the Euro-Council partly with an eye to drawing in campaign subscriptions from farmers. In one or two cases Chambers of Commerce seemed to have made some efforts to affect the selection but in general the testimony of those involved was of genuinely open selections.

Candidates had to make some desperate choices when two interviews occurred on the same day. One who chartered a plane found himself grounded and unable to reach a selection conference where he was well-favoured. A week later he was chosen for a constituency he much preferred. Some candidates enjoyed this hectic selection process but most found it distasteful to rush around selling their personalities in constituency after constituency. One likened himself to Coriolanus, having to show his wounds to the populace, and described what was going on as 'second rate people looking for third rate candidates who they could patronise'.

A certain fraternity developed among the candidates as they bumped into each other in one waiting room after another, and sometimes they exchanged helpful hints. Something of a consensus evolved about their rivals' merits. It was widely felt, at the end, that almost all the best candidates had in fact found a suitable berth. But in the process there were humiliations for leading figures. Sir Henry Plumb, Lady Elles and Jim Scott-Hopkins were each rejected by two constituencies before being chosen for a third.

The most eminent failures were those seeking a dual mandate. Among members of the European Assembly, Lord Reay, Charles Fletcher-Cooke, Sir Derek Walker-Smith, John Osborn and John Corrie, were unsuccessful at selection conferences and one or two others withdrew when they saw how the land lay. There were also a number of Westminster members who tried and were rejected. The most conspicuous, of course, was Paul Channon, with his defeat in Essex North East; Eldon Griffiths in Suffolk, who might have led the delegation, was another well-publicised failure, even though at the last moment he was willing to say that, if selected, he would give up his Westminster seat. Other MPs who were rejected included John Page, Kenneth Warren, John Hunt, Jasper More, Sir John Rodgers and Sir Frederick Bennett. The four MPs who secured a dual mandate were all already members of the European Parliament. Jim Spicer (West Dorset) and Elaine Kellett-Bowman (Lancaster) were chosen for the Euro-constituency which contained their Westminster constituency. Tom Normanton was chosen for one immediately adjacent to his Cheshire seat, while Sir Brandon Rhys-Williams got London South East, which, though no great distance from his home or his Kensington seat, was not adjacent. Jim Scott-Hopkins was defeated in a couple of constituencies that were not near his Westminster seat of Derbyshire West, and when he was chosen for Hereford and Worcester it was only on the understanding that he had abandoned any intention of staying on as an MP. Lord Bethell and Lord St Oswald, among current members of the European Parliament, and Lady Elles and Lord O'Hagan, among former ones, were also chosen.

Conservative selection committees chose quite a wide range of people including a few of considerable substance from outside the ordinary range of politicians. Sir Fred Catherwood, Sir David Nicholson, Sir John Stewart-Clark, Madron Seligman, Basil de Ferranti and Sir Henry Plumb representing large industrial and farming interests, were of a

Table 4. Conservative candidates

	36 Con-servative seats★	42 Labour seats†	All (78) Con-servative candidates	(Labour comparison)
Occupation				
Businessman	11	18	29	(5)
Banker	2	2	4	(1)
Lecturer/teacher	1	3	4	(29)
Journalist	4	4	8	(5)
Lawyer	3	6	9	(2)
Politician	3	1	4	(3)
Professional technician	1	4	5	(13)
Eurocrat	3	2	5	(1)
Public Service	2	1	3	(9)
Farmer	6	1	7	(–)
Union official	–	–	–	(6)
Manual worker	–	–	–	(4)
Age				
Median	48	40	43	(41)
Oldest	60	66	66	(67)
Youngest	27	30	27	(27)
Other qualities				
Peer, VIP, ex-candidate for Commons	26	15	41	(33)
Councillor or ex-Councillor	2	13	15	(41)
Obvious Euro-connections	26	5	31	(3)
Already resident in Euro-seat	8	13	21	(46)
Women	2	8	10	(8)
In *Who's Who 1979*	26	2	28	(4)

★ These seats are the 36 in which Conservative candidates for Westminster, in combination got more votes than Labour candidates in October 1974.

† These seats are the 42 in which Labour candidates for Westminster in combination got more votes than Conservatives in October 1974.

type that has largely disappeared from the House of Commons since 1945. Twenty-eight of the 78 candidates were already in *Who's Who*. There were also 10 present or former members of the European Parliament and four Brussels officials, in addition to a large number who had business or professional connections with Europe. It was a cumulative process. People with European interests were more likely to put themselves forward, more likely to get past the Central Office screening process and more likely to recommend themselves to Europe-minded selection committees. The contrast with Labour selections was very sharp.

The Conservative candidates' characteristics are summarised in Table 4. The occupational pattern was not sharply different from those who stood in May 1979 for Westminster though businessmen were a little more prominent and professional men a bit less: women fared slightly better but there were still no representatives of the working class.

There was surprisingly little difference in the categories selected for the safer and the less promising seats. The peers and MPs got better seats and women got worse ones. Local councillors were strong in the worse seats, mainly urban ones, while those with clear European links fared particularly well.

All in all the Conservative hierarchy were quite pleased with the selections. 'There are only three or four who really oughtn't to be there' was one comment. But though the candidates had high qualifications in languages and business and often in technical expertise about Europe, there was some anxiety about their political inexperience and the absence of anyone with real weight in the British political scene.

CHAPTER SIX
Others

The Liberals were the most unequivocally pro-European of parties. There were virtually no unbelievers among the party hierarchy and a number were full-blooded federalists. The party saw Europe as a large stage to work on. There were flourishing Liberal parties in most of the other Community countries, thanks to proportional representation, and the Liberal International offered an outlet for some talented British Liberals. The Liberal European Action Group, with Aza Pinney as its Secretary, was the Liberal wing of the European Movement and it, more than any other group, maintained an explicitly federalist stance.

Moreover the party, believing that its advance in Britain depended on a change in the electoral system, was eager to take part in elections to a Parliament which was supposed to move to a common electoral system by 1984. One of the rewards of the Lib-Lab pact of March 1977 was Government sponsorship of a form of proportional representation in the European Assembly Elections Bill. When that came to nothing the Liberals knew that they were doomed to having virtually no members in an elected European Parliament. But they still saw the contest as a propaganda opportunity: they could sell the cause of Europe; they could publicise their Westminster candidates by giving them prominence as Euro-candidates; and they could make play with their grievance over the electoral system.

When the Liberal Party formally decided to contest the European elections at their Special Assembly in January 1978, their selection procedure had already been planned by the candidates committee under Alan Beith, with the main work being done by David Penwarden and Philip Goldenberg. Despite their limited resources they put one official, Tom Dale, virtually full-time onto European elections for six months or more. They recommended that a list of approved candidates be drawn up very strictly. Only Liberals who had already been approved as Westminster candidates were to be considered and they would have to show familiarity with at least one European language and some knowledge of European affairs. Only 150 candidates satisfied these tests. The number approved turned out to be too small to allow every constituency (the Liberals were the only mainland party to fight in Northern Ireland) a full choice between three strong contenders, since many were only prepared to be considered locally and many were selected early by one constituency and were unavailable for later selection meetings.

The Liberals tried to democratise their procedure so that all party members could take part. The contenders from the approved list went together on a circuit over a week or so to meetings in each Westminster constituency (though often for convenience two or three Westminster constituencies met jointly), and then there was a postal ballot using the single transferable vote. The meetings were knowledgeable and earnest, and in many parts of the country were quite well attended. Each candidate spoke and answered questions, and then, in some cases, there was a joint brains trust. There were no rows over the final selections, though one or two delays occurred when all the candidates dropped out late in the day. The first selection was completed on 26 January and the final one only at the last moment in early May.

Some unhappiness was expressed about the dual mandate, but since Russell Johnston, MP for Inverness who had been a member of the European Assembly since 1973, was determined to stand in the one seat where the Liberals plainly had the best chance, objections were silenced. Indeed there was talk of John Pardoe standing for Cornwall if the Westminster elections were out of the way soon enough.

The 79 Liberal candidates had more electioneering experience than their rivals. The 79[1] included 67 who had stood for Westminster, 33 of them in May and 17 of these in constituencies within their Euro-constituency. In Lord Gladwyn, at 78, they had the oldest of all the candidates and among their other standard bearers there were more with widely known names than the Labour Party could muster.

In addition to Russell Johnston MP, there were three ex-MPs – Lord Mackie, Christopher Mayhew and David Austick, and three peers – Lady Seear, Lord Mackie and Lord Gladwyn.

The Liberals made a virtue of fighting on the manifesto of the European Liberal Democrats and not a mere national appeal. The fact

---

[1] The Liberals fought Northern Ireland and boasted of being the only party fighting every seat in the UK.

that the Liberals were pro-European was one of the few widely recognised attributes of the party. In a less anti-European period this might
have been a major electoral asset. As it was, the party went into the
election with determination but without any special popular support or
any expectation of success.

Most of the fringe parties at the Westminster elections were anti-
European and had anyway exhausted their resources in the 3 May fight.
The National Front, the Communists and the Workers' Revolutionary
Party all decided to put up no candidates.[2] The only challenge to the
major parties came from the Ecologists and from a scattering of anti-
Market candidates. The Ecologists, fighting three seats, felt they got
enough publicity to justify their lost deposits. The anti-Market candidates found it difficult to get much of a hearing and any co-ordination of
their activities was on the most limited scale.

Particularly when the Regional List was under discussion various
well-known figures explored the possibility of standing as independents
– the voting system would have given a famous name quite a chance of
winning a seat in one of the large multi-member constituencies. But
with the switch to single member seats an awareness of the odds against
success was a fatal discouragement. Lord George-Brown declared his
intention of fighting Derbyshire as a pro-Marketeer where he had held a
Westminster seat for 25 years, but in early May he decided against
intervening, partly perhaps because none of the major party candidates
in Derbyshire was anti-Market.

It is notable that a month after a general election in which there were a
record number of minor party candidates (583 who were not associated
with the three big parties or with the Scottish or Welsh Nationalists
stood in the 623 seats in Britain), the European election brought
out only 22 in the 78 seats. The fact that the deposit was £600 not £150
may offer one explanation but the timing of the Westminister election
was probably equally important. If the confidence vote on 28 March
had gone the other way and it had seemed that Labour would soldier
on till the autumn, it is certain that interest in the Euro-elections
would have been greater, and probable that a number more fringe
candidates would have taken the opportunity to get publicity and test
the electoral mood.

The Scottish National Party had had a slightly ambivalent attitude
towards Europe. By a narrow margin it had recommended a NO vote
in the 1975 Referendum and it had made much of the under-representation

---

[2] The Communists had named five candidates in March and decided to allot £1,000 to
each of their campaigns but they changed their minds. One of the candidates, S. Hill in
Cleveland, none the less stood as an independent.

of Scotland in the European Parliament by comparison with Ireland or Denmark. But Winnie Ewing had been a member of the appointed European Parliament and the party had opened up an office in Brussels. The European Community offered a forum where Scotland's problems could be aired; and it was also a source of regional aid. The SNP's attitude to Community membership was far from flat hostility, and European elections were always seen as offering a platform for taking the SNP's message to the Scottish people. As early as 27 May 1977 the party committed itself to fighting the elections. But the Scottish devolution referendum absorbed all the party's energies and it did not start choosing its eight Euro-candidates until March. There was no great rush to stand, though for some of the nominations there were two or three aspirants. Those who were finally chosen, one or two of them at the last minute, were all substantial figures on the Scottish scene, and with some international experience. No objection was made to Winnie Ewing seeking a dual mandate by standing for Highlands and Islands (although, in fact, by June she had lost her Moray and Nairn seat at Westminster).

Plaid Cymru's position towards Europe had something of the same ambivalence as the SNP's. Independent membership of the Community might be appropriate to an Independent Wales. But with their socialist and their 'small is beautiful' traditions they were temperamentally unsympathetic to many aspects of the Community. They fought all four Welsh seats, but, devastated by the result of the 1 March Referendum and set back by the May election, their heart was scarcely in the battle.

Two long-established bodies naturally took a keen interest in the European elections. The European Movement, dating back to 1948, had expanded greatly during the struggles over British entry. It had in 1978 a nominal membership of 4,000–5,000 and 100 branches, and its active supporters were deeply committed to full participation in the European Community's affairs. The European Movement provided an umbrella for party activities. Its headquarters in the National Liberal Club were shared by the Conservative Group for Europe, the Labour Committee for Europe, and the Liberal European Action Group. Its Director, Ernest Wistrich, had played an important role in the Britain in Europe campaign in the 1975 Referendum. In 1979 he himself was largely engaged in his own efforts in seeking a Labour nomination and then in fighting the Cleveland Euro-seat. But the office provided a clearing house for information. Its regular journals were quite widely circulated and it prepared a large amount of background literature for general distribution.

ELEC, the European League for Economic Cooperation, had flourished since 1948 as an élite discussion and pressure group. Its crest of importance had come when it had largely provided the cover under which the YES campaign in the 1975 Referendum was master-minded through 'Britain in Europe'. During the year before the European elections, ELEC, with Douglas Hurd as its Research Director, arranged one day briefing conferences for 75–150 local notables in each of 10 regional centres. It also prepared a lucid handbook on Community problems, which was published in March 1979 and distributed generally to candidates of all persuasions.

Some observers had foreseen that European elections would offer a rare opportunity for outside organisations possessed of national networks to intervene in the selection process and in the campaign, since the Euro-constituencies extended so far beyond the ordinary party boundaries and established contacts. But this did not in fact happen. In a wide range of encounters with party officials and candidates, we found very few traces of outside interference. The TUC took no obviously active part, and only one or two of the unions seem to have had any positive policy. Where union activity was observed it was usually the work of an individual, a committed general secretary or research officer, rather than a co-ordinated effort by a union as a whole. On the other side of industry the CBI proclaimed an interest in European elections. They had encouraged one or two prominent figures to put their name forward, but whether their activities were decisive in any single instance is not clear. The CBI had long had arrangements for the briefing of MPs on relevant issues and they extended these to candidates; in April they held a one-day conference to educate their members on European questions. But there was no evidence that their regional structure, the largest private network of paid officials of any national organisation, intervened significantly in selections or elections.

The National Farmers Union was the next most obvious organisation to play a part in the European elections. Three quarters of the Community Budget was devoted to the CAP; and NFU was firmly committed to Community membership and plainly had an enormous interest in the shaping of Community policies. Its President, Sir Henry Plumb, had resigned in order to seek a Conservative nomination. But the Council of the NFU had decided not to get involved in the nominating process, though their members in one or two areas, notably Devon and Norfolk, were not so forbearing. However NFU members were advised to make contact with the candidates once they were selected.

There were one or two scattered stories of local Chambers of Trade organising on behalf of particular Conservative aspirants, and of signs of interest by the Road Transport Lobby and the food manufacturers, but there was no significant evidence of their achieving anything, and indeed granted the structure of the selection process, it is difficult to see what any such bodies could have done to much effect. Campaign contributions (which were meagre enough) could have earned a small modicum of goodwill later on. But the selection process was too broadly based to be significantly fixed or influenced and, when the campaign came, no group could deliver any measurable number of votes. Candidates, like MEPs, would in the nature of things listen politely to any significant interest group in their constituency and offer help if they reasonably could, but they could hardly expect any immediate electoral payoff.

In a new and flexible situation where interest was low and established procedures were absent, some observers had expected that outside bodies might move in on the political scene. But, in the event, interest groups and fringe parties cannot be said to have mattered much in the period before the European campaign or in the campaign itself. It was essentially a party affair.

CHAPTER SEVEN
Constituency campaigning

'A most dispiriting campaign', wrote a newly-elected Labour MEP soon after the votes were counted. 'As [a] candidate it felt very much like "the loneliness of the long-distance runner".' Few put it as graphically. Many must have felt the same. At the constituency, as at the national level, the first European election campaign in history posed a whole range of unfamiliar problems. Some sprang from the inescapable fact that it was a European, and not a national election; others from the particular circumstances in which the election was fought. Almost all bore more heavily on the candidates than on anyone else.[1]

The chief problem was inherently insoluble. As a strongly anti-Market Labour MEP pointed out after the election: 'Most elections are won or lost on overall views, i.e. anti- or pro-Government.' It is around that cardinal principle that a general election campaign is organised – at constituency, no less than at national level. Candidates from the opposition parties attack the record of the incumbent Government; candidates belonging to the governing party attack the proposals put forward by the opposition parties. Though such questions as the personal record of the sitting member sometimes play a part in constituency campaigning, it is generally a small part. Typically, the constituency

---

[1] After the election we sent a very informal but confidential questionnaire to all Conservative and to all Labour candidates, to half the Liberals and to one or two others. We did not use any follow-up to press those who did not reply but in fact 60 of the 78 Conservatives and 49 of the 78 Labour candidates did so; 19 of the 39 Liberals replied. A fair number more had in fact talked to us on the telephone or in person during or after the election. In the absence of ordinary newspaper reports, we have based this chapter to a very large extent on what they wrote in their very full and often uninhibited answers to the questionnaire. There was no obvious pattern to the non-response and we record the result in percentage terms to facilitate comparison. But the response rate should be borne in mind when considering the percentages we quote, particularly for the Liberals.

campaign is a national campaign in miniature. The candidates in their speeches, and the party workers in their canvassing, concentrate on national issues, albeit with a local slant. They are the local chorus in a national drama, designed to convince the electors that their personal futures will be critically affected by the colour of the next Government.

In the European election, they were a chorus without a play. The Community had no Government; support for the opposition to a Government could therefore play no part in the campaign. Nor was it a second Referendum. Not even the most virulently anti-Market Labour candidate could plausibly argue that a vote for him would be a vote to leave the Community. Not even the most passionately 'European' Conservative or Liberal could convincingly argue that a victory for his party would change Britain's European destiny. Some candidates tried to persuade the electorate that the British results would have a decisive impact on the composition of the new European Parliament. The argument contained an element of truth. Since the British elections were fought on the traditional first-past-the-post basis, while the elections in all other Member States were fought on one variety or other of proportional representation, quite small swings of opinion in the United Kingdom could, and indeed did, have disproportionate consequences at Strasbourg and Luxembourg. But that argument was a poor substitute for the dramatic, black-versus-white, life-or-death rhetoric of a Westminster campaign. The fact was that the voters were *not* choosing the future Government of Europe, and that everyone knew it. They were being asked to register an opinion, not to take a decision; and to many of them, the mere registration of an opinion seemed pointless. 'Telling people they had an opportunity to take part in a historic exercise cut no ice whatsoever', wrote a successful Conservative candidate when the campaign was over. 'People vote on bread and butter issues, and these are the prices of bread and butter. They could not see what relevance the Parliament had and were only aware of the limitations of its power.' That mood enveloped the campaign from the beginning, and would almost certainly have made itself felt whenever it had taken place.

To make matters worse, many voters evidently felt unqualified to register opinions on the issues involved, perhaps even to hold them. On the day before the vote, the *Yorkshire Post* ran a story summarising the results of a straw poll in Leeds and Bradford. This showed that only half of those questioned knew that the elections were taking place on the following day; that only a quarter knew the name of any Euro-candidate; that no one questioned knew the names of all the candidates in his or her constituency; and that only a tiny minority of those questioned had any detailed knowledge of the issues. A certain Dennis Pridmore explained: 'It is a lot of rubbish. I know nothing about it and I don't care. I doubt that I shall bother to vote'. He knew nothing of the campaign, he told the *Yorkshire Post,* except that it concerned 'Belgium or something'. There were many Mr Pridmores in Britain in the summer of 1979. Few candidates detected much voter interest in the election, though most thought that the level of interest had improved during the campaign. One Conservative candidate wrote,

In the first week the typical comment was: 'Go home, don't you know the election's over.' The second week: (glazed look in eyes) 'Oh yes, I think I have heard something about it.' Third week: *Everyone* had heard there was an election but 'I don't know anything about it.' Fourth week: 'You're the only candidate I have met. I have had no literature from anybody.'

One or two candidates had more cheering experiences. 'When we spoke to voters they were interested but very confused', wrote a Labour candidate. 'The response was much more polite and enquiring than usual.' Such experiences were rare. 'There was public interest which increased towards the end of the campaign,' wrote a Conservative candidate, 'but the main questions were "What is it all about", or "We don't understand it".' A successful Labour candidate went further, detecting 'Very little interest. Mostly of the sort "Well I didn't vote to go there in the first place, and hell mend those who did. Let them get us out of this mess".' A successful Conservative candidate, who had conducted one of the most energetic constituency campaigns in the country, consoled himself for a low turnout with the thought that

most abstentions reflect(ed) a perfectly reasonable conclusion on the part of many people that there was not sufficient evidence about the nature of the European Parliament and its likely effectiveness to enable them to make an intelligent choice. They therefore stayed away.

He may have been right, but the mood he detected did not make for lively campaigning.

These difficulties faced candidates of all three parties. Labour candidates faced additional built-in difficulties as well. What precisely *were* the opinions between which the electorate was being invited to choose? The Conservatives fought the election on the propositions that Britain should remain in the Community; that there was, however, a great deal wrong with the Community; and that the Conservative Party, by virtue of its basic commitment to the Community, was in a better position to put the wrong things right than was the Labour Party. These were fairly simple propositions; and the first two of them, at any rate, were in accord with the electorate's own instinctive assumptions.

Faced with Conservative opponents taking that line, Labour candidates found it hard to decide on their replies. One possible choice was to 'out-European' the 'Europeans': to differentiate themselves from their Conservative opponents by calling for a stronger European Parliament, for more European integration and for new Community policies beneficial to this country. But although that choice existed in theory, it did not exist in practice. Only a few Labour candidates were, in any sense, more 'European' than their Conservative opponents; only one Labour candidate (Ernest Wistrich of the European Movement) came near to playing that card. Even where the Labour candidate was a pro-Marketeer, moreover, there were usually strong anti-elements in at least parts of his Euro-constituency party. One moderately 'pro' Labour candidate in a Midlands constituency which would have gone Labour on the general election figures wrote ruefully that 'a not unusual' response to an appeal for help to the Secretary of a party branch had been:

'You won't get much help here I'm afraid. Most of them are violently anti and won't have anything to do with it, and the others wanted X (a very pro-EEC man, and local) to get the candidature.' So there remain big divisions. One of the Labour MPs in my area was advising people not to vote. A local Labour councillor wrote to the press saying the same thing. The majority Labour voice was on the 'get-out' side. There were one or two who would like to see a Federalist Europe, but this view, even where held, is not expressed much – it would not be a healthy thing to do. I was lucky in that none of the eight constituencies refused to do anything at all, but at least three of them had some debate before deciding.

For Labour candidates in such a position – and many Labour candidates found themselves in positions fairly close to that – the 'European' card as played by Mr Wistrich was simply not available. In any case a 'European' line would have been quite inconsistent with the Labour Party's line at the national level; and, for that matter, with the centralised election address on which all but two Labour candidates had to rely. Only two other options were left, both of them unsatisfactory. One was to steal the Conservatives' lines: to echo the propositions that Britain should remain in the Community, and that the undoubted defects of Community membership should be put right, but to insist that Labour would be better placed to correct them than the Conservatives. The other was to adopt a markedly more 'anti-European' position than the Conservatives, in particular by promising withdrawal from the Community if the 'reforms' put forward in the Labour manifesto were not carried out. The first of these two options was difficult to sustain, since the Conservative Party had already pre-empted it. The second exposed those who took it to the charge that they were trying to go to Strasbourg under false pretences.

After the election, some Labour anti-Marketeers concluded that their party would have done better to fight a full-bloodedly anti campaign. A veteran of the Labour Safeguards Campaign, who had been elected for a safe Labour seat, wrote

If the Labour Party nationally had made itself more clear that we would *seriously* consider withdrawal if drastic changes were not made, we would have secured a much higher vote and won more seats.

He may have been right. Though poll data do not suggest that withdrawal *per se* would at the time have been popular, many candidates were surprised, and in some cases even shocked, by the strength of the anti-Community feeling which they encountered. 'The only fact about the EEC known universally is that the EEC sells butter to the Russians . . .' reported the successful Conservative candidate for an outer London constituency; 'Many people [said] "I voted YES in the Referendum but I was wrong".' A Liberal who had contested one of the Welsh Euro-constituencies thought the reluctant attitude towards the Community was 'a sort of indulgent ignorance. . . . I don't know and I don't want to know'. Another Liberal, who had fought a seat in outer London, thought that: 'What was most striking and most depressing, was the generally sour attitude by the ordinary voter towards the Community. It [has] for so long been used as a scapegoat for our own ills, so consistently been divided in the popular press, that one found little or no positive approach towards it.' But in the absence of a national campaign for withdrawal, no individual candidate could argue credibly for it, for the obvious reason that no individual MEP could deliver it, even if elected. To call for withdrawal in these circumstances was to invite the charge of hypocrisy or careerism. Yet to take a strongly anti line while stopping short of a call for withdrawal was to sound half-hearted, or sulky, or both.

By a curious paradox of the electioneering process, the difficulties facing Labour candidates had unexpected echoes in the Conservative Party. Whatever else it may be, an election is, first and foremost, a contest; and it is difficult to arouse interest in a contest from which one of the contestants has apparently withdrawn in a huff. Jaded Conservative Party workers, tired after their general election efforts, might have been stimulated to new efforts by a vigorous Labour campaign; apathetic Conservative voters might have been prodded into voting by the sound of the enemy in action. These stimuli were absent; and more than one Conservative candidate felt the lack of them. 'The total absence of a

Labour campaign was damaging', wrote a successful Conservative candidate for a Home Counties constituency, 'nothing motivates a campaign like seeing the opposition in full cry.' Another concluded:

the only way . . . that participation could have been significantly increased would have been (a) A much more positive approach over the years and during the campaign proper by the Labour Party, and (b) an infusion into the debate of national political tensions – even by barn-storming on the part of the two main party leaders.

A third candidate noticed a more disturbing phenomenon. One of the main features of the election, he recalled, had been:

The almost complete non-participation of the working-class vote, Labour or Tory. In the General Election, committee rooms were reporting high turnouts on council estates, for example; and previous canvass returns indicated that almost 50% were voting Conservative. On June 7 the same polling stations were reporting turnouts of as low as 10%.

A more strident Labour campaign might have stimulated working-class Conservatives to vote as well as working-class Labour supporters.

These problems would have arisen in one form or another, in any event. They were exacerbated by another set of problems arising from the particular circumstances of the campaign. Chief among these was the size of the Euro-constituencies. Had the election been fought on the Regional List basis favoured by the Labour Government, the political parties, candidates and party workers would have been obliged to recognise that they were engaged in an exercise of a quite different kind from that involved in a normal Westminster election. They might or might not have been able to devise satisfactory tactics for that new situation, but they would have had to recognise that a new situation existed. Once the House of Commons decided that the election should be fought on a first-past-the-post basis, however, it was all too easy for those concerned to imagine that the task facing a candidate for a Euro-constituency, with an electorate of half a million, differed only in degree, and not in kind, from the task facing a Westminster candidate, fighting a constituency with an electorate of 60,000.

Yet, in reality, Euro-candidates faced at least two big problems, to which Westminster experience was almost irrelevant. The basic purpose of a British political party is to return members to the House of Commons. Thus, the basic unit in British electoral politics is the Westminster constituency party. There are smaller units within Westminster constituency parties, of course, but these are, in practice, branches of the Westminster party tree. Westminster constituency parties have accumulated reservoirs of loyalty; they also control the organisation of the party within their own territory. The new Euro-constituencies, on the other hand, were artificial creations, with no histories behind them; and the Euro-constituency organisations were bound therefore to seem shadowy and unreal to the average party member. They were not structures with lives of their own, independent of the election which had given birth to them. They were temporary alliances of independent chieftains, assembled on a particular occasion to meet a particular need, and not a deeply felt need at that.

The 'internal' problem of how to organise a satisfactory Euro-constituency party structure was compounded by the 'external' problem of how to make effective contact between the candidate and the electorate in such a huge area. Even in Westminster elections, much of the candidate's activity has a symbolic rather than a practical value. On the assumption that one can canvass one household in three minutes, and that there are two electors per household, it would take 1,500 hours to canvass an electorate of 60,000. On the assumption of a ten-hour day spent canvassing, that would mean 150 days. In practice, the average Westminster campaign lasts for around 20 days. Public meetings are even less 'cost effective'. On the generous assumption of 50 people a meeting, a candidate who addressed three meetings a night for an entire election might speak to 5 per cent of a total Westminster electorate. All the same, an active Westminster candidate, employing the familiar techniques of meetings and canvassing, supplemented by street 'walk-abouts', and backed by an enthusiastic party machine, can, at least in theory, make direct contact with around 15 per cent or perhaps even 20 per cent of his or her electorate. The task facing Euro-candidates was of a quite different order of magnitude. One exceptionally active Conservative Euro-candidate claimed to have spoken personally to 25,000 electors. In a Westminster constituency, that would be around one third of the total electorate; on the assumption that the encounters were shrewdly distributed geographically, it would mean that a substantial proportion of the electorate had at least had a vague notion of the candidate's presence. In a Euro-constituency, even that feat still left 95 per cent of the electorate unaccounted for.

Timing caused more difficulties. The Euro-constituency boundaries were finally decided only in November 1978; thus the process of candidate selection could not begin until a few months before the election campaign itself. Whereas Westminster candidates are normally selected somewhere around half-way through the life of a Parliament, the Euro-candidates had at most a few months to make an impact on their electorates. Even if the general election had been held in October 1978, or had been postponed until October 1979, this would have been a formidable task. There is no doubt that it was made much more formidable by the fall of the Government at the end of March 1979, and by the holding of the general election over the next six weeks. The general election took up the time and energy of party workers, which might otherwise have gone to the Euro-campaign, and absorbed money which might otherwise have been spent on the Euro-election. In many cases, it also denied candidates an opportunity to get to know party workers before the Euro-campaign started; at least two Labour candidates in the North East complained that in May they had to take time off from campaigning in order to meet ward parties which they had intended to meet in April. Moreover, it meant that the European Commission's information programme had to be aborted see p. 111. More than one Euro-candidate thought that this had had a damaging effect on the level of public knowledge and interest. As a successful Conservative candidate in a safe Home Counties Conservative Euro-constituency put it:

In retrospect, it was absurd to expect that any candidate could make even a marginal impact on 500,000 voters between March and June of one year, or that any information campaign could enable voters to 'identify' in under six months. The General Election also had a much more serious effect than I thought it would at the time. I had thought certain organisational advantages might exist: e.g. an up-to-date marked register. These were, however, overwhelmed by the disadvantages: (a) the bathos of yet another campaign following the Conservative general election victory, (b) the difficulty of mobilising party workers (many, esp. YCs, take leave for elections, and had none left for 7 June), (c) the virtual elimination of the £1 m 'neutral' information programme, (d) the 'switching off' of the media (when we complained, the reasonable reply came back that readers/viewers were 'fed up with politics'), (e) the reluctance of leading national politicians to participate while forming a government – trying to regroup.

As his comment implied, the coming together of the two elections caused a further problem as well. Before the Euro-campaign started, many had assumed that it would be largely a 'media campaign'. But it could only be a 'media campaign' if the media were prepared to make it so. To the candidates themselves, it often seemed that the media were bending over backwards to do the opposite. To be sure, the responses of candidates after the election suggest that most were reasonably well treated by radio and television. Of the Conservatives who completed our questionnaire only 12 per cent had had no radio or television exposure; 10 per cent had only appeared on television and 36 per cent only on radio; 50 per cent had appeared on both. Of the Labour respondents, only 9 per cent appeared on neither medium; 9 per cent had appeared only on television and 30 per cent only on radio; 63 per cent

93

had appeared on both. The Liberals had fared about as well. Of the Liberal respondents 11 per cent had had no radio or television exposure; 16 per cent had appeared only on television and 5 per cent only on radio; 69 per cent had appeared on both.

Press coverage was a more complicated matter. Candidates from all three parties believed that the local press had provided much better coverage of the campaign than had the national press. Eighteen Conservatives complained specifically about the bad quality of Fleet Street coverage, while only three expressed approval of it. On the other hand, 25 seemed reasonably pleased with their local press coverage, whereas only one complained. He was a successful candidate, who wrote in something close to anguish. 'The big problem was that the local press gave very poor coverage so that there was no way to communicate to the electorate.' Much the same was true of Labour and Liberal candidates. Twenty-one of the Labour respondents were critical of the coverage given by the national press, as against only one who seemed content with it. On the other hand, 19 seemed reasonably satisfied with the local press, while only eight were critical. Eleven Liberal respondents criticised the national press and none seemed satisfied with it; nine seemed satisfied with the local press as against five who were critical.

Even among the majority who conceded that they had been fairly treated in terms of column inches, however, there were criticisms of the quality of local press coverage. The main local paper, wrote the successful Labour candidate for an industrial constituency in the North East, 'published press releases from the candidates every day for the ten days before the election. Other papers gave a reasonable coverage, but in a dull way, describing the institutions of the EEC rather than looking at the candidates and their opposing policies.' Another Labour candidate, this time for a safe Conservative seat, put it more succinctly. 'Locals', he wrote, 'did their usual yawn, yawn about this sort of thing.' In any case, even good coverage by the local press, supplemented by the occasional radio or television appearance, seemed inadequate to candidates trying desperately to break through a wall of public indifference and hostility. 'The election should have been fought largely through the media, as elections are in constituencies of this size in the USA', wrote a successful Conservative candidate for a Home Counties constituency. 'I believe our media were tried and found miserably wanting.' He spoke for many. Another successful Conservative candidate, also from a Home Counties constituency, commented scornfully: 'The national media showed scant interest (on polling day the fact that the elections were taking place was featured on the 5 p.m. news *after* the news of the retirement of James Hunt from motor racing).' 'There was hardly any enthusiasm shown by the media to bring out in the open the important issues. . . .' wrote a Labour candidate for a safe Conservative seat in the south of England. 'They were rather more interested in describing the powerlessness of a European Parliament and the pay packets of the successful candidates.' Another unsuccessful Labour candidate, in a constituency which Labour might have won in a better year for the Labour Party, criticised not only the quantity of media coverage but the way in which the coverage was given:

The *candidates* should have been allowed to speak for themselves . . . People who were not standing in the election should not have occupied the centre of the stage. To that extent, the media displayed lazy, 'clubby' attitudes and contributed to the notion that no one knows the candidates – how could they when the air time was monopolised even at regional level by people who were not standing anyway.

Such were the problems. How well were they overcome? The vast majority of candidates of all three parties spent the campaign period working full-time in their Euro-constituencies; they campaigned strenuously though often single handedly. It is not clear how far their efforts were well-judged. Though many recognised uneasily that the Euro-election was not a Westminster election writ large (or, for that matter, writ small) few broke decisively with Westminster precedent. Most devoted themselves to the customary Westminster rituals, though with less emphasis on canvassing and more on 'walk-abouts' of various kinds. But it is doubtful if many of these 'walk-abouts' were well-organised. One Conservative Party official suggested a few months before the campaign that, if the Euro-candidates were to make an impact, their 'walk-abouts' would have to be organised in a much more professional way than is normal in a British general election. Instead of sending the candidate into a shopping precinct with a few party workers to keep him company, he thought it should be a systematically organised 'blitz' on the area to be covered, with lots of workers accompanying the candidate to drum up interest, working to a carefully prepared plan. He doubted whether anything of the kind would be done: the travels of even national figures like Denis Healey and William Whitelaw were not yet organised in this way. His scepticism was almost certainly borne out by the event. 'Taking all into consideration I enjoyed the exercise and found it very educational', reflected, the Labour candidate for a safe Conservative seat in East Anglia, 'but it was a "loony" election. No one knew what the election was for or when it was, you never saw your opponents except at joint meetings – and for one we had to go to a canteen to get an audience, there were very few posters about and virtually nothing in the papers.' That was in a safe Conservative seat, where the Labour Party was virtually divided and the local press unusually uninterested; it would be wrong to take it as the norm. But it was almost certainly closer to the norm than would be any vision of high-pressure, American style razzamatazz.

There was an enormous variety in the number of meetings held, and in the attendances achieved. Among Conservatives who responded to our questionnaire, the average number of meetings held in each Euro-constituency was ten, but this average conceals a variation from no meetings in an industrial constituency in Wales, to 60 in a rural constituency in Scotland. Only one candidate had no meetings, and only three had one. At the other end of the scale, only four had more than 20. Attendances were equally varied – so much so that it is meaningless to work out an average figure. The largest attendance at any constituency meeting of which we had a report was 3,000 – that secured by Harold Macmillan when he spoke for Lord St Oswald in Yorkshire West. The lowest figure recorded was nought, and more than one candidate recorded attendances as low as one. Two Labour respondents eschewed meetings altogether; the highest number recorded was 25. The average figure, however, was six. As with the Conservatives, attendances varied enormously as well. The lowest attendance was one and the highest (for the final Labour Party rally in Leeds with Jim Callaghan and François Mitterrand) was 2,000. Five hundred people came to hear Tony Benn in Sheffield, 180 listened to Shirley Williams in London West. The smallest number of Liberal meetings reported to us was two and the largest 32; the (rather meaningless) average figure for the 19 Liberal respondents was ten. Attendances varied from ten to 300.

Some candidates tried to inject life into the campaign by using less conventional techniques. Altogether, 29 of the 60 Conservative respondents to our questionnaire claimed to have used campaign 'gimmicks' of one sort or another. Most of them, it must be admitted, were fairly unambitious. Characteristic examples are a decorated Land Rover, a campaign coach, 'girls in T shirts', an open-top bus, and sponsored walks by Young Conservatives. One or two, however, were more ambitious. One enthusiastic candidate said that he 'used a campaign bus with one of the official films on the Community to be seen inside, a Land Rover decked out with the flags of the Community and with a tape cassette of musical passages, interspersed with messages from myself (the Land Rover plus cassette was very successful), and we had a twenty foot advertising balloon one hundred and fifty feet up in the air. . . . We also had carrier bags, T shirts and childrens' balloons printed "X for Europe".' A large number had visiting speakers from

Europe, mostly from the CDU. Their Labour opponents were more austere, or less imaginative. Thirty-two of our Labour respondents said that they used no 'gimmicks', as against 13 who employed them. One Labour candidate wrote sadly: 'As far as I know there were no Labour gimmicks. I was alone most of the time.' Another wrote that he had used no gimmicks, but added: 'There was a wide distribution to Asian houses of 10,500 copies of a leaflet in Urdu and Punjabi, except in one suburb where it was vetoed by the CLP, although requested by Asian members of the Party.' A few were more ambitious. A strongly pro-Market candidate for a northern constituency used a decorated caravan with loudspeaker and recorded music; he also had five continental visitors, though he added sternly that this was: '*not* a gimmick'. The Labour candidate for Leeds had three European visitors speaking at the regional 'Euro-Rally' there, including François Mitterrand. Another, slightly less ambitiously, 'put a float into a local carnival. It got third prize in its class'.

The Liberals were more energetic, or perhaps more desperate. Twelve said that they did employ gimmicks and only seven that they did not. The gimmicks employed varied. One Liberal candidate in outer suburbia, for example, 'used a horse box/cattle wagon – sides coated with ply wood, painted orange with slogans "X FOR EUROPE" – symbols and posters superimposed. Mobile display boards and literature were carried inside and brought out in markets, shopping centres for information and electioneering.' A university teacher, standing as a Liberal candidate in the north of England, was even more energetic. 'I walked the whole length (22 miles) of the constituency on Spring Bank Holiday', he wrote, 'I had Belgian and Dutch Liberals campaigning for me.' On the other hand, the ex-candidate for a Welsh constituency had to confess – 'I wanted to do a bicycle relay around the constituency, but no one would organise it. I was the only gimmick available.' Another rather moving failure was that of the Liberal candidate who: 'Hoped to use the Belgian Liberal Euro-Squirrel but [was] defeated by customs delays'.

Decorated caravans, continental visitors, sponsored walks and Euro-squirrels could give zest to an otherwise dreary campaign. They could not man polling stations or mark up an electoral register. On this more mundane level, candidates of all three parties fared badly in comparison with their Westminster counterparts. Though the Euro-election was fought, ostensibly at any rate, on different issues from those on which the general election had been fought, and although some voters might therefore have been expected to vote differently from the way they had voted on 3 May, few Euro-parties were well enough organised to conduct new canvasses to elicit the voters' Euro-intentions. Only about a fifth of our Liberal respondents, 17 per cent of their Labour counterparts and 16 per cent of the Conservatives claimed to have done additional canvassing, and most of these implied that it had been fairly rudimentary in character. Most (73 per cent of the Conservatives and 57 per cent of the Labour respondents, though only 26 per cent of the Liberals) had relied on the canvass returns left over from the Westminster election. Some had to make do without canvass returns altogether.

Much the same was true of organisation on polling day, though here there was a sharper difference between the parties. Perhaps reflecting real differences on the ground, perhaps only reflecting the euphoria of victory, Conservative respondents to our questionnaire seemed markedly better pleased with the way their parties had behaved on polling day than did their Labour or Liberal counterparts. One-fifth of the Conservatives implied that their parties had been well organised on polling day, and two-fifths that the level of organisation had been fair. Only a minority (albeit a substantial minority) implied that it had been sketchy or bad. Labour and Liberal respondents were much more critical. Only 4 per cent of the Labour respondents, and none of the Liberals, implied that they had had satisfactory polling day organisations; only 12 per cent of the Labour respondents and only 5 per cent of the Liberals, implied that the level or organisation had even been fair. The rest implied that it had been sketchy or bad.

Even Conservative comments, however, were far from enthusiastic in tone. One Conservative wrote smugly that his polling day organisation had been 'very good'; another that it had been 'fully comprehensive'. Much more typical, however, was the comment of the successful Scottish candidate, who wrote that his organisation had been: 'Good in parts. But no Westminster constituency manned every polling station – let alone manned it all the time. Many helpers out, but well below General Election standards.' Labour and Liberal comments were less enthusiastic still. One characteristic Labour response was that polling day organisation had been 'non-existent'; another read: 'No polling day organisation'. Those were in hopeless seats, but the situation was not much better in the party's good seats. One candidate in such a seat seemed representative of many when he wrote that his polling day organisation had been: 'A bit patchy. Well organised to full standard in some areas, almost non-existent in others.' A typical Liberal comment from a prominent member of the party, who had campaigned in East Anglia, was that: 'We only had partial polling day organisation in two of the constituencies.' Another Liberal from a south of England constituency, wrote that he had had 'none'. A third wrote, perhaps even more revealingly, that, so far as his polling day organisation was concerned, it was 'impossible to tell, but disappointing'. The candidate for a Welsh constituency wrote simply: 'Ugh. No polling day organisation. I went on a drive-about.'

Bad organisation was, to some extent, a function of lack of finance. The cost of the constituency campaign was modest, considering the number of electors. Taking all candidates in Britain together they only spent 30 per cent of the permitted maximum (just on £15,000 in a seat with 500,000 electors). None came within £1,500 of the maximum for their constituency. The three highest spenders were Peter Price £14,691 (Con., Lancashire West), Stephen Bundred £13,309 (Lab., London South East) and Richard Blackburn £13,502 (Lib., London East). But Conservatives in general spent more. Of the 19 candidates who exceeded £10,000, 14 were Conservative, three were Labour and only one was Liberal; Winnie Ewing £11,044 (SNP Highlands and Islands) was the one Scottish candidate to exceed £10,000. On the other end of the scale Peter Freitag who fought South Tyne and Wear on £187 was far the most economical of the seven Liberals who spent under £1,000. The ten Labour candidates who spent under £3,000 included two victors, Winston Griffiths £2,556 in South Wales and Janey Buchan £2,725 in Glasgow, but the most economical was Dennis Hunt £1,975 in Midland Central. Only two Conservatives spent less than £4,000. Adam Fergusson won Strathclyde West on £4,717 and Moira Carse lost Strathclyde East on £3,478. Of the 14 Conservatives who spent less than £6,000 five were successful.

The extremes, of course, came from other parties. The Federalist in Northamptonshire spent only £14 besides his deposit and Viscount Weymouth, the Wessex Regionalist, spent £36. On the other hand in Northern Ireland, with twice the electorate of any mainland constituency, James Kilfedder (Independent Unionist) spent £22,041 and John Hume (SDLP) £20,888.

Not only were Conservative candidates better served by their local party organisations, at any rate on polling day; they were also better served by party headquarters. Among our Conservative respondents 41 per cent gave answers about this, that could be classified as 'good' and 21 per cent, that could be classified as 'fair'. Only 25 per cent gave answers which implied that party headquarters had given bad or sketchy service. The replies themselves were very varied. One respondent wrote that Head Office had served him 'very well indeed. Pre-campaign arrangements were excellent. The Euro-researchers could not have been more helpful.' Another wrote that he had been served 'moderately – only sign of their existence was information material. Let down on speakers – Reg Prentice cancelled day of public meeting, no substitute.' Another wrote more philosophically: 'Well served, but HQ really irrelevant in a campaign.' One of the critics wrote that: 'They overwhelmed me – and the postman – with largely useless information. The value of assistance, in practical terms, nil.' Liberal ex-candidates were more critical, but on the whole fairly tolerant of the shortcomings of an overworked and under-staffed Head Office on the morrow of a general election. A Liberal candidate from the East Midlands thought that: 'With their limitations (financial and human) he had been served "adequately".' Another said that he had been served 'quite well, but I used it very little'. A third was much more critical. 'Headquarters were irrelevant except in their role of channelling material from the ELD (European Liberal Democrat) Federation', wrote a Liberal respondent who had fought a seat in the West Country, 'all of which arrived too late for maximum use.' Another West Country Liberal was equally grudging. 'Apart from organising literature from the ELD', he wrote, 'HQ were for this election almost no help at all.' A more blunt and succinct comment from a Liberal candidate in the south-east of England was that he had been served 'poorly'.

From the pens of Labour ex-candidates, by contrast, came a long litany of complaints, some of them quite savagely phrased. Of the Labour respondents who commented on the service they had received from Transport House, only 29 per cent were favourable, as against 71 per cent who were critical. A leading Labour anti-Marketeer who had campaigned successfully in the north of England wrote that his constituency had been served 'pretty well, in view of shortage of funds and the general lack of enthusiasm for the EEC in the Labour Party'. A respondent who had contested a seat in East Anglia wrote, in rather similar terms, that 'considering the basic argument in London' he had been served 'very well indeed'. The ex-candidate for a safe Conservative seat in the South of England constituency, whose responses to other questions suggest that he should be counted as a moderate pro-Marketeer, wrote that although it had been late in starting, Transport House had done 'quite well in later briefing and sending me to candidates' conferences in Luxembourg and Birmingham'. Another tolerant Labour respondent, who had fought a Home Counties constituency, found the service 'excellent from the point of view of having the addresses printed and delivered to us. In the last few days, very well with *Europe Today*. Well, from the point of view of Labour candidates' meeting.'

But these were exceptions. More typical was the comment of the London anti-Marketeer who wrote: 'Transport House was a joke. Herbert Morrison House [Headquarters of the London Labour Party] was superb.' Another, middle-of-the-road Labour respondent who had fought wrote that the service from Transport House had been: 'B. awful!!!! Received a box of car stickers after count was completed on Thursday night. Press releases arrived on Wednesday before election day.' A mild pro-Marketeer who had campaigned unsuccessfully thought he had been served 'very poorly – we received, unheralded, some cash for the campaign only one day before polling day when it was too late to spend'. Another, North Western, comment was that the service had been: 'Too little – too late – too negative'. A staunch anti-Marketeer from the Midlands was equally scathing. Transport House, he wrote, had served him: 'Not at all'. A strongly pro-Market London candidate thought: 'Transport House useless. We dreaded their press conferences. Their absurd "model" press releases arrived two days after the final local press edition!' A mildly anti-Market candidate in the West Country wrote that he had been served 'very badly (but I was not surprised by this!)'. A moderate anti-Marketeer who had fought a seat in the North West wrote that the service from London had been: 'Far too little and too late'. A candidate for an East Anglia seat thought the 'Briefings from Transport House of no use, except to very anti EEC candidates'. During the campaign, more than one anti-Market Labour candidate reported, with some embarrassment, that he depended for briefing material on the Labour Committee for Europe.

By the same token, Labour candidates were far more critical of their party's national campaign than were their Conservative or Liberal opponents. Many Conservatives would have liked to see a more active campaign nationally, sometimes on grounds of European principle rather than on grounds of party advantage, but several conceded that such a campaign would have won fewer seats, and even those who deplored the demure approach adopted by party headquarters did so in moderate terms. 'With a very few exceptions the national campaign was a non-event', wrote one idealistic Conservative critic, 'and too many of the events organised tended to trivialise the Euro-elections. No issues other than which party could do the best job for Britain emerged.' Another enthusiastic European complained: 'Mrs. Thatcher did one youth rally, one press conference, and I believe, one TV commercial. Mr. Callaghan sounded embarrassed. Mr. Steel bleated. No wonder public interest was low.' Another complaint, from a successful candidate for a Home Counties seat, was that:

the Prime Minister did not appear on TV herself and appealed to those who voted Conservative in the General Election to put their trust in her and vote in the Euro-Election. Also, some decisions taken during the Euro-campaign (particularly price rises) definitely hurt us. I got the impression London had forgotten, or ignored, the fact that there was still an election campaign going on. There was no attempt to build up interest over a period of weeks and it was most unfortunate that the bulk of the campaigning was left to Mr. Heath who, to put it bluntly, commands very little affection among my party workers because of his attitude to Mrs. T. and because HE took us into the EEC.

More typical of Conservative attitudes, however, was the robust comment: 'Given the General Election in May we had to fight as we did. The low turn-out was a definite plus in terms of Conservative seats. High profile campaigns were counter-productive, e.g. Lord St. Oswald in Yorkshire.' 'I did not like the silent strategy at the time', confessed another successful candidate, elected for a marginal London constituency, 'but it worked.'

Labour attitudes were very different. 'Nationally the campaign did not befit an international election', wrote the defeated candidate for a safe Conservative seat in the south of England. Another defeated candidate, for a London constituency, thought the 'behaviour of the national leadership created an impression among Labour supporters at all levels that it didn't really matter whether we won or lost'. A Labour respondent who had fought in the West Country complained that, because of the Labour split on Europe, 'no effective agreed message could be got across, and what did come over only confused the line I was taking in the constituency.' Others were angrier. A strong pro-Marketeer, who had fought in London, described the national campaign as 'a disgrace', and thought it 'confused the voters who did not know why we were standing since we appeared to be against the whole idea'. Another pro-Market Labour respondent, this time from the North West, described his party's national campaign as:

a disaster 1. Negative election address imposed on all. 2. Negative spokesman. 3. Jim Callaghan publicly driven away. 4. Little TV coverage. For Labour voters it was an invitation *not* to vote.

At the Labour Party Conference in October 1979, these reactions came into the open. Ivan Taylor, the defeated Labour candidate for Central Lancashire, reminded the delegates that 'most of us did not want to see Labour members returned to a European Parliament at all'; because the party 'could not make up our bloody minds', the elections had only been 'half fought'. Jeff Hopkins, Euro-candidate for Salop and Stafford, was more critical of the party leadership. Labour's campaign, he argued, suffered from a 'lack of vision'. The issue put to the electors was 'whether you were for the Common Market or against the Common Market; the more important question of Labour's relationship with the other democratic Socialist parties in Europe had been forgotten'. Bill Duncan, candidate for Wessex, was more critical still.

It was a disaster, what the NEC did. They produced manifestos, many of which arrived too late. Other candidates know as well as I do that there were thousands and thousands of election addresses which stayed in constituency offices and were never delivered to people. Thousands of pounds were wasted in changing one word in the manifesto . . . Even though the Confederation of Socialist Parties in Europe had been working on a manifesto for months and months, the Labour Party refused to participate. They sent along observers, but would do nothing to help formulate that policy. I remember phoning up Transport House and getting no information at all. As for posters, you were lucky if you could get hold of them. In Wessex we had to end up doing it ourselves. Their performance on television was apathetic. I think this was a great historic issue for Britain for all the important issues which have been mentioned by the last speaker – but we were apathetic about it. That indifference mattered; it mattered, because a lot of Party workers did not turn out to help on the day. Now, comrades, I have been in the Labour Party for a long time, but I was close to becoming ashamed during the European elections.

Nationally, as the defeated Conservative candidate for one of the safest Labour seats in the country put it, the campaign was a 'one-horse race'. It was a one-horse race in most constituencies as well, at any rate, so far as policy was concerned. Nearly all Conservative candidates stuck firmly to the position which their party had pre-empted from the beginning: that Britain's interests could best be protected by vigilant protection from within the Community structure, and that Conservatives alone could offer the vigilance which was needed. Labour and Liberal candidates had to adjust themselves to the Conservative position as best they could.

In all three parties, the candidates' election addresses contained a middle section, common to all the candidates of the party concerned. Conservative candidates added a personal message on the front page; Labour and Liberal candidates put their personal messages on the back. The common middle section of the Conservative addresses contained about 600 words of text, interspersed with pictures of Harold Macmillan, Edward Heath and Margaret Thatcher. Conservatives, it promised, would 'press for an end to unnecessary "harmonisation", for reducing wasteful surpluses arising under the Common Agricultural Policy, and for fairer contributions to the Community Budget'. The common section of the Labour address was headed: 'Points from Labour's manifesto'. It contained slightly more text than the equivalent section of the Conservative address, much less attractively presented, and no pictures. It began by reminding readers that, 'The Labour Party warned of the dangers of EEC membership'; insisted that Labour would 'restore to the Commons the power to amend or repeal legislation applicable to Europe'; demanded 'radical changes in the Community budget' and 'fundamental reform of the CAP'; and ended by reiterating the manifesto commitment that 'if the fundamental reforms contained in our manifesto are not achieved within a reasonable period of time, then the Labour Party would have to consider very seriously whether continued EEC membership was in the best interests of the British people'. The central section of the Liberal address contained ten points, taken from the manifesto of the European Liberal and Democratic Federation, stressing, among other things, the Federation's commitment to Economic and Monetary Union, to industrial democracy, to equal opportunities for women and to decentralised decision-making.

All this meant that individual candidates had less opportunity to stress their personal attitudes than in general election addresses. None the less, they could and did add personal messages to the common section prepared by their party headquarters; and these provide the best source for the themes put forward at constituency level. Many Conservatives attacked the Brussels bureaucracy and what Eric Forth, the candidate for Birmingham North, described as its 'idiotic rules and regulations'. Some attacked the Common Agricultural Policy and promised to press for stable prices and smaller surpluses. Conservatives in coastal constituencies called for a policy to protect fish stocks and, at least by implication, deplored the Community's failure to adopt such a policy. More than one attacked the Regional fund – either on the grounds that the aid it had provided had gone to areas other than the one in which the attacker was standing, or on the grounds that, as John Weait, the candidate for Northumbria put it, 'smaller, private sector businesses' had not benefited sufficiently. At least one (Beata Brookes, the candidate for North Wales) reminded her prospective constituents that: 'Despite Labour's boast of having "renegotiated" Britain's terms of membership . . . the British contribution to the Budget is still unfairly large.'

There was as much variety in the choice of positive proposals. Many Conservative candidates stressed the defence implications of Community membership; some urged, implicitly if not explicitly, that the Community should acquire a defence dimension. John Ling, the candidate for Midlands Central, promised to use his influence to: 'Restrict imports from Japan and Eastern Europe when they compete unfairly with Midlands industry'; Christopher Jackson, the candidate for Kent East, called for 'freer trade . . . to encourage smaller businesses'. William Hopper, the candidate for Greater Manchester West, stressed the Community's role as 'the greatest free enterprise zone in the world'; Alastair Hutton, the candidate for Scotland South, devoted the entire front page of his election address to a catalogue of the grants received by different parts of his constituency from Community Funds. Anthony Simpson, the candidate for Northamptonshire, promised that he would 'seek to increase the influence of the European Parliament in order to do a better job for you'; Richard Cottrell, the candidate for Bristol, stressed that the European Parliament 'is not a rival to Westminster and never must be'.

These, however, were variations on a common theme. Albeit in different accents, all the Conservative candidates had the same story to tell: that they were both better Europeans and better Britons than their rivals, and that they were better Britons because they were better Europeans. As Lord Bethell, the candidate for London North West who had sat in the nominated European Parliament, put it in his election address:

The tradegy of our six years in Europe is that the last five have been wrecked by the internal disputes and broken promises of the British Labour Government. The Labour Party has still not made up its mind whether it is in Europe or out of it.

Naturally their confusion causes even greater confusion in the minds of our European partners. They see little point in making concessions to Britain under Labour. Why should they? Why give anything to a so-called partner, who spends most of his energy putting a spanner in the works or threatening to break the agreement altogether?

We Conservatives are trusted in Europe. We negotiate hard, but we keep our word.

It was a simple, coherent and credible story; and Labour candidates did not find it easy to frame an answer. Many replied by trying to tell essentially the same story, only in Labour language. More than one Conservative candidate noticed that, as the logic of the campaign went home, the position of the two main parties converged. One Conservative MEP commented that even an 'unattractive, left-wing, anti-market Labour candidate did not openly advocate getting out'. 'In the end', reported another, 'everyone was saying the same thing.' 'General convergence', boasted a third, 'I occupied that ground from the beginning.' More significantly still, some Labour anti-Marketeers were conscious of the same phenomenon. One of the leading members of the Labour Safeguards Committee wrote that he was 'genuinely surprised by the hostility to the EEC shown by many of the thousands of people I met', but added: 'Almost everyone actively concerned agreed with the same political line – i.e. very critical, but accepting that membership was not an issue.' The defeated Labour candidate for a constituency in the south of England noticed a 'convergence' in the attitudes of parties and voters, adding that it was 'a pretty despairing convergence'. The successful, and hitherto strongly anti-Market, candidate for a London constituency noticed: 'A general convergence. Very few people believed that getting out is a realistic alternative. Federalism is very unpopular except with the educated radical middle class, and there it is very popular. I tried to keep people's feet on the ground and steer a middle course. Largely, I feel, I was successful.'

The extent of this convergence should not be exaggerated. In Humberside, John Prescott, MP for Hull East, accused the Conservative candidate, Robert Battersby, a principal administrator in the Commission Directorate-General for Fisheries, of 'selling out' local fishing interests. The Conservatives threatened to seek criminal prosecution, and distributed 4,000 copies of a reply accusing the Labour party of 'selling out' British fishing interests in the 'Cod War' with Iceland. Exchanges of this sort were unusual, but a number of Labour candidates were at pains to stress their differences from the Conservative line. The successful anti-Market Labour candidate for a Scottish constituency wrote:

The Liberal did the full frontal Federal bit to no avail. In no way did I find any sizeable group of people in the latter grouping. I found the most pathetic type of response was, largely from working class women, 'Well, I admit I voted YES because I was frightened that we wouldn't get jobs here – but look what has happened to us. It is awful. We were really told a lot of lies.' I found I could persuade even such disillusioned people about the wisdom of voting but the size of constituency and the time factor defeated any chance of that.

Another anti-Market victor, this time in the north of England, attributed one of the best Labour results within the country to the fact that 'I took a highly critical line. Many people told me they were not going to vote because they did not want anything to do with the Common Market. I persuaded them with the reply: "Try to change it, and if we fail, give the British people another chance to come out".' A third reported that he had 'pursued a strong anti-EEC campaign, i.e. a loose confederation with major changes or fight to come out'. In his election address Alf Lomas, in London North East, declared that he 'fully support(ed) the Labour Party in saying that if we cannot achieve our aims in a reasonable time, then we shall have to seriously consider whether we can remain a member'. Reg Scott in Devon pledged himself 'to continue to fight against EEC policies which are damaging Britain and the West Country, and to go on fighting until Britain's freedom of action is restored – or we get out'. Such explicit calls for withdrawal were rare, but many Labour candidates referred to the Community in language even more hostile than that of the manifesto. To Tony Hart, in London South West, it was 'an economic nightmare'. Terry O'Sullivan in Midlands East was 'disgusted' by it. Janey Buchan, in Glasgow, found the

Common Agricultural Policy 'a moral outrage'. Myles Mackie, in Cambridgeshire, denounced it for destroying 'good food' – something he considered 'criminal'.

There were limits to convergence even when the Labour candidate was a pro-Marketeer. One Labour pro, elected for a northern industrial constituency wrote that 'considerable differences emerged between myself and the Conservative candidate on devaluation of the Green Pound and Europe's relationship with the Third World and defence'. Some Labour pro-Marketeers took pains to differentiate themselves from their Conservative opponents. 'We can't risk the Tories', declared Jim Daly, the Labour candidate for London West, in his election address, 'their anxiety to please the French farmers has already cost us dearly in high food prices.' Others made it clear that their support for the principle of Community membership did not imply approval of existing Community policies. 'I voted "yes" at the referendum. . . .' wrote Jim Honeybone, the candidate for the Cotswolds. 'However, I am most unhappy as indeed are so many British people about the way the Common Market is working at the moment.'

As befitted their party's policies and attitudes, Liberal candidates were more internationalist. Many stressed the exceptional nature of the Euro-election, above all the fact that, as Andrew Phillips, candidate for Essex North East put it, 'We are not choosing a *government* at this election. . . . We are electing a representative for this half of Essex to make the best of a great opportunity.' Christopher Mayhew, in Surrey, stressed another, related, common theme. 'For the first time', he wrote, 'Tory and Labour electors can vote Liberal without any fear of bringing in a government they dislike and oppose into power. They can at last break away from party politics and judge the candidates on their merits.' A third favourite was to stress the Liberal Party's links with continental Liberals, and to suggest that, by virtue of these links, Liberals were in a better position to change the Community from within than were either of the big parties. Many echoed Alan Butt-Philip, candidate for Somerset, in arguing that the Community's faults could only be put right from within and that

the British Conservatives and Socialists stand virtually without allies in the rest of the Community. We Liberals think the only way to change the Common Market is to persuade other Europeans to our point of view: the Liberals' close political ties with other parties enable them to do this. The Liberal MPs in the European Parliament are also a much bigger force than the Conservatives.

Yet it is doubtful if these differences counted for much beside the gross facts that the candidates of all three parties were proposing to participate in the work of the Parliament if elected; that none advocated immediate withdrawal; and that all saw defects in the Community, which they hoped to correct from within. It was certainly a partial convergence, and may have been a 'despairing' one. It was convergence all the same.

CHAPTER EIGHT

National campaign

For Britain, the European election was completely overshadowed by the Westminster election and the change of Government at the beginning of May. From 28 March, when the Government was defeated in the House of Commons, until 4 May when Mrs Thatcher took up office, all attention was on the Westminster campaign. Because of the Easter break, this was of exceptional duration. Apart from the Euro-candidates themselves, there were few who thought about what was to happen on 7 June. Once the Westminster election was over, a new Government was taking office, drafting a Queen's Speech and making preparations for its first Budget, due five days after the Euro-vote. A further distraction was the Jeremy Thorpe trial which ran from 8 May to 22 June occupying many column inches which might otherwise have been given to politics. It is not surprising that the European election was about as inconspicuous as could be imagined. As *The Economist* wrote on 2 June 'The British political establishment is not taking this election seriously'.

It is interesting to speculate on what might have happened in the Euro-campaign had the Westminster election been held in October 1978 or, indeed, in October 1979. In either case the European election would have turned into a general trial of strength between the parties, as seems to have happened in France. The parties would have seen it as an opportunity to test their machines and to draw attention to their arguments. The run up to the campaign would have been much longer. Candidates would have indulged in publicity-seeking gimmicks and the European Commission and Parliament advertising campaign would have made electors more aware of what was about to happen. The media would have been much more interested in this Euro-novelty. In practice it proved an anti-climax, even a Euro-bore; it does not follow that it would have done had the timing been different.

One other possibility should be mentioned. If the Westminster election, too, had taken place on 7 June, as many Labour strategists desired, the European election would have been almost completely submerged in the domestic battle; the linkage with the main issue – which party should be in Downing Street for the coming years – together with the larger turnout would almost certainly have given Labour a better result in the European elections. It is, of course, arguable whether Labour would have benefited more from its more anti-European stance than it would have lost from its manifest disarray on the subject and from the Conservatives' exploitation of the conflict between its Westminster manifesto and its Euro-manifesto.

Returning Officers actually had to issue notices of the Euro-election on Wednesday, 2 May and the period for nominations closed on Saturday, 12 May, a week after the general election. This may be one of the reasons why there were so few fringe candidates.

Another reason for the flat nature of the campaign was the general expectation of a Conservative landslide. On 9 May the *Guardian* published figures showing that, if everybody voted as they had done on 3 May, the Conservatives would get 48 of the seats and Labour 30; and it was generally expected that, with a lower turnout, Labour would do even worse. Two weeks later on 1 June the Gallup poll further dampened Labour's spirits by showing that in the Government's honeymoon period there had been a 5 per cent swing to the Conservatives. Moreover, throughout the campaign worries about turnout were widely publicised. Would people bother to vote so soon after a general election, especially in a contest for a Parliament with few powers and in which there was no needle excitement about who would win? There were no clearly identified marginal constituencies on which to focus and there could be no sense of theatre about who would win locally or nationally. Hardly any opinion polls were conducted during the campaign and there was no sense of a mounting climax. Even the finale was muted by the fact that people were voting on Thursday but would not be allowed to know the result until Sunday or Monday.

The press devoted little space to the campaign. *The Times,* as the only paper giving major coverage to the European Parliament, might have been expected to treat the election seriously, but it was in the middle of its eleven-month stoppage. The *Guardian* devoted up to a page daily to the election over the last ten days and there were regular stories in the *Daily Telegraph*. But even in the quality papers the Euro-election seldom reached the front page. In the popular papers it got almost no coverage at all. The provincial papers gave it rather more attention – but hardly made it a major feature. In their last issue before the poll neither of the quality Sunday papers thought the election worth an editorial.

The two political stories of the period were first (and far the more prominent) how the new Government was doing, and, secondly, the development of recrimination within the Labour Party. Coverage of the European election tended to be used as an illustration to these themes rather than as a subject of interest in its own right.

The largest amount of space in the press came early in the campaign with the £600,000 display advertising sponsored jointly by the European Parliament and the European Commission. This was very low key and simply told people of the scale of the Community and the fact that an election was to take place on 7 June. It was all that was left of the £1,100,000 effort launched in February which had been suspended early in April so as not to impinge on the Westminster election. At their London office in Kensington Palace gardens, the European officials who designed the scheme felt very frustrated.

The portable exhibitions costing £150,000, which were intended for display on 190 sites in population centres around the country, had only been seen by a limited audience before they had to be abandoned. Another £150,000 was allotted to publications, and a certain amount of literature was distributed in minority languages among the ethnic communities. The European Parliament Office supplied speakers for 350 meetings and arranged for a phone-in service to answer questions about Europe, but there was a saddened recognition that the efforts before 7 April were relatively ineffective. After 3 May, only the press advertisements (three full-page displays in every daily paper between 10 May and 24 May) made much impact.

There is some evidence that the press advertisements helped considerably to add to the number of people who were aware of the European election. At the beginning of May an NOP survey found 14 per cent of people knew that there would be an election in June. By the end of the month, after the advertising campaign, the number had risen to 56 per cent. It is not unreasonable to attribute part of the increase to the advertisements, since so little else about the European election reached the great mass of the electors. This publicity effort had started with two goals – to make people aware of the election and to motivate them to vote; but it later acquired a third, negative, goal – simply to avoid political involvement. Those running it talked about keeping a low profile, but even so there were protests from anti-Marketeers that the propaganda was pro-European and therefore anti-Labour.

In some recent elections, the broadcasting authorities had been accused of 'overkill' and they were very sensitive to the charge. They

Yes. Have your say on June 7. Use your Eurovote.

You have a new vote. A vote you can use on Thursday June 7.

You can then elect your member of the European Parliament (also called the European Assembly).

Before you use your vote, here are some facts you need to know.

Why is this a new vote?

Up to now all the members of the European Parliament have been nominated from the national parliaments of the countries in the European Community.

But now they will be directly elected–by voters in each of the nine Community countries. Between June 7-10, 180 million Europeans will be able to vote together for the first time.

In fact, June 7 will see the world's first international elections.

What will my vote do?

It will give you a say about who represents you in the European Parliament – your European MP, who will have an influence on those Community matters which affect you.

What does the European Parliament do?

The Parliament helps to shape decisions taken by the Community. It has an important say about how much it spends, and on what.

It keeps a close eye on those who take decisions, and on those who carry them out–the Council of Ministers and the Commission.

What can my European MP in the Parliament do for me?

Your Member of the European Parliament will be able to raise any issue about the work of the Community that affects you.

Many of its decisions concern you directly. They affect, for example, employment, prices and the cost of food.

The Community has a major say in world trade agreements which affect your job and wage packet.

The European Community.

1. Belgium
2. Denmark
3. Fed. Rep. of Germany
4. France
5. Ireland
6. Italy
7. Luxembourg
8. Netherlands
9. United Kingdom

The Community spends its funds to help our poorer regions, to create new jobs and to help retrain workers. It is also concerned with the interests of the consumer and protecting the environment.

Your European MP will be there to keep an eye on your interests in all these matters.

How many European MPs will there be?

You will be helping to elect 81 British Members. France, Germany and Italy will also send 81 each; the Netherlands will send 25, Belgium 24, Denmark 16, Ireland 15 and Luxembourg 6 – a total of 410.

Who will be able to vote?

All those who have a vote in a general or local election.

Where and how can I vote?

You will vote at your nearest polling station in the usual way. In Northern Ireland voting will take place by the transferable vote system used in local elections.

What choice will I have?

Candidates will be put up by political parties or stand as independents.

How can I get more information?

Call in at your local authority offices or public library.

EUROPEAN ELECTIONS JUNE 7

Published by the European Parliament and the Commission of the European Communities, 20 Kensington Palace Gardens, London W8 4QQ.

also believed that the public had been bored by the extent to which politics had been allowed to dominate the airwaves. Particularly after the Westminster election they were reluctant to face a similar charge and the amount of broadcast coverage given to the European election was limited accordingly. Coverage was cut down for other reasons as well: lack of enthusiasm was manifest much earlier. A proposal was actually made by the broadcasting authorities that there should be no party broadcasts at all during the Euro-election, though this was later over-ruled. The broadcasters complained of a lack of planning time, since all their relevant producers had been engrossed in the Westminster election. In the end most of the main current affairs programmes devoted one or two editions to covering some aspect of the European election and each party was allowed one party political broadcast. But the contrast between the coverage of the European contest and the coverage of the Westminster election a month before was very marked indeed.[1]

Jay Blumler quoted a News Editor

I'm in a difficulty because my roles as a broadcaster and a journalist point me in different directions. As a journalist, my instinct is not to be interested at all, because the European elections lack the inherent drama of the UK General Election. You don't get the same polarisation: Will it be Jim or Maggie? Although it may grow, the influence and power of the European Community to change people's lives is also not great. As a broadcaster, one says, though, that this is one of the early steps towards what ultimately could be a profound road. And I've some duty at least to explain the process being started. So I have to force myself to be more interested than I naturally am.

He cited other programme makers saying 'What campaign?' 'Nothing is happening.' 'The general air of unexcitement' to justify their limited coverage.

Mallory Wober made the same point in a different fashion,

As the campaign unfolded, it became evident that little 'theatricalisation' was taking place. No principal characters standing for readily recognisable stereotypes were emerging, or indulging in any orchestrated series of playlets to build up adversarial momentum which would be resolved in the mass participant class of voting day. . . . There was no European government to be elected so there were few goals of the clarity to which the voting public is accustomed, to mobilise their attention. . . . The theatrical function of the broadcast enterprise . . . to generate a sense of excitement and participation among those who, without such busking would not join in, was also a failure.

[1] For a fuller discussion of the broadcast coverage see: J. Blumler, 'Communication in the European Elections: the Case of British Broadcasting', *Government and Opposition* (Autumn 1979); M. Wober, *The Election to the European Parliament* (IBA paper, October 1979).

Ironically, the evidence suggests that the broadcasters underrated public interest. The IBA survey found that 51 per cent of viewers thought there had not been enough European election coverage and only 15 per cent thought there had been too much. Alistar Burnet commented:

It may very well be that by playing it low-key we helped to make the election not only dull but incomprehensible. The responsibility for the low turnout may lie just as much at our door as at the politicians' door.

The programmes dealing with the election got a high appreciation rating except for Lord Grade's oddly conceived TV spectacular, a 'Eurogala' entertainment on 3 June. But less than half the viewers remembered seeing any programmes showing life in European countries. About a third recalled the party broadcasts, put out simultaneously on all channels (37 per cent mentioned seeing the Conservative effort, 33 per cent the Labour one and 20 per cent the Liberal one).[2] The main television news programmes averaged one election item per night over the final three weeks. The attempt to make the whole affair a European occasion met with limited success. The BBC morning radio programme *Today* was put out on successive days from the capitals of the Community. There were reports on campaigning in other countries but the plans for Europe-wide broadcasts largely came to nothing. The most newsworthy programmes were probably the radio phone-ins each morning, with Robin Day in the chair, in which listeners interrogated Ted Heath, Tony Benn, David Steel, Margaret Thatcher and Jim Callaghan: there were no gaffes but the man in the street's questions managed to highlight the strains within the major parties.

In the Labour Party the campaign marked the opening of the party's internal war. The National Executive, which had acquired control of the writing of the manifesto in January, also took control of the campaign. The NEC held a contentious meeting on 23 May to decide how to relaunch the manifesto. At one stage Mr Callaghan complained that he had not been consulted about the arrangements: 'I am not a wheel-horse to be wheeled on a platform when my support is needed.' In the end, on 24 May, Ron Hayward took the chair at the first press

[2] In the Institute of International Communications survey after the European elections, 54 per cent of British electors recalled watching some TV programme about them; 36 per cent remembered reading some newspaper report on the subject; 25 per cent claimed to have read election material sent to their door; 19 per cent to have listened to a radio programme; 19 per cent to have noticed a newspaper advertisement and 17 per cent a poster; 33 per cent said they had discussed the election with family or friends but only 5 per cent had been canvassed or spoken to party workers and only 2 per cent had attended a public meeting.

conference which had been delayed for two days while these matters were smoothed over. Mr Callaghan said that the question of leaving the Market was not going to arise because there was a Conservative Government in Britain. As for his own position, he would not have been at the launch of the manifesto unless he was able to give it 'his general support'. However, the newspapers continued to be on the watch for signs of conflict between Mr Benn and Mr Callaghan as they expressed their differing views on the European question, and at the end of the campaign Mr St John-Stevas attacked Mr Callaghan for letting Mr Benn preside over Labour's efforts 'like a political commissar'.

At an earlier NEC meeting the purists in the party had insisted on the scrapping of the election addresses that had been prepared, because the slogan on the front page was 'Labour for Europe' instead of 'Labour in Europe'. The press variously estimated the cost of this change between £27,000 and £60,000, all taken from the grant from Community funds (which were not supposed to be used for campaigning). Another unfortunate feature of the Labour campaign was a candidates' conference in Birmingham on 12 May, Cup Final Day. Tony Benn and Joan Lestor, the leading figures in the NEC European Liaison group, found themselves unable to attend; Frank Allaun, the Party Chairman, came alone to face a barrage of complaints from pro- and anti-Marketeers. As Ann Clwyd Roberts, an anti-Market candidate, wrote in *Labour Weekly* on 18 May,

Both candidates and agents voiced anger and frustration over the NEC's apparent wish to pretend that direct elections were a mirage which might, with luck, disappear as quickly as they appeared. It was suggested that the NEC's hostility towards the EEC had been directed towards its own candidates: there was a lack of finance; a lack of planning; a mishandling of money made available for the party's election information programme and general disarray.

'We have been treated as though we were the enemy for standing at these elections,' said one candidate.

It was said that the NEC had even refused at first to allow John Prescott, the leader of the Labour delegation in the previous European Parliament, to come to address the conference.

In general the mood of many people in the Labour party was one of resentful embarrassment about the election. They could hardly wait to get it over. They knew they were going to fare badly and there was a great potential for trouble. There were plenty of other things to worry about. But that did not prevent the critics of the Market from trying to get across to the faithful at public meetings and in the columns of *Tribune* and *Labour Weekly* and in Union journals and, in a fragmentary way, to the wider broadcast audience, the alternative approach to

Europe reflected in the NEC manifesto. The leading pro–Market Labour figures were somewhat muted, partly it was suggested because the Shadow Cabinet elections were due on 14 June: with a predominantly anti-Market parliamentary party, a degree of silence might be prudent.

The Conservatives went into the election better prepared and without internal divisions. They had their background documents and their campaign literature written and their manifesto was ready to be launched. The party was in high spirits because of its victory in the Westminster election. All it had to do was to coast along and avoid mistakes. Lord Thorneycroft presided over the campaign as a minor repeat of the general election. He faced few problems. The local crises and panics which are such a feature of general elections were absent. Each member of the Cabinet dutifully gave a speech; Mrs Thatcher appeared at three of the five press conferences. She had dominated press conferences during the Westminster election and, now that she was Prime Minister, questions were even more apt to focus on her. It was notable that although one of the most important issues in the election was agricultural policy, when the new Minister of Agriculture, Peter Walker, appeared on the platform with Mrs Thatcher, not a single question was addressed to him.

The Conservatives' biggest campaign effort was the occasion of Mrs Thatcher's only public speech. They held a large and successful youth rally near Birmingham on 3 June attended by 3,000 enthusiastic Young Conservatives who had been brought from a wide area to cheer their new Prime Minister. Mrs Thatcher said that although the Conservative party was committed to Europe, this did not mean that it would not 'argue tenaciously for our national interests when these are at stake'.

The Liberals had long planned a complex European campaign and were particularly frustrated by the obstinate inattention of the media. They made a virtue of holding three of their nine national press conferences outside London. David Steel launched the manifesto at the first one on 16 May; he complained of the injustice which would almost certainly deny the Liberals any representation in the European Parliament although in terms of popular percentage they were one of the strongest Liberal parties in Europe. He appealed to voters to take advantage of the situation when they were not choosing between a Labour and a Conservative Government but were free to express other sympathies. Although he only attended one other press conference he was the most energetic of the party leaders. He made a number of speeches and conducted two campaign tours but he attracted only local attention until his attack on the Conservative and Labour parties as 'grudging Europeans' in the party's broadcast on 3 June. Russell Johnston, who was the only Liberal candidate with real hopes of victory, was the party's strategist and spokesman in Scotland. The Liberals were very conscious of making the campaign a European affair: they saw it as starting with the great rally in Luxembourg on 7 April to which they sent over several planeloads of supporters and they arranged speeches or mini-tours for several eminent European Liberals including Guido Brunner, the EEC Commissioner. The European Liberals arranged a seminar in Inverness to help Russell Johnston's efforts. The British Liberals also sent over speakers to campaign in Europe, including David Alton, the new MP for Edge Hill.

They were much more energetic than the other parties, starting with a 'Eurofest' in Westminster on 8 May and arranging a daily telephone link with all their candidates and a telex link with the European Liberal parties. But except in local radio they won very little reward for all their ingenuity. The comment in the Party's Annual Report is worth quoting:

These Elections were held in the tired aftermath of the General and Local Elections, without any preparatory public information campaign (in contrast to the 1971 Great Debate and 1975 Referendum), with absurdly cumbersome and in many cases ill-drawn constituencies, an offensive voting system, unnecessarily expensive rules, deliberately low-key campaigns by Conservative and Labour and almost total disinterest by the media until the consciences of television, radio and the serious press were eventually pricked in the final ten days. Little wonder that the turn-out was only 32% in Britain and that our candidates and their helpers in the field and our small campaign team at HQ found it was like pounding dough.

The Scottish National Party fought the most anti-European campaign, arguing that membership of the EEC had done no good to Scotland. One of its candidates, Gordon Murray, argued that while the EEC reported Scottish wages at half the German or Belgian level

Scottish oil is expected to pay the bill for the UK contribution to the Community budget at the end of the day.

But they pointed out that the Euro-elections gave the Scots their first opportunity to by-pass Westminster – and that the EEC was much involved in the key Scottish issues – fishing, oil and regional aid. Yet they had difficulty in differentiating their stand on these issues from the other parties in Scotland. There was a general convergence on the need to fight for the country's interests at Brussels and Strasbourg – and the perception of what those interests were differed much less between the parties than it had done at the time of the 1975 Referendum. It was hard to give a Scottish dimension to the campaign, and, except in the north of Scotland where Winnie Ewing attracted attention, planehopping about her vast constituency, there seems to have been no more media interest in the campaign than there was south of the border.

There were one or two stories about the Ecology Party's campaign, with its spokesman's claim 'The major parties are ignoring the significant issues. . . . A fundamental change is going to occur in the life style and economies of the Western World.' There was also an occasional mention of Mebyon Kernow's efforts in Cornwall, but the lesser parties were largely ignored in the national coverage.

Fringe groups took some part in the campaign. The European Movement was active through its political wings. The Conservative Group for Europe, the Labour Campaign for Europe and the Liberal European Action Group sent briefings to candidates (and one Labour anti-Marketeer commented that it was more use than anything he received from Transport House). One effort, supported by the European Commission office in London, which attracted some attention was a service in Coventry Cathedral on the final Sunday of the campaign, in which representatives of the major parties participated in a 'Vision of Europe' service.

The European campaign was a totally different affair in Northern Ireland. The province was a single constituency and the use of proportional representation meant that it was everyone for himself in a contest where all the main contenders were, at least locally, celebrities. Ian Paisley, whose Democratic Unionists had made a considerable advance in May, was able to develop his assault on the Official Unionists, fortified by being an unequivocal anti-Marketeer in the area of the United Kingdom which, with the exception of the Scottish Islands, had yielded the largest NO vote in the 1975 Referendum; the Independent Unionist MP, James Kilfedder, reinforced the Unionist assault on the Official Unionists, Harry West and John Taylor, who were much more ready to defend the Community and in particular to speak up for what the Common Agricultural Policy had done for Northern Ireland farmers. On the other side, John Hume of the SDLP and the 'anti-repression' Bernadette Devlin-McAliskey, fought as old rivals but both with the avowed intention of using the European Parliament as a forum for solving, or at least publicising Ireland's problems. There was so much scope for expressing fine shades of preference within the rival Orange and Green camps, that there was little room left for the somewhat forlorn campaign of the moderate Oliver Napier of the Alliance Party.

Naturally the election was about 'the Irish dimension'. It was involved in all the European issues. The Common Agricultural Policy, the Green Pound, and the Regional Fund were each matters of great local interest and all became victims of sectarian argument. Ian Paisley could argue 'the EEC puts Your pound in Dublin's pocket' and that EEC membership gave £146 a year to each Eire citizen and took £20 from each UK citizen. John Taylor could reply that Northern Ireland farmers benefited particularly from the CAP but it was an argument that would not appeal to the urban half of the Ulster electorate. Moreover, the fact that European schemes benefited both sides of the Border could be an embarrassment. Ian Paisley, although ready 'to milk the EEC cow', could warn against 'annexationist EEC policies' originating in Dublin. He pointed out that the Community recognised the Republic's Constitution with its claim to sovereignty over all Ireland. John Hume, on the other hand, saw the Community as a means of 'peace and reconciliation'.

Enoch Powell campaigned belatedly for the Official Unionists but his appeal to British electors to vote Labour to dish the Common Market offered more comfort to Mr Paisley and Mr Kilfedder than to Mr West and Mr Taylor.

Northern Ireland moved from having the lowest turnout in the 1975 Referendum to having the highest turnout in June 1979. It is plain that the European election could stir up excitement. In Northern Ireland it may have been a parochial battle over familiar personalities and issues, but the novelty of the election, and the special local rules under which it was fought, developed fresh slants to the weary Orange and Green argument.[3]

Manifestos play a key role in British electoral politics. The drafting of the manifesto occupies every party, particularly if it is in opposition, for years in advance of the election, and a Westminster campaign necessarily centres around the themes of the manifesto. Usually few electors read the manifestos; even so, the central promises are known and publicised. Manifestos are powerful weapons in the politics of the years that follow as the Government is attacked or praised for breaking or fulfilling its promises. The parties duly produced manifestos for the European election but the documents had none of the importance of Westminster manifestos and they made little impact in the campaign. The candidates could not, in the nature of things, be bound by them; no Government was going to emerge from the election to be judged by its adherence to its promises.

However, the writing of the manifestos had considerable importance, at least on the Labour side. We described in Chapter 4 how the Labour NEC produced its manifesto on 24 January and how Tony Benn, on behalf of the Labour Party, also signed a Euro-socialist declaration of

[3] For a full discussion of the Northern Ireland campaign see P. A. Hainsworth, 'The European Election in Northern Ireland', *Parliamentary Affairs* (Autumn 1979).

principles. The manifesto, re-launched at the press conference on 24 May, contained two points which did play some part in what little campaign argument there was: the manifesto envisaged the possibility of leaving the Community and it demanded the return to Westminster of powers surrendered in 1973, (powers which, in fact, could not be returned without a fundamental renegotiation of the Treaty of Rome).[4]

The Conservative manifesto was drawn up by Sandy Walker and Michael Fallon in the Conservative Research Department during the winter of 1978–9, but, though it was virtually completed in February, it was not published until Mrs Thatcher launched it at a press conference on 18 May; some small late revisions had been made, designed to underline the fact that the new Conservative Government would work with a Conservative delegation in improving the European Community. The manifesto was an optimistic, but unexciting, document, which stressed the virtues of European membership and the need for the European Parliament to keep the Community under democratic control. Above all it emphasised the need to foster free enterprise in the shaping of Europe over the next 20 years.

The Liberal party made a virtue of fighting on the manifesto prepared by the Federation of Liberal and Democratic Parties of the EEC. It added only a short UK supplement to the document. The whole stress was the most optimistic and European-minded of all the manifestos, with an underlying commitment to federalism.

The SNP manifesto argued more briefly for the importance of SNP representation in the European Parliament.

The SNP alone among the political parties in Scotland warned the Scottish voter in the 1975 referendum that Common Market membership would mean higher food prices, more unemployment, subsidies for butter mountains and wine lakes, and severe damage to Scottish fishing interests.

Its record of opposition to the present form of the Common Market qualified it uniquely to speak for Scotland in the European Parliament:

SNP members in the European Parliament will spell out to the Common Market that Scotland rejects a status that condemns her to only *eight* MPs, while Denmark with the same population has *sixteen*. They will insist in front of European opinion on Scotland's right to join the international community as a free and equal nation.

Lying within the manifestos can be found the issues on which such serious argument as there was took place during the campaign. The high price of food and the disillusion with the Common Agricultural

---

[4] A full text of the Labour, Conservative and Liberal manifestos, as well as those of the European democrats and the European Socialists, is printed at the end of *The Times Guide to the 1979 European Parliament* (London 1980).

Policy were undoubtedly the matters that stirred people most. The idea that the Community was a device for robbing the British tax-payer to subsidise French farmers was used quite widely by the more anti-Market Labour candidates. Mark Hughes pointed out, moreover, that 14 of the 20 Conservatives standing for the safest seats had substantial farming interests and that they would not be there to fight for the consumers of Britain. It is unlikely that many people understood the subtleties of the Common Agricultural policy, but there is no doubt that it was used as the most potent symbol of the unsatisfactoriness of the EEC.

The issue of sovereignty was of course exploited by many, most notably Mr Benn and Mr Powell, but Mr Healey, too, argued that Labour was most to be trusted to resist the federalist tendencies in the Market. One or two people spoke of the Community as a safeguard against war. David Owen was provoked to an eloquent speech arguing that the Community must never be allowed to become involved in defence arrangements. It was an economic not a military Community. Mr Heath described Mr Benn and Mr Powell as out of date: 'They will find themselves washed up on the sands of time.' In some regions stress was laid on the aid that had come from the Market. It was argued, for example, that Scotland was a net beneficiary as a result of regional grants.

The critics who said that the election lacked a theatrical aspect and provided no clear confrontations were fully justified. Mrs Thatcher and most of her ministers each made a single speech.

Mr Macmillan, at 85, emerged from retirement to speak to his pre-war constituency of Stockton and then in Bradford. He had decided

to play some small part in the first elections to a European Parliament in the true sense . . . The next decade will see not Britain reproached for being in decline but as she has always been in her great periods, when true to herself, proud and strong as a lion

and he praised Ted Heath for 'the everlasting glory' of having taken Britain into Europe. This drew a characteristic retort from Michael Foot

He roared into Suez like a lion and came out like a lamb. I don't think he is the best person to advise us . . . Some Conservatives look upon the market as a kind of substitute for the British Empire which they were so successful in losing.

After the first press conference, Mr Callaghan was little in evidence. But, despite discouragement from some in the NEC, he went on 27 May to a rally of Socialist leaders in Paris.

The limelight for most of the campaign fell on two newsworthy politicians. Edward Heath was incomparably the most energetic Conservative, appearing on platforms throughout the country and visiting 39 constituencies. When he was asked why he was doing so much more than the official leadership of the party he tactfully said that they were all busy with their departments. None the less, his vigorous and strongly pro-European stance put a stamp on the whole campaign. In Trowbridge on 29 May he recalled the hot May of 1945

when we celebrated VE Day. That was the time many of us decided to go into politics to prevent the same thing happening again. I don't think any of us thought that only 34 years later, in every country, friends and foe alike, we would be going to the polls together. Europe needs us to show them how to make the new democracy work.

In a debate at the Cambridge Union three days before the poll Mr Heath denied that direct elections in any way affected national sovereignty and told his audience

You will look back and say 'I was there on June 7, 1979, when European democracy was created.'

He carried the motion against Enoch Powell who suggested that his undergraduate audience might even have to fight for the right to remain a sovereign state

It is a question which cannot be argued about. It is a question which can only be felt about, acted about, and in the last resort fought about . . . There are few in this chamber who have personal experience of the sensation of what it is to respond to the threat to national existence . . . The question of nation or no nation is the most important and fundamental question that people can ask themselves. I believe we shall be a nation still.

The Labour campaign was clearly led by Tony Benn. He may have been reluctant for Labour to fight the election but once the battle was joined he did not spare himself. In some places he only got small audiences but he was still quotable and attracted far more publicity than any other Labour spokesman. In a broadcast on 4 June he said

It is the first election in human history demanded by the people at the top and not wanted by the electorate as a whole. Every other election has been demanded by the people and resisted by the government. It is, I think, because the commission wants a sort of fan club to support their own demands for greater federal control. . . . [The election was about choosing whether] you want Britain to govern itself or have a federal Europe.

The role of the new Conservative ministers was very much linked to their new bargaining position. They were trying to reassure a sceptical electorate that their past pro-European stance did not mean that they would be pushovers in any negotiations with the rest of the Community. They were also trying to pass the same message in a more sophisticated way to their European colleagues. George Younger, the new Scottish secretary, proclaimed a strong stand on British fishing interests 'If all else fails the government reserves the right to take unilateral action', and Peter Walker, the new Agriculture Minister, indicated his intention of getting fundamental changes in the CAP. Francis Pym stressed that defence lay outside the EEC's purview 'The Treaty of Rome does not provide for common policies on defence' and Douglas Hurd, for the Foreign Office, called for the voice of British common sense to be injected into the working of the EEC

Unlike Labour, we Conservatives understand and support the aims of the Community. That should put us in a stronger position to advance our own interests as part of Europe.

But perhaps the most significant intervention in the election came from Enoch Powell who urged his own voters in Northern Ireland to support the Ulster Unionists but asked electors in Britain to vote for the Labour party because there was a far greater chance of Labour members fighting for the United Kingdom to regain the sovereignty she had 'so wantonly lost' in 1973.

It was supposedly a European election and several distinguished Europeans, mainly Liberals, came to take part. Mr Callaghan spoke jointly with François Mitterrand to a final rally in Leeds. These incursions from across the channel, however, drew little publicity.

Mr Callaghan in a message to candidates on 5 June wrote

Britain no longer has a government determined to defend with the greatest energy, the interests of ordinary people, here or in the Community.

Mr Whitelaw retorted that Mr Callaghan

is trying hard to pretend that the party is united on Europe. But in reality the only thing on which Labour can unite is the foolish threat to withdraw if our partners do not do exactly as they are told by Mr. Benn and Mr. Silkin.

Mr Silkin had said that Common Market membership would soon prove insupportable for Britain without changes in the Community's agricultural arrangements and, in his final speech, Mr Callaghan added that if the Conservatives did not achieve such a reform

they deserve to be kicked from here to Land's End. The Community as it is shaped at the present time – perhaps because we were late entrants to the Community – does not fit many of the problems that we have in this country [But Labour was not threatening to withdraw from the EEC] We did not go in to it saying we will come out if we don't get what we want.

That last phrase was taken as a deliberate comment on the passage in the Labour manifesto which suggested that if reforms were not achieved within a reasonable period of time 'then the Labour party would have to consider very seriously whether continued EEC membership was in the best interests of the British people'.

Anxieties about the turnout were expressed from many quarters. Roy Jenkins came over from Brussels to speak on 1 June. He warned:

A low British turnout will make it more difficult for Britain to get the changes it wants. It is easy but dangerous to find false reasons for non-participation . . . The argument that Europe has run itself into the sand and lost its momentum, if true, should mean action, not non-participation.

Joan Lestor, the Labour chairman, urged anti-Marketeers not to abstain.

There is a job to be done in the EEC in bringing about a better deal for Britain . . . As the campaign has gone on the Tory party has latched on and begun to exploit the very criticisms that many of us made about the EEC from the very beginning. It seems to me that the Tory party has recognised the apprehensions of many people. Their own voters are beginning to acknowledge that many of our criticisms were in fact valid.

Mrs Thatcher at her final press conference on 6 June summarised her approach to the election

We want a good turnout because we have a chance of being the largest single group in the new Parliament. That of itself would give the British tremendous influence . . . The Centre and right wing parties must stick together . . . Every single free country in the world is largely a free enterprise country.

Any verdicts on the European election campaign in Britain must be set in the context of its timing. It could not have come at a worse moment for exciting the interest of the parties or of the public. The country was sated with electioneering: there had been the Scottish and Welsh referendums and the local government contests before the Westminster campaign – and that had been hanging over the nation since the previous summer and, when it came, had been elongated into a five-week drama. The experience had exhausted the appetite of the media for following a new campaign. The parties, too, had little incentive to stir things up. It was too soon to use the contest to prove the popularity or unpopularity of the new Government. The Westminster election had left the Conservatives too busy and the Labour Party too shocked to give them any zest for a fight which in any case would have been hard to dramatise unless as an aspect of the domestic party battle.

What, in Britain, was the European election about? Voters were asked to choose between more grudging Europeans and less grudging

Europeans – but the lines were not clearly drawn. Since the issue of staying in or leaving was not at stake, the question was to decide which personalities or tactics would secure what almost every candidate demanded – the reform of the Common Agricultural Policy and the lessening of Brussels bureaucracy. It is hard to discuss with a mass electorate the subtleties of negotiating tactics, but some voters seemed to have doubts about sending declared sceptics about the Common Market to work as parliamentarians for the reform of Community Institutions.

The campaign may also have been muted by the unfamiliarity of the situation. The parties and the media had to learn how to cope with a new type of contest. Constituencies with 500,000 electors could not be tackled like constituencies with 50,000. It is arguable that even Westminster constituencies have long outgrown those rituals of electioneering still preserved from nineteenth-century contests (when there were only 5,000 or even 500 voters to persuade). One candidate commented acidly on his difficulty in persuading a BBC producer that he would not be filmed canvassing because he was deliberately doing no canvassing; he saw it as a wasteful and irrelevant activity when, by driving slowly through shopping centres on top of a bus, he could draw the attention of 5,000 to 10,000 people per day. That, and the relentless pursuit of the local press and broadcast outlets, had to be the nature of Euro-campaigning.

But few people in the parties or the media had really thought about the nature of a European election. On the whole, they tried to make it like a low key Westminster election. Hugh Thomas described the Europe-wide elections as 'national elections with a European face'. But in Britain even the European face was missing and, as a national election, it lacked the spark that can make national elections exciting. There were, it is true, replicas of all the activities tht characterise a national election – press conferences, leaders' speeches, canvassing, loudspeakering and party political broadcasts. But these were on a small scale. The national politicians were not themselves candidates; most of them only gave a day or two to the European contest. The customary exchanges between party leaders at successive press conferences and in nightly speeches did not take place. There was little argument between the parties on the nature of Britain's role in Europe or the real advantage of voting for one party or the other. Most politicians saw it as a tired and lack-lustre affair, and it sparked neither eloquence nor enthusiasm in them.

Yet it can be argued that an opportunity was missed. Fire could have been put into the campaign. As one reporter commented on the eve of the poll 'When Mr. Macmillan spoke, we knew what we had been missing'. In his two speeches the old actor had offered something of the theatre that had been so conspicuously absent. Mr Heath and Mr Benn and a few other leading figures had campaigned vigorously and with some passion but their utterances had not been widely covered. The press conference exchanges which have for 20 years provided the staple of Westminster campaigns hardly took place. The politicians were not trying very hard. One reason for this was that the media were not reporting them or encouraging them to think the public was interested (although the media could riposte that it was the politicians' fault for not saying or doing newsworthy things). But the public was not quite as apathetic as some people suggested. As we showed on pp. 113–4 they felt that the broadcasters gave insufficient time to the European elections – and they felt this more strongly than the electorate in any other Community country.

The Conservatives fought the election without any great gusto. It is true that the party has always had a much more efficient machine, centrally and in the constituencies than the Labour Party; and in the summer of 1979 they had no serious internal divisions on the European issue while their activists included a significant proportion of Euro-enthusiasts. Therefore it was natural that they should put on a far more organised campaign than their opponents. But Chapter 7 showed, and as their limited success in fund raising in the constituencies confirmed, there was no vast enthusiasm for the affair. At the centre the leadership was preoccupied with taking office and making a success of Government.

In addition there was a fear – that could not be voiced – of winning too overwhelmingly. If turnout was going to be as selective between pro- and anti-Market voters as some polls suggested, there was a possibility that Labour might only get one or two seats. Apart from misgivings about the quality of some of the Conservatives who would then emerge as MEPs, strategists were aware that a delegation to Strasbourg composed almost entirely of Conservatives might not be in the national interest. Apart from the indignation that such an outcome would generate about the unfairness of the electoral system, it would serve to drive Labour into a still more anti-European stance and it would not help relations with Community partners, half of whom had a socialist party represented in their Government.

But there was another inhibition to the Conservative campaign. The country was not in a pro-European mood and attacks on the Labour Party for its half-heartedness or hostility to the Common Market were hardly likely to win over votes. Moreover, the new Government was learning how serious were going to be its problems over the British contribution to the European Budget. At a time when public opinion might have to be rallied behind a firm stand against the Community, it was inappropriate to offer hostages to fortune by praising what the EEC had done or would do for Britain. Apart from the ebullient Europeanism of the backbench Mr Heath, it was a *sotto voce* campaign by the Conservatives. They did the minimum necessary in a competent way but they won few headlines and stirred no passions.

The Labour Party was in disarray, not just because it had lost the Westminster election, but also because Europe had in so many ways become the symbolic battleground between left and right, between NEC and Cabinet, between the mass party and the élite. Perhaps no compromise was ever possible, but the NEC exacerbated the situation by refusing for so long to accept that there were going to be elections and that the Labour Party must in the end fight them, and by using the writing of the Euro-manifesto so explicitly as a weapon in the battle over control of the Wesminster manifesto. If the decision to fight the European elections had been made early in 1978 (when it was plain that the necessary legislation was going to get through Parliament), Transport House and the constituencies would have been much better prepared. If the decision to fight had not been followed by a rearguard obstructionism, many of the frustrations chronicled by Labour candidates in Chapter 7 would have been obviated. But the blame does not lie exclusively with the NEC. It can be argued that the pro-Marketeers and the front-bench also failed to give appropriate priority to preparing for the campaign. Their tactics in resisting or debating the NEC manifesto in January 1979 were, as Chapter 4 showed, ill managed. And when the campaign came, they were not much in evidence. The Shadow Cabinet had far more free time than the Cabinet but Shadow ministers, with one or two exceptions, were as inactive as ministers on the hustings. The right wing of the party was painfully aware that the Common Market was the one big issue on which public opinion was more sympathetic to their opponents in the party than to themselves.[5]

[5] It is worth recording the attitudes to the Market at the time of the vote.

The last EEC monitor poll before the election (30 May–4 June) found the public believing 37 per cent–34 per cent that EEC membership was currently good for UK. Future membership was favoured 43–25 per cent.

In an ORC survey the day after the election day ITN found 40 per cent saying YES and 47 per cent saying NO to the question 'Generally speaking are you in favour or against Britain being a member of the Common market?' Those who had actually voted were 57 per cent to 34 per cent in favour but those who had not were 28 per cent to 55 per cent against. When asked whether Britain's future interests would be better served by staying in the Common Market or by getting out, the full sample by 50 per cent to 36 per cent thought staying in was better. By 34 per cent to 33 per cent they thought the European Parliament 'should have more power'.

The Liberals put energy and ingenuity into the battle but their arguments were not popular arguments; in any case they went largely unheard, thanks to the harsh judgements of news editors about what the public wanted to see or hear or read. The Scottish Nationalists admit that their campaign lacked the zest that had been put into earlier battles.

The contest could not be about detailed policies. The public, and even some of the candidates, were too ignorant about the details of the Common Agricultural Policy and of how monies could be secured for local purposes from the Regional Fund and the Social Fund for there to be any serious argument about the matters on which MEPs might really be able to exercise some influence.[6] And on the more general question of Britain's involvement in the Community, candidates in all parties were pressed towards some convergence. The hedging process that had begun during candidate selection continued. The election never became a re-run of the Referendum. There were far more votes to be lost than won by being either stridently anti-Market or ardently federalist. It was worth pursuing the support of middle of the road voters. And so it was hard for the public to see what the campaign was about. At the national level those who campaigned and those who reported the campaign did little to help them.

A NOTE ON THE COSTS OF THE ELECTION

As we showed on p. 99 candidates reported spending on average £4,581 each. The grand total of expenditure by Conservative candidates was £613,000, by Labour candidates £346,000 and by Liberals about £210,000. All candidates put together returned an outlay of £1,318,823.

The other costs of the election are harder to measure. Of the £1¼ m. allocated to publicity by the Community £600,000 was spent during the campaign on press advertising. The total administrative costs of the election, including Post Office costs for distributing free of charge election addresses, were reckoned to be about £12 m, almost all in monies paid to Returning Officers. The broadcasting authorities can offer no estimate of the cost of putting on the party broadcasts; they might be regarded as part of their general service. But in commercial terms that amount of air time has a considerable notional value.

[6] The Conservatives set up a special three man office in Eaton Place to deal with campaign queries but very few came in. Ron Hayward told the Labour Conference that Transport House Research Department received barely half a dozen enquiries.

The central expenses of the parties raise particular difficulties. How much of their ordinary costs during the campaign should be charged to it? Moreover, there is a problem of double counting since substantial sums were distributed to the regions or the constituencies which also appear in the candidates' returns of expenses.

The Conservatives estimate that they spent £232,000 between 10 May and 10 June on the European elections. It came out of the money raised by their general election appeal. About £45,000 was spent on general establishment, additional personnel, postage and the like; £55,000 went on printing the manifesto and the election guide and £80,000 on publicity, including the television broadcasts; £50,000 was allocated to cash grants to the needier constituencies.

The money that the Conservatives received from Brussels (£460,000 over the two years 1978 and 1979) financed most of their Euro-activities to 10 May since these could largely be classed as informational. But they claim that after 10 May they were scrupulous to charge nothing to this source.

With the Labour Party it was different. Norman Atkinson, the Treasurer, had told the Labour Conference on 3 October 1978 that 'there will be no money at all for the European elections than can come from central funds' and that was largely adhered to: the minimal costs of managing four press conferences and arranging leaders' travel came from the routine Transport House budget. Almost all other expenditure seems to have been met out of the £230,000 which the Labour Party received from Brussels in 1978 and 1979 through the Confederation of Socialist Parties for 'information purposes'. A lot of this was devoted to printing the manifesto and the election addresses – including those pulped because they said 'Labour for Europe' instead of 'Labour in Europe'. But in the end the party did make available £25,000 for grants to the constituencies.

The Liberals, too, depended heavily on European money. In 1978 they received £75,000 and in 1979 £100,000 through the European Liberal Democrats.[7] The 1978 contribution was spent on information and education in the embryo Euro-constituencies. So was a part of the 1979 contribution. The balance, together with a small sum from party funds, was devoted to grants to regions and to constituencies (£62,000 – each constituency receiving £600, the equivalent of the deposit) and to central expenses during the campaign (£9,000 – mainly literature).

The SNP received no Euro-funds and used 'less than £5,000' on its

[7] For figures on the overall allocation of money to the European parties see pp. 223–5 *The Times Guide to the European Parliament* (London 1980).

central campaign, although Winnie Ewing in her Highlands and Islands campaign spent more per capita (3.6 p.) than any other candidate in the country.

These party figures are not strictly comparable but they give at least an indication of the amount of central effort put into the campaign. It should, however, be recorded that the different parties interpreted the 'information purposes' condition to the European grants in very different ways. It was very hard to discover from Community sources how the money was spent or audited. As the first example of the public subsidy of mass (as distinct from parliamentary) political activity, its arrangements remain a source of some mystery.

CHAPTER NINE
Outcome

The weather on polling day was mixed. But the intermittent rain was not sufficient to explain the extraordinarily low level of party activity and the reports of empty polling stations. The election had not supplied the main headline in any national newspaper on 7 June. All mentioned it, but usually in the tone of the *Daily Telegraph* story 'LABOUR FEARS OF EURO POLL ROUT'. On 8 June, however, much attention was paid to the negligible turnout and there was gloomy head shaking about its implications. Yet the most colourful story came from Brussels, where some British nationals, protesting at not having a vote, set up a polling station in a bus and encouraged their compatriots to sign a petition to Mrs Thatcher demanding the franchise.

As the ballots were checked in Westminster constituencies[1] on Friday, 8 June, it became apparent that the participation was even lower than the worst expectations. Only in Northern Ireland did the turnout reach 50 per cent; in the Scotland-Exchange division of Liverpool only 16 per cent voted. Nationwide the figure was 32.1 per cent. Turnout was markedly higher in Conservative rural seats than in urban areas but, as John Curtice shows in the Appendix, the explanation that Labour's poor performance was simply due to the party's supporters' staying at home does not accord with the figures.

The formal count of votes was not allowed to begin until 9 p.m. on 10 June when the last polls had closed in Europe (five of the nine countries were voting on the Sunday). Helped by a promise of overtime payments from the Home Office 49 of the 78 Returning Officers counted on Sunday night. By the time the first UK result was available at 10 p.m., much of the European outcome was plain (only the

---

[1] In Devon they were checked in local government areas.

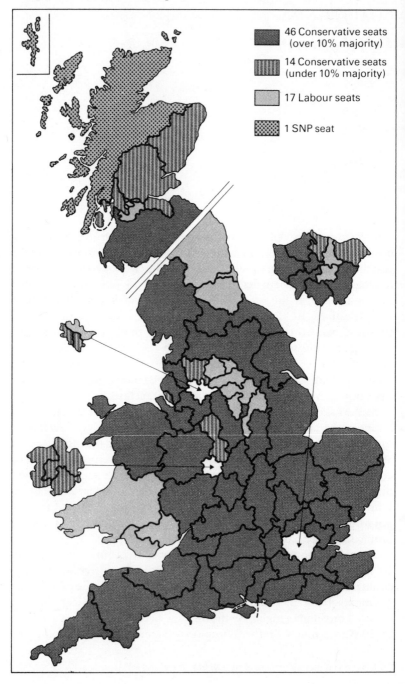

46 Conservative seats
(over 10% majority)

14 Conservative seats
(under 10% majority)

17 Labour seats

1 SNP seat

Netherlands and Ireland waited until Monday to count). The early results from various parts of Britain showed that Labour, though faring very poorly, was not being annihilated as some had feared.

When the final figures for Britain were in by lunchtime on Monday the Conservatives had won 60 of the 78 seats they fought and Labour secured a mere 17. Mrs Ewing was returned for the SNP in Highlands and Islands and the three Northern Irish seats were divided between Ian Paisley (DUP), John Taylor (OUP), and John Hume (SDLP) representing the three largest tendencies in Ulster politics. The Liberals with 13 per cent of the UK vote got no seats (though Russell Johnston ran Winnie Ewing fairly close, and pushed the Conservatives into third place).

Geographically, Labour's performance was very patchy. The North-South divide, so evident in the Westminster elections in May, looked even more extreme. Labour's only English successes south of the Nottinghamshire-Yorkshire coalfields were in two Inner London seats. Labour won three seats in Wales and two in Scotland. Of their 17 MEPs, 9 came from the 12 seats east of the Pennines between Northumberland and Nottingham.

There was a 5 per cent swing to the Conservatives compared to the Westminster elections – but it was unevenly spread. One or two results might have personal explanations. Of the two slight swings to Labour, one (0.2%) was in Greater Manchester North where Barbara Castle was displaying her North Country force and charm. Not far away Liverpool showed the largest swing to Conservative (11.3%), perhaps because Terence Harrison, the Labour candidate, was a much-publicised member of the Trotskyite Militant tendency. Ernest Wistrich, Director of the European Movement, in Cleveland, suffered the next biggest anti-Labour swing (8.7%), partly perhaps because of his efficient and well-publicised pro-European campaign and partly because of the intervention of an anti-Market left winger who got 3.3 per cent of the vote.

Three well-known Liberals fared exceptionally well. Lord Mackie in Scotland North East (24.5%, an increase over May of 15.2%), Chris Mayhew in Surrey (29.7%, +9.9%) and David Cobbold in Hertfordshire (24.2%, +10.0%). None of the independent anti-Marketeers made much impact although Air Marshal Bennett got 6.1 per cent of the vote in Cotswolds. A notable minor party vote was Mebyon Kernow's 5.9 per cent in Cornwall and Plymouth (if a Cornish Nationalist had no appeal in Plymouth, that represented 9% of the vote in Cornwall).

There was one small irony flowing from the British insistence on making European elections rules as similar to Westminster ones as

Table 5

		Rank order of safety §	Turnout (%)	Con. (%)	Lab. (%)	Lib. (%)	Nat. (%)	Other (%)	Swing May_ June 1979††
England									
London									
London C.	Sir D. Nicolson (Con.)	33	30.5	54.4	29.3	12.2	–	E4.1	7.5
London E.	A. Tyrrell (Con.)	11	29.5	48.8	40.7	10.5	–	–	1.8
London N.	J. Marshall (Con.)	14	28.5	49.7	39.7	10.6	–	–	3.5
London N.E.	A. Lomas (Lab.)	(15)	20.4	34.1	57.5	8.3	–	–	–1.9
London N.W.	Ld Bethell (Con.)	30	31.3	55.3	31.1	13.6	–	–	5.4
London S.	J. Moorhouse (Con.)	40	33.4	58.9	27.0	14.1	–	–	4.4
London S.E.	Sir B. R.-Williams (Con.)	29	34.3	55.0	32.0	12.5	–	0.5	1.7
London S.Inner	R. Balfe (Lab.)	(5)	27.3	43.6	48.8	7.6	–	–	2.7
London S.W.	Shelagh Roberts (Con.)§§	23	31.4	52.0	32.2	13.2	–	2.2, 0.4	4.6
London W.	B. Hord (Con.)	17	33.0	51.0	38.3	9.7	–	0.9	4.0
South East									
Hants. E. & Wight	S. Johnson (Con.)	57★	34.5	64.7	17.6	17.8	–	–	–
Hampshire W.	B. de Ferranti (Con.)	54★	33.6	58.9	17.7	23.5	–	–	–
Hertfordshire	D. Prag (Con.)	31	36.9	50.2	25.6	24.2	–	–	3.3
Kent E.	C. Jackson (Con.)	55	32.4	64.7	22.1	11.1	–	2.1	7.9
Kent W.	B. Patterson (Con.)	47	32.9	60.8	24.8	14.5	–	–	6.3
Surrey	Mquis of Douro (Con.)	53★	37.8	54.3	13.8	29.7	–	A2.1	–
Sussex E.	Sir J. S.-Clark (Con.)	56	35.1	65.7	17.4	16.4	–	–	5.4
Sussex W.	M. Seligman (Con.)	60★	35.3	65.9	13.5	17.9	–	A2.7	–
Thames Valley	Lady Elles (Con.)	52	33.2	63.1	22.7	14.2	–	–	4.7
Upper Thames	R. Jackson (Con.)	48	33.0	59.4	22.9	17.7	–	–	5.7
South West									
Bristol	R. Cottrell (Con.)	27	35.1	54.2	32.1	13.7	–	– M5.9	6.4
Cornwall & Ply.	D. Harris (Con.)	44	35.0	55.2	21.4	13.5	–	E3.0 A1.1	–
Devon	Ld O'Hagan (Con.)	58★	38.5	61.8	18.2	20.0	–	–	–
Somerset	Sir F. Warner (Con.)	48★	38.4	57.0	19.9	23.1	–	–	–
Wessex	J. Spicer (Con.)	59★	37.2	63.3	15.1	20.8	–	0.8	–
East Anglia									
Bedfordshire	P. Beazley (Con.)	38	33.7	58.8	27.9	12.6	–	0.7	7.2
Cambridgeshire	Sir F. Catherwood (Con.)	42	32.2	59.0	26.3	14.7	–	–	5.6
Essex N.E.	A. Sherlock (Con.)	51	32.5	60.7	20.5	16:1	–	A2.8	5.0
Essex S.W.	D. Curry (Con.)	26	30.5	53.9	31.9	14.2	–	–	3.2
Norfolk	P. Howell (Con.)	36	34.1	59.8	30.4	9.8	–	–	7.1
Suffolk	A. Turner (Con.)	43ʹ	32.3	60.4	27.0	12.6	–	–	6.8
East Midlands									
Derbyshire	T. Spencer (Con.)	15	30.1	50.9	39.2	9.9	–	–	6.6
Leicestershire	F. Tuckman (Con.)	25	32.5	55.1	34.7	10.2	–	–	4.2
Lincolnshire	W. Newton-Dunn (Con.)	46	31.3	61.5	26.3	12.3	–	–	7.2
Midlands E.	J. M. Taylor (Con.)	24	32.3	55.3	35.1	9.6	–	–	5.8
Northants	A. Simpson (Con.)	41	32.8	59.6	27.1	13.3	–	–	6.2
Nottingham	M. Gallagher (Lab.)	(1)	28.6	44.8	45.9	9.4	–	–	2.7
West Midlands									
Birmingham N.	E. Forth (Con.)	9	26.6	47.8	42.0	10.2	–	–	2.4
Birmingham S.	Norvella Forster (Con.)	5	27.3	47.5	43.7	8.8	–	–	2.7
Cotswolds	Sir H. Plumb (Con.)	50	36.5	58.6	20.3	15.0	–	A6.1	7.2
Hereford & Worcs.	J. Scott-Hopkins (Con.)	39	34.8	58.5	27.5	14.0	–	–	2.5

Table 5 (cont.)

		Rank order of safety §	Turnout (%)	Con. (%)	Lab. (%)	Lib. (%)	Nat. (%)	Other (%)	Swing May– June 1979††
Midlands C.	J. Ling (Con.)	37	34.0	57.9	28.5	9.7	–	E3.9	6.9
Midlands W.	R. Simmonds (Con.)	3	27.3	47.3	46.0	6.7	–	–	1.7
Salop & Staffs.	C. Prout (Con.)	35	32.2	57.5	28.9	10.5	–	3.1	5.4
Staffs. E.	R. Moreland (Con.)	7	28.4	48.7	44.2	7.2	–	–	4.5
North East									
Cleveland	Sir P. Vanneck (Con.)	22	28.2	50.6	34.2	12.0	–	A3.3	8.7
Durham	R. Boyes (Lab.)	(12)	27.7	35.1	54.2	10.6	–	–	3.8
Humberside	R. Battersby (Con.)	18	30.1	51.7	36.8	11.5	–	–	5.4
Leeds	D. Enright (Lab.)	(7)	28.6	37.7	45.6	14.6	–	–	0.9
Northumbria	G. Adam (Lab.)	(4)	32.2	39.9	44.8	15.3	–	–	5.3‡
Sheffield	R. Caborn (Lab.)	(9)	29.4	42.1	50.7	7.2	–	–	5.4
S. Tyne & Wear	Joyce Quin (Lab.)	(3)	29.8	44.9	49.2	6.0	–	–	7.3
Yorkshire N.	N. Balfour (Con.)	45	34.5	57.1	24.8	16.1	–	–	5.6
Yorkshire S.	B. Key (Lab.)	(17)	27.0	32.6	58.3	9.1	–	–	1.7
Yorkshire S.W.	T. Megahy (Lab.)	(11)	29.0	35.9	51.9	12.3	–	–	1.5
Yorkshire W.	B. Seal (Lab.)	(2)	33.3	44.4	46.2	9.3	–	–	0.4
North West									
Cheshire E.	T. Normanton (Con.)	32	31.7	56.1	31.5	12.5	–	–	6.0
Cheshire W.	A. Pearce (Con.)	34	32.6	56.8	28.7	14.5	–	–	7.9
Cumbria	Elaine K.-Bowman (Con.)	28	34.8	56.4	33.7	9.0	–	0.9	4.9
G. Manchester N.	Barbara Castle (Lab.)	(10)	31.7	39.2	50.2	10.6	–	–	–0.2
G. Manchester S.	Ld H-Nicholls (Con.)	8	29.8	47.5	42.5	10.0	–	–	5.0
G. Manchester W.	W. Hopper (Con.)	1	29.4	43.3	43.1	13.7	–	–	2.7
Lancashire C.	M. Welsh (Con.)	21	31.6	54.1	31.7	8.2	–	–	3.9
Lancashire E.	Ed. K.-Bowman (Con.)	13	33.2	49.9	40.6	7.9	–	1.6	3.3
Lancashire W.	P. C. Price (Con.)	16	28.0	51.2	38.7	7.8	–	2.2	7.3
Liverpool	Gloria Hooper (Con.)	10	23.7	45.2	38.7	16.1	–	–	11.3
Wales									
Wales Mid. & W.	Ann Clwyd (Lab.)	(6)	38.2	36.0	41.5	9.4	12.2	1.0	2.9
Wales N.	Beata Brookes (Con.)	20	35.9	41.9	26.3	12.4	19.3	–	5.3
Wales S.	W. Griffiths (Lab.)	(8)	32.9	37.9	44.1	10.1	7.9	–	7.4
Wales S.E.	A. Rogers (Lab.)	(16)	31.1	30.3	54.8	6.2	7.3	1.3	5.9
Scotland									
Glasgow	Janey Buchan (Lab.)	(14)	28.2	27.3	49.0	7.3	16.4	–	5.3
Highlands & Is.	Winnie Ewing (SNP)	†	39.4	26.1	9.2	30.7	34.0	–	–
Lothians	I. Dalziel (Con.)	4	34.9	35.6	32.6	15.8	16.0	–	6.7
Scotland Mid. & Fife	J. Purvis (Con.)	6	35.0	35.1	31.2	9.6	24.1	–	6.7
Scotland N.E.	J. Provan (Con.)	12*	32.7	33.0	24.2	24.5	18.3	–	–
Scotland S.	A. Hutton (Con.)	19	34.5	43.0	27.7	10.8	18.5	–	7.6‡
Strathclyde E.	K. Collins (Lab.)	(13)	31.3	28.6	49.8	7.1	14.5	–	3.2
Strathclyde W.	A. Fergusson (Con.)	2	35.6	37.2	36.1	10.2	16.5	–	6.3
Northern Ireland									
	I. Paisley (DUP)						29.8**		
	J. Hume (SDLP)		55.7				24.6**		
	J. Taylor (OUP)						11.9**		

For notes to table see p. 136

possible. Shelagh Roberts who was elected for London South West found that, as an unpaid member of the Occupational Pensions Board, she held technically 'an office of profit under the Crown' at the time of the poll and was therefore disqualified. If she had been elected to Westminster, Parliament could have passed an indemnifying Act to put the situation right. But retrospective legislation would not have been acceptable to the European Parliament and so, at considerable expense, a by-election had to be held in September. Miss Roberts was returned with a reduced majority.

The Conservative vote of 51 per cent marked the first time since 1931 that any British party had secured over half the votes in a national election.[2] The British turnout of 32 per cent was sharply at variance with that of her Community partners though the turnout everywhere was lower than is customary in national elections.[3] Only in Denmark (47%) was it below 60 per cent. It was notable that Northern Ireland, with proportional representation and a personality contest between well-known leaders, had a turnout of 56 per cent, far higher than the most enthusiastic British constituency (Highlands and Islands, 39%).[4]

[2] The 54 per cent won by the National Government in 1935 should also be mentioned but the Conservatives only received 48 per cent. The 1931 election when the Conservatives won 55 per cent of the vote was in fact the only occasion since 1900 in which one party secured over 50 per cent of the vote.

[3] An interesting footnote to the British turnout is offered by the postal vote. Because of the recent general election an exceptional number, 800,000 (2 per cent of the total electorate) were on the postal register, 64 per cent of them valid votes.

[4] Highlands and Islands normally has exceptionally low turnout in Westminster contests. The battle between the well-known Winnie Ewing and Russell Johnston may offer one explanation.

---

* The Liberals came second in these seats. If the ranking had been by majority over the second party, the position of Scotland North East would have been unchanged; Somerset would have been 44th and 49th. All the other starred seats would have stayed among the safest ten.

† Highlands and Islands was won by the SNP and the Liberals came second.

‡ For these calculations two votes in May 1979, Scottish Labour in South Ayrshire and Independent Labour in Blyth, are counted with Labour.

§ The rank order of safety is based on the percentage difference between Conservative and Labour votes. The most marginal Labour seat (Nottingham) is marked (1) and the safest (Yorkshire South) is marked (17). The most marginal Conservative seat (Greater Manchester West) is marked 1 and the safest (Sussex West) marked 60.

§§ In the by-election on 20 September 1979, Shelagh Roberts was again elected. The turnout was 19.3 per cent and the party percentages were Con. 41.2 per cent, Lab. 32.7 per cent, Lib. 23.9 per cent, anti Common Market 1.9 per cent and 0.3 per cent. There was a 5.7 per cent swing from Conservative to Labour.

** Share of first preference votes.

†† The swing is 'total vote swing', i.e. the average of the overall Conservative gain and Labour loss in overall percentage between the Westminster election of 3 May 1979 and the European election of 7 June 1979.

Table 6 Northern Ireland.

Name	Party	1st Count Votes	2nd Count Transfer of Paisley's surplus	Result	3rd Count Transfer of Bleakley's, Brennan's, Cummings's, Devlin's, Donnelly's and Murray's votes	Result	4th Count Transfer of Devlin-McAliskey's votes	Result	5th Count Transfer of Napier's votes	Result	6th Count Transfer of West's votes	Result
Bleakley, David	UCC	9,383	+218	9,601	−9,601	–	–	–	–	–	–	–
Brennan, Brian	Repub Clubs (0.6%)	3,258	+5	3,263	−3,263	–	–	–	–	–	–	–
Cummings, Eddie	UPNI (0.7%)	3,712	+125	3,837	−3,837	–	–	–	–	–	–	–
Devlin, Paddy	UL (1.1%)	6,122	+25	6,147	−6,147	–	–	–	–	–	–	–
Devlin-McAliskey, Bernadette	Ind (5.9%)	33,969	+7	33,976	+2,130	36,106	−36,106	–	–	–	–	–
Donnelly, Francis	RCMP (0.2%)	1,160	+4	1,164	−1,164	–	–	–	–	–	–	–
Hume, John	SDLP (24.6%)	140,622	+55	140,677	+5,396	146,073	–	146,073	–	146,073	–	146,073
Kilfedder, Jim	UU (6.7%)	38,198	+12,424	50,622	+3,364	53,986	+638	54,624	+14,760	69,384	+3,174	72,558
Murray, James	Liberal (0.2%)	932	+16	948	−948	–	–	–	–	–	–	–
Napier, Oliver	Alliance (6.8%)	39,026	+378	39,404	+6,299	45,703	+5,561	51,264	−51,264	–	–	–
Paisley, Ian	Dem U (29.8%)	170,688	−27,628	143,060	–	143,060	–	143,060	–	143,060	–	143,060
Taylor, John	Off UU (11.9%)	68,185	+9,044	77,229	+2,979	80,208	+198	80,406	+16,001	96,407	+57,059	153,466
West, Harry	Off UU (10.0%)	56,984	+4,179	61,163	+789	61,952	+188	62,140	+3,776	65,916	−65,916	–
Non-transferable:			1,149	1,149	+4,003	5,152	+29,521	34,673	+16,727	51,400	+5,683	57,083

There were 13,744 spoilt papers (2.4 per cent of valid votes).

137

Table 7. UK results by region.

Region	Seats Con.	Lab.	Other	% voting	Change in % voting	Con. %	Lab. %	Lib. %	Nat. %	Other %	Swing Since May Lab. to Con.
London	8	2	–	34.0	–41.5	51.0	36.7	11.4	–	0.9	4.0
South East	10	–	–	34.5	–42.8	60.7	19.7	18.9	–	0.7	5.6
South West	5	–	–	36.9	–41.8	58.5	21.1	18.5	–	1.9	4.4
East Anglia	6	–	–	32.6	–45.9	58.9	27.3	13.3	–	0.5	5.9
East Midlands	5	1	–	31.3	–46.7	54.8	34.3	10.9	–	–	5.7
West Midlands	8	–	–	30.8	–44.8	53.5	34.2	10.5	–	1.8	4.9
North East	3	8	–	30.0	–44.7	43.5	44.9	11.3	–	0.3	4.6
North West	9	1	–	30.7	–45.6	50.3	38.4	10.9	–	0.4	5.3
England	54	12	–	31.8	–44.1	53.5	32.5	13.3	–	0.8	5.3
Scotland	5	2	1	33.6	–43.2	33.7	33.0	14.0	19.4	–	5.5
Wales	1	3	–	34.4	–45.0	36.6	41.5	9.6	16.7	0.6	5.8
Great Britain	60	17	1	32.1	–44.1	50.6	33.0	13.1	2.6	0.7	5.3
Northern Ireland	–	–	3	55.7	–12.0	–	–	0.2	–	99.8	–
United Kingdom	60	17	4	32.7	–43.3	48.4	31.6	12.6	2.5	4.9	4.9

The outcome was seen as part of a general swing to the right in Europe. Table 8 shows the composition of the new Parliament.

Table 8

	Christian Democrats	Lib.	Con.	Socialists	Comm.	Progressive Democrats	Others	Total New	(old)
United Kingdom	–	–	61	18	–	1	1	81	(36)
France	9	17	–	21	19	15	–	81	(36)
Germany	42	4	–	35	–	–	–	81	(36)
Italy	30	5	–	13	24	–	9	81	(36)
Netherlands	10	4	–	9	–	–	2	25	(14)
Belgium	10	4	–	7	–	–	3	24	(14)
Denmark	–	3	3	4	1	1	4	16	(10)
Ireland	4	1	–	4	–	5	1	15	(10)
Luxembourg	3	2	–	1	–	–	–	6	(6)
	108	40	64	112	44	22	20	410	(198)
(Old Parliament)	(53)	(23)	(18)	(66)	(18)	(17)	(3)	(198)	

In Germany, Britain, Belgium, Holland and Denmark the result was decidedly to the right of the previous general election. In Italy and Luxembourg general elections held in the same week as the Euro-election showed a strong swing to the right. Only Ireland and France resisted the tendency. It is doubtful how far Irish politics can be classified in right–left terms: in France the parties of the left made no net advance compared to March 1978. All reports suggested that in other countries, as in Britain, the election reflected domestic political battles rather than a view on the way in which Europe should develop.

The outcome underlined how the balance in the European Parliament depended on Britain and the exaggerations of her majoritarian electoral system. Apart from Luxembourg (with three Christian Democrats out of six members) no other country gave any one party more than 43 per cent of its seats:[5] the Conservatives got 74 per cent. In the European Parliament the left (Communists and Socialists) elected 156 members and the centre-right (Christian Democrats, Conservatives, Liberals and their allies) 216.[6] If the British members had been divided 17 to 60 instead of 60 to 17, the result would have been left 199, centre-right 173. Yet the swing needed to produce such a reversal in Britain has often been seen over the last two decades in opinion polls and in by-elections.

[5] In Germany the CDU got 42 per cent of the seats but with the CSU it got 52 per cent.

[6] This leaves the 22 Progressive Democrats and the 20 non-aligned MEPs out of consideration.

Most of the issues facing the European Parliament cut across left–right divisions; moreover, the large transnational party groups contained so many ideological tendencies that it was sometimes hard to classify them in left–right terms. None the less, the ideological tone and mood of the new Parliament was strikingly different from those of the old. The difference owed much to the fact that the British Conservatives now constituted easily the biggest single national party group.

The characteristics of the candidates were discussed in Chapters 4 and 5. But it is worth stressing certain characteristics shared by the British members. Far fewer had dual mandates than was the case with any other country, except Holland; only four MPs were elected as MEPs, though there were also four peers. It contained fewer politicians of weight – one ex–Cabinet minister (Barbara Castle) and three ex–junior ministers (Jim Scott-Hopkins, Basil de Ferranti and Lord Harmar-Nicholls), who were also the only ex-MPs in the delegation. It contained a certain number of people with substantial business or administrative experience – notably Sir Fred Catherwood, Sir Henry Plumb, Sir Fred Warner and Sir David Nicholson. Seven Conservative MEPs had been employed by Community Institutions; more had strong European connections. On the Labour side many had played significant roles in local government. Yet, in contrast to the representatives from other large countries, it was not a very outstanding group. The German Social Democrats sent a strong team, headed by Willy Brandt. Among the Italian members were included Signor Colombo, President of the last nominated Parliament and Signor Berlinguer, Secretary General of the Italian Communist Party. The French sent two former Prime Ministers, Michel Debré and Jacques Chirac, as well as George Marchais, the leader of the Communist Party and François Mitterrand, the leader of the Socialists.[7] Altogether the new Parliament contained nine former Prime Ministers. Of the British only Barbara Castle could begin to be considered in their league. Ironically Northern Ireland redressed the balance slightly, sending three of the largest fish from its small pond.

The British press greeted the outcome as sourly as they had covered the campaign. Much of the comment centred on the low turnout.

Britain's low poll . . . is disturbing . . . [But] the new MEPs have no need to be despondent: they have a vital role to play even if non-voters at this first international election failed to understand it.

Observer, 10 June

It is not at all surprising that the poll should have been so low. Only when top

---

[7] However, M. Mitterrand promptly resigned his seat, nominally in protest against a recount by which the Socialists lost one seat.

politicians are prepared to put their careers behind this new institution can ordinary people be expected to give it their votes.

Sunday Telegraph, 10 June

The EEC has failed, like many an urban district council, to get its usefulness across to all of its ordinary folk.

The Economist, 16 June

It is being said that the low poll . . . effectively deprives our elected representatives of any parliamentary mandate. The massive British abstention is, the argument continues, tantamount to a massive anti-EEC vote. Well, perhaps the argument has some truth in it – who can tell? But the point is that these people have been elected by a not derisory number of voters in an open democratic election. . . . It is cheering that, in contradistinction to the feeble, outgoing nominated Assembly, this new more vigorous Parliament will have a clear majority of Centre-Right parties . . .

Daily Telegraph, 12 June

Conservative candidates were ready to blame the other side for the low turnout. One wrote

The total absence of a Labour campaign was damaging – nothing motivates a campaign worker like seeing the opposition in full cry.

Another commented

I think Labour's attitude was too destructive and divided, and they do govern the thinking of half the population.

One Labour candidate's observations were similar

The national campaign never got off the ground because of the fundamental differences of opinion among the party leaders about the Labour party's policies on the EEC.

But another argued

If only Transport House had fought an anti-Market campaign, we would have had something approaching the Westminster vote.

A third Labour candidate asked about the campaign riposted

'What national campaign? Please send details.'

The *Guardian* looked more broadly:

The elusive nature of the cause and the campaign and the failure to put up candidates of a Brandtian or Berlingueresque eminence, seems to have had something to do with the apathy. . . . No wonder there was such bitterness yesterday against the British Labour party among some continental socialists. By their failure to come to terms with these elections long after they had become inevitable, by their weak and mean spirited campaign, by their failure to recruit more than a handful of candidates of any previous note they had diminished the Socialist representation in the new Parliament.

Guardian, 12 June

But the last word should not be left with the press for, as one victorious MEP wrote to us:

The election should have been fought largely through the media as elections are in constituencies of this size in the USA. I believe our media were tried and found miserably wanting. Not a single one of the country's newspapers tried to get a real election controversy going.

CHAPTER TEN
Aftermath

The directly-elected Parliament assembled for the first time in Strasbourg on 17 July in an atmosphere of mingled euphoria and confusion. The press of Europe was present in force; television cameras and portable tape recorders seemed everywhere. The bars, corridors and galleries were packed: one newly-elected Conservative MEP commented sardonically that it was like being at Gatwick Airport when all the flights to Ibiza had been cancelled. For the MEPs themselves it must have been an exhilarating, yet at the same time a daunting, moment. They were making history, but no one could tell what kind of history it would turn out to be. To some extent, of course, the same would be true for newly-elected Westminster MPs at the start of a new Parliament. But, however bewildered he may be, the new boy in the House of Commons is, at any rate, a new boy in an old school. Newly-elected Westminster MPs generally know what part the House of Commons is supposed to play in British politics, and what part they themselves will be expected to play at Westminster and in the constituencies. None of this was true of the new MEPs. Only eight of them had served in the old, nominated Parliament: in any event, lessons drawn from the nominated Parliament would be unlikely to have much relevance to the elected one. None could know with any degree of certainty what job he had been elected to do, what problems he would have to overcome in order to do it, or what resources he would have at his disposal.

As we saw, (p. 34) it had already been decided that the salaries paid to Strasbourg members should be the same as the salaries paid to the members of the respective national Parliaments. Thus, the British contingent did at least know what salaries to expect. But the level of allowances had deliberately not been decided before the election, and there was no way of telling precisely what that level would be. In addition, the new MEPs would have to work out how to organise their personal and constituency lives and what kind of relationship to establish with their constituency parties, with their voters, with pressure groups, with the press, and with radio and television. On none of these questions were there precedents of any value. Even in mundane organisational terms, the new MEPs were like non-swimmers, thrown suddenly into the deep end of an alarmingly large pool. It would be up to them to decide whether they sank or swam and what kind of stroke to adopt.

They also faced a more daunting range of political questions. The new Parliament's first task was to elect its own President. As in most continental Parliaments, the post is of much greater political importance than that of the Speaker of the British House of Commons. The President of the European Parliament does not merely preside over debates in the hemicycle. He or she is also the head of the Parliament's own executive, and presides over the meetings of the enlarged Bureau, which manages Parliament's business. It is as though the Speaker of the House of Commons were also the Leader of the House, and at the same time the head of a separate bureacracy, independent of Whitehall. In the old nominated Parliament, the President had often played an important political role; few doubted that the Presidency would be even more important in the early years of the new, directly-elected Parliament than it had been in the past.

The major political groups had already begun to sound out the ground before the new Parliament assembled; as part of a move to create a centre-right alliance, the Christian Democrats had already decided to support the candidate put forward by the Liberals. The Liberals had voted amongst themselves; Gaston Thorn, the former Prime Minister of Luxembourg, had been defeated by Madame Simone Veil, until the election Health Minister in France, and now President Giscard d'Estaing's candidate for the post. The chief political questions facing the new Conservative MEPs were whether or not they should take part in the emerging centre-right *bloc* of Christian Democrats and Liberals, and, if so, whether or not they should vote for Madame Veil as President. She visited the Conservative Group at a meeting in Luxembourg the week before the Parliament assembled; though there was a certain amount of muttering within the group, partly because of her role in reforming the abortion laws in France and partly because some members feared that Conservative Associations in Britain would take it amiss if their representatives at Strasbourg voted for a Liberal, it was agreed that the Conservatives would support her. Some suggested that Conservative support for her should be made conditional on a promise that when her term of office came to an end, the Liberals should support a Conservative as her successor, but the group decided to support her unconditionally. But, although the Conservatives, Liberals and Christian Democrats combined were easily the strongest block within the new Parliament, they did not have enough votes to elect Madame Veil on their own. The European Progressive Democrats – a group dominated by the French Gaullists – ran a candidate of their own against Madame Veil, in order to demonstrate to the French Government that its candidate for the Presidency could not win without Gaullist votes; and although Madame Veil was comfortably ahead on the first ballot, with 183 out of 380 votes, she did not have an overall majority. The Gaullist candidate then withdrew. On the second ballot Madame Veil polled 192 votes, securing a narrow overall majority. She would not have won so soon without the 60 British Conservatives; conceivably, she would not have won at all.

Another aspect of the Conservative Group's involvement in centre-right European politics was its decision, also taken at the meeting in Luxembourg before the Parliament met, to change its name. It decided to stop calling itself the Conservative Group and to describe itself instead as the European Democratic Group. The reason for the change of name was revealing. Many of the Conservative members of the old nominated Parliament had come to the conclusion that the name 'Conservative' was a barrier to establishing close relationships with right-wing groups on the Continent, where the word has different connotations from those which it has in the United Kingdom. Christian Democrats in particular would find it difficult, so it was argued, to make a formal alliance with a group describing itself as 'Conservative'. Against this it was argued that local constituency Associations would not understand why their members had suddenly abandoned the historic name of Conservative as soon as they crossed the channel, and that, in any event, all the right-wing political tendencies in the Community were in varying degrees idiosyncratic, that Christian Democracy is a different animal from Conservatism or Liberalism, and that a worthwhile centre-right alliance would have to be based on mutual recognition of these differences. Despite these arguments, however, majority feeling in the Group was in favour of the change of name, and the objectors were fairly easily overruled.

Meanwhile, the Labour members were also being introduced to the intricacies of Strasbourg Group politics. Before the election, some Labour candidates had feared that it might be difficult to reconcile the Labour Party election manifesto with the statement put out by the Confederation of Socialist Parties, and that Labour members at

Strasbourg might not be able to work harmoniously with much more pro-European Socialists from other Member States. Despite these fears, however, no one had suggested that the Labour members should do anything other than join the Socialist Group. They were, of course, a much less important element in the Group than they had been in the nominated Parliament. Before June, the British Labour members had provided the largest single national contingent in the Socialist Group. Now they had less than half as many members as the German SPD, slightly fewer than even the French Socialist party. In striking contrast to their nominated predecessors (see pp. 26–7), they decided that, in future, the Labour Group would take binding policy decisions before Group meetings. For the moment, however, that decision was of symbolic rather than operational significance. The only important issue to be decided in this first week was the presidency of the Socialist Group itself. Ludwig Fellermaier, the outgoing German president, ran for re-election and was opposed by the Belgian Socialist, Ernest Glinne, as well as by the Dutch Labour politician, Anne Vondeling. There had been a good deal of muttering against Ludwig Fellermaier's chairmanship among the nominated British members of the old Parliament, and it was not altogether surprising that the Labour members of the new, elected Parliament decided to vote for Ernest Glinne instead. The new German delegation was probably somewhat to the left of the old one and it may well be that some Germans also voted for Glinne against Fellermaier. In any event, Ernest Glinne was elected, and almost certainly elected with British support.

As well as electing its president, the new Parliament had to choose its vice-presidents and committee chairmen. The British had two vice-presidents – Basil de Ferranti for the Conservatives, and Allan Rogers for the Labour Party. The Conservatives were also allocated two committee chairmanships, Sir Henry Plumb becoming chairman of the powerful Agriculture Committee and Sir Frederick Catherwood of the Committee on External Economic Relations. Ken Collins of the Labour Group became chairman of the Environment Committee and Michael Gallagher became vice-chairman of the committee on energy and research and Barry Seal of the External Economic Relations Committee. As well as their two chairmanships, the Conservatives also had three vice-chairmanships – Basil de Ferranti (Economic and Monetary Affairs), Amédée Turner (Legal Affairs) and Stanley Johnson (Environment, Public Health and Consumer Protection). Other notable committee assignments were those of Barbara Castle to the Agriculture Committee and of Richard Balfe, Robert Jackson and John Taylor to the Budgets Committee.

In the next few months, some of the uncertainties of the early days were resolved. During the summer the salaries of Westminster MPs were raised from £6,897 to £12,000 (in 1981); MEPs had the same increase. They did not, however, receive any of the British MPs' travel or other allowances, and there was some ill feeling about attempts in Westminster to deny the four dual mandate members any pay for their European role.[1] Secretarial and other allowances were fixed at generous levels; apart from salaries MEPs were allotted 900 European units of account (about £600) per month to run their offices of which 400 (£266) was fully accountable. Although an MP receives a sum of money out of which he himself pays his secretary's salary, the European Parliament adopted a different procedure in order to prevent abuse. It was decided that MEPs should nominate a secretary or secretaries, who would then be put on the Parliament's payroll and receive a salary direct from the Parliament; the money not going through the member's pocket.

Like their predecessors in the nominated Parliament, MEPs had two committee assignments – which meant that they received *per diem* allowances for nearly twice as many days for committee work as they would have had if allocated to only one committee. It seemed clear that, with these allowances, all MEPs were getting by reasonably well, though some Conservatives who had given up high-salaried jobs needed to supplement their salaries by other work. Some Conservatives were rich men, some were farmers, one or two were journalists or solicitors and able to combine their normal profession in some measure with their work as MEPs. But some needed to get consultancies and the like. It is however, worth noting that at least one, who was given a consultancy by a merchant bank, refused to take any salary from the bank because he found that he had no time to give in his first months as an MEP. For him, it was a completely full-time job, just as it was for all his Labour colleagues as well, none of them having significant outside sources of income.

Not only was the job more full-time than many had expected before being elected; it also involved much more travelling. One week a month was given up to the plenary session, and there were often group meetings in one of the other weeks. On two or three days a week in the remaining weeks members would have to attend committee meetings in Brussels. Constituency loads, on the other hand, were not onerous. No Strasbourg member had anything approaching a Westminster MP's constituency workload, for the obvious reason that the European

---

[1] However, MEPs received a daily allowance of 90 units of account (£60) for time spent abroad on Community business. It was alleged that some extra committee assignments were to be explained by a desire to qualify for these allowances.

Parliament had no competence to deal with the kind of matters about which individuals press for the redress of grievances. Particularly in rural or semi-rural constituencies, however, MEPs found that they received quite a lot of letters and circulars from interest groups of different kinds. This was most obviously true of MEPs with agricultural constituencies, but was also true of MEPs in constituencies with non-agricultural interests with a Community dimension. Others, however, faced little or no constituency pressure for activity; by the end of the first six months, constituency workloads varied from around two to three serious constituency letters a week to around 40 to 50. Even MEPs with big post bags, however, received few letters from individuals. Letters arrived from interest groups which had come to the conclusion that the MEP could be a useful channel of influence, a conclusion which seemed to relate to the MEP's committee assignments more than to any other tasks, though it was also affected by the extent to which the MEP managed to publicise his activities. A number of MEPs produced a newsletter to their local activists and often to their local newspapers. A couple of small agencies worked for two or three Conservative MEPs at the same time, generating news which could produce more demands on the MEPs. But not even the most active and publicity-seeking Strasbourg member could hope to rival the 'Ombudsman' role of his Westminster counterpart.

The same was true of press coverage. When it resumed publication in November 1979, *The Times* continued to publish regular reports on the plenary sessions of Parliament; *The Economist* maintained its excellent coverage of Community affairs. Otherwise the British press remained as insular as before; not even the *Guardian* or *Daily Telegraph* made serious attempts to offer their readers a continued report of Strasbourg activities. Radio and television were no better. Facilities for television coverage do exist in the European Parliament. The cameras are present during plenary sessions, and regional television stations in this country could easily broadcast shots of the regional members at Strasbourg, taking part in activities on the floor when issues of concern to that region are debated. Little of the kind was done, and radio was equally unadventurous. As we showed in Chapter 7, candidates during the European election felt very aggrieved at the poor coverage which the campaign received from the media. It was the same story after the election as it had been before and during it.

The area in which early expectations were most thoroughly belied was that of relations with Westminster. Initially, MEPs had been much concerned about their relationship with the House of Commons collectively, and with their respective Westminster parties. They felt humiliated by having no more right of access than a member of the ordinary public to the Palace of Westminster; more seriously, they also assumed that they would need close contact with Westminster MPs and the Westminster structure to do their jobs properly. The issue of whether they should be allowed to use Westminster facilities, let alone attend Westminster party and parliamentary committees, was discussed in a leisurely fashion; it was November before MEPs were allowed free copies of *Weekly Hansard*. Little by little, however, most lost interest in the issue. They recognised that their life was not closely linked to that of Westminster. Many of them had no London base and did not naturally travel through London or in normal circumstances have occasion to attend Westminster meetings. Some – notably Barbara Castle, and some London-based Conservatives – continued to agitate for more access and some central London base, but these were a minority. Meanwhile, the European Parliament was itself anxious to obtain office premises more central than their old office at Kensington Palace Gardens. In the end they obtained the lease of a building in Queens Gate, not 300 yards from Parliament. But these premises were only large enough to provide an office for the leaders of the two delegations and a very limited amount of other space for their followers; for the average MEP it was less a base than a perch.

The same applied to the relationship between the Strasbourg members and their Westminster parties. Conservative subject groups appear to have welcomed the presence of Strasbourg members from the start, and there seems to have been no difficulty in a Strasbourg Conservative attending a subject committee in the field of his Strasbourg competence. Predictably, the Labour party was less welcoming. The Foreign Affairs group of the Labour Party unofficially invited members of the Labour Group at Strasbourg to attend a meeting of the Foreign Affairs Committee. This was done on the personal authority of the chairman of the Committee, Tam Dalyell, who had, of course, himself been a member of the European Parliament before direct elections, and who felt considerable sympathy for the predicament of the new directly-elected members. The Labour Group in Strasbourg thought very carefully about this invitation, and decided that it would be tactically unwise to send a large number of members to this meeting with the PLP Foreign Affairs Committee, for fear that they might swamp it and upset the antis in the PLP. So they sent two of their members only, one pro-Marketeer and one anti-Marketeer; and these two attended the Foreign Affairs Committee. By the end of the year, however, this was the only subject committee which had made a gesture of this kind. The practices of regional groups within the PLP varied considerably. The Northern group was quite welcoming to Strasbourg members, and one or two Strasbourg members attended its meetings. Other regional groups, by contrast, were very cold in their attitude, and rebuffed attempts from Strasbourg members to attend.[2]

Far overshadowing all the other political issues with which the newly-elected British members had unexpectedly to cope within a few months of their election was the intricate, highly technical and increasingly explosive question of the 1980 Community Budget. This had a double significance – one particular to Britain, and one common to the Community as a whole. When Britain joined the Community in the early 1970s it had been assumed that the proportion of the Community Budget devoted to agricultural expenditure would gradually fall as new policies were developed in other fields. This had not happened, partly because few new policies were developed, and partly because of the inexorable tendency of agricultural spending to increase. The result was that Britain, which derived little benefit from the Community's agricultural spending, found that once the transitional arrangements which had been made to ease her entry into the Community had come to an end, her net contribution to the Community Budget rapidly grew. As we have seen, many Labour candidates in the election had devoted space to this problem in their election manifestos. Conservative candidates had said little about it, but the Conservative leadership in the Westminster Parliament was less reticent. Partly because of its own domestic problems and its determination to cut domestic public expenditure, the new British Government would not tolerate a situation in which Britain was contributing net to the Community Budget something approaching 2 per cent of British public expenditure. By the time the newly-elected Parliament had assembled in Strasbourg it was already clear that Mrs Thatcher and her colleagues were determined to make a substantial reduction in Britain's net budgetary contribution one of their chief political priorities.[3]

[2] Many of the relevant problems are discussed in the 25 July 1978 Report of the House of Lords Select Committee on the European Communities 'Relations between the United Kingdom Parliament and the European Parliament after Direct Elections' (H.L. 256, 1977–8).

[3] Mrs Thatcher made the net British contribution to the EEC the central theme of Summit meetings throughout her first year in office, much to the irritation of the other Community members. She pointed out that Britain, the third poorest country in the Community, made the second largest contribution to its funds, on balance paying out at least £1,000 million more than she received. At the Dublin Summit at the end of November 1979, she firmly refused an offer that would cut this by £300 million. At the Luxembourg Summit in April 1980 she spurned a compromise that would reduce the net contribution by £700 million on the ground that it was for only two years. At Brussels on 30 May Lord Carrington negotiated a deal worth slightly more and lasting three years and this she reluctantly endorsed at the Venice Summit on 14 June 1980.

That was the British aspect of the question. There was also a wider, Community aspect. It, too, sprang from the apparently boundless appetite of the agricultural sector. As we have seen, the Luxembourg Treaty, which created the 'own resources' system, also made the Community financially independent of Member Governments. But there was a ceiling to the Community's 'own resources'; and by the end of the 1970s it was becoming clear that, if agricultural spending continued to increase at its existing rate, that ceiling would soon be reached and even exceeded. The Commission had tried in vain to hold down agricultural spending by putting forward modest or nil price increases, but the farm ministers, who actually decide the level of agricultural prices, had consistently overridden the Commission's prudent proposals. The Member Governments were thus confronted with an intolerable state of affairs – no more tolerable for being their own creation. Agricultural expenditure was growing remorselessly; but the only way to keep it within bounds was to stop the agriculture ministers from increasing prices, and this the Governments (including the British Government) dared not do. Instead they consistently cut back on Commission proposals to increase expenditure in other areas – notably on the Regional Fund, on the Social Fund, on energy and on industrial policies in general. This had perpetuated the imbalance in the Community Budget, from which the British were the chief sufferers; it had also prevented the Community from moving forward into new policy areas. In 1977 the Commission had seen the Budget Council emasculate its draft Budget for 1978; in 1978 it saw the Council emasculate its draft Budget for 1979. On each occasion, the European Parliament had backed the Commission, and had tried to restore the cuts in non-agricultural spending made by the Council. On each occasion, however, the net result had been a compromise, much closer to the Council's position than to the original Commission draft.

Though few realised it at the time, the elections of June 1979 had thus taken place at a peculiarly critical moment in the development of the Community. In May the Commission had prepared its draft Budget for 1980 in the normal way, and had sent it in the normal way to the Council of Ministers. It had proposed an increase of 13 per cent in 'commitment appropriations' and of 9 per cent in 'payment appropriations'. The increases were concentrated in the non-agricultural, so-called 'non-obligatory' sector. That sector of the Budget was to be increased by approximately 40 per cent, the increases being devoted to a substantial increase in expenditure on the Regional Fund, to increases in the Social Fund, to increases in expenditure on research, industry and energy, and to increases in development aid to the Third World. In

June, however, the farm ministers had proceeded to increase farm prices yet again, with shattering effects on the Commission's draft. The effect of their decisions was to increase the Budget's 'commitment appropriations' by 22 per cent as against the Commission's original proposal of a 13 per cent increase, and, in doing so, to drive the Community Budget very close indeed to the ceiling on Community revenues. The implications were stark. Either the Community cut back its swelling agricultural expenditures or it could not afford even modest extensions in non-agricultural spending proposed by the Commission. If the Commission's proposed increases in regional, social, energy, industrial and development expenditure were struck out of the Budget, agricultural spending would be even more predominant than it was already. The role of the European Parliament, whose powers over the 'non-obligatory' sector are, of course, much greater than over the 'obligatory' sector would be diminished. The Commission's authority would be undermined. Most important of all, the Community would be unable to devise new instruments to deal with the central economic problems facing it in the 1980s.

The Budget Council had been due to consider the Commission's draft in July, but postponed consideration of it until 11–12 September. It then made sweeping cuts in the Commission's draft, all of them in the 'non-obligatory' sector. The total draft Budget was cut by 11 per cent. Where the Commission had proposed increases of around 40 per cent in 'commitment appropriations' in the non-obligatory part of the Budget, the Council cut the increase to 5 per cent. Where the Commission had proposed that 1,370 million units of account (just under £1,000 million) should be spent on the Regional Fund, the Council, after a bitter all-night session, agreed to a figure of 850 million – a lower figure than the 1979 Budget's 945 million. For the first time in the Community's history, in other words, the Council was proposing that less should be spent on regional aid in the year ahead than was being spent in the current year. Expenditure on the Social Fund was cut by 170 million units of account. The 'Davignon Plan' for industrial re-structuring was scrapped, as were credits for coal and for energy research, as well as all the Commission's proposed increases in development aid. On 12 September, Christopher Tugendhat, the Budget Commissioner, expressed formal reservations to the Council, warning that its cuts in the Commission's draft would jeopardise the proper working of the Community. Next day, the Commission supported his reservation, and for good measure decided to urge Parliament to restore what the Council had struck out.

Parliament needed no prompting. Partly for reasons of institutional prestige, partly for reasons of democratic principle, partly to prove to their electors and the world that direct elections had not been a waste of time, most MEPs would, in any case, have been anxious to assert their budgetary rights as fully as possible. Moreover, the Council's proposals were objectionable in substance to most members of the two biggest transnational Groups, the Socialists and the European Peoples Party (the Christian Democrats). Most Socialists were in favour of higher regional, social and industrial spending for its own sake; apart from the French, most of them also believed that agricultural spending took up too much of the Budget and wanted to bring it under control. Though most EPP members were in favour of the Common Agricultural Policy in principle, many feared that, if agricultural spending continued to increase at its existing rate, the CAP would collapse under its own weight; these fears had made them increasingly sympathetic to the suggestion that agriculture's share of the Budget should be reduced. As the most solidly 'integrationist' group in the Parliament, they were also instinctively sympathetic to the suggestion that the Community had to develop new policies, of the sort which the Council's cuts had ruled out. Of the remaining Groups, the European Progressive Democrats could be relied upon to support the Council, while the Liberals and Communists were divided. The French Republicans, who belonged to the Liberal Group, would be reluctant to engage in a battle with the Council, if only because theirs was the party of the French President. The non-French Liberals shared the attitudes of the EPP and the Socialists. The same division was apparent in the Communist and Allies Group – the Italians fervently in favour of restoring the cuts made by the Council and of asserting Parliament's powers, the French doggedly anxious to confine Parliament's role to the minimum.

That left the Conservatives, now the European Democrats. As they had shown in the election of Madame Veil, their numbers gave them a pivotal position in the new Parliament, and it was clear from an early stage that much would depend on them. Few Conservatives shared the instinctive Socialist view that higher regional, social and industrial spending was inherently desirable or believed, as a matter of principle, that the powers of the European Parliament should be increased. On the other hand, they had an even stronger incentive than their continental colleagues to prove to a sceptical electorate and party leadership that Strasbourg mattered, or could be made to matter. Above all, they had a strong incentive to prove that it could be made to matter in a way which would benefit the United Kingdom. The CAP was the most unpopular aspect of Community membership in Britain, and Britain's most important Community interest was to reduce her net budgetary contribution. The European Parliament could not reform the CAP or remove the imbalance in the Community Budget all by itself. But if it restored the cuts which the Council had made in the Commission's draft Budget, and if it curbed agricultural spending at the same time, it would go some way towards doing both. If it did that, it might help to break down the mixture of hostility and indifference which had produced the low British turnout in the election, and would almost certainly help to raise the Strasbourg Group's status in the Conservative Party at home.

On 14 September, the Conservative leader, Jim Scott-Hopkins, told his constituents that there had 'simply got to be a change in the Community Budget, so that the balance is no longer tilted against Britain', that the Council's proposal to cut regional spending was 'not acceptable' and that, if necessary, Parliament might have to take 'the ultimate step . . . and that ultimate step is for the Parliament to reject the Budget'. It was the first move in a remarkable exercise in coalition politics. On 24 September, Parliament assembled for its second plenary session. In a general debate on the Budget, Pieter Dankert, the Dutch Socialist rapporteur on the 1980 Budget, declared that the Budget could not be approved in its present form, attacked the distinction between obligatory and non-obligatory spending as a 'trick' with which ministers evaded parliamentary control and urged Council and Parliament to 'build a barrier together' against excessive agricultural spending. Altiero Spinelli, a former Italian Commissioner and now a member of the Communist and Allies Group, warned that if the Council rejected any proposals from Parliament to increase spending, the Budget would have to be rejected at the December session. John Taylor, one of the Conservative members of the Budgets Committee, described the Budget as amended by the Council as 'bad for Europe'.

These were sighting shots. The battle lines did not take shape until October, at a series of meetings of the Budgets Committee. At these meetings, the committee decided to put forward a series of amendments to the Budget as it now stood, so sweeping in character as to amount to an alternative Budget. The alternative contained three main elements. In the first place, the committee proposed that the cuts which the Council had made in the Commission's proposals for expenditure on regional policy, social policy, energy research and development aid should be reinstated. Secondly, it proposed that Community lending and borrowing should be included within the Budget, thus subjecting them to parliamentary control. Thirdly, and most importantly, it proposed that Parliament should make a direct attack on the swollen dairy Budget. This was to be done in two ways – by cutting expenditure on milk products by 380 million units of account, and by raising the tax on milk production (the so-called 'co-responsibility levy') from 0.5 per cent to 2.5 per cent.

In proposing this, the Budgets Committee was doing three things. Hitherto, the European Parliament had concentrated on increasing non-obligatory spending, over which it had the last word, and had made little use of its power to propose modifications in the crucial obligatory sector. In practice, obligatory spending had been left to national Governments. The volume and pattern of the agricultural Budget had been determined by producer-oriented farm ministers, who knew that, no matter what prices they fixed or what level of production ensued, someone else would always find the money. Now the Budgets Committee was trying to insert the European Parliament, the representative of the Community's tax-payers and consumers, into the process. In doing so, it was trying to give a Community Institution a say in what had previously been an overwhelmingly intergovernmental affair. Above all, it was giving notice that Member Governments could no longer be sure that the outcome of the intergovernmental process would be automatically approved – a warning which it underlined on 5 November, when it adopted a motion for a resolution proposed by Pieter Dankert, declaring, among other things, that Parliament would adopt the budget only if

the unjustified cuts carried out by Council for non-compulsory sectors are overturned, and if the first moves to control agricultural expenditure have been achieved, and if the European Development Fund and all the Community's lending and borrowing activities are included within the Budget.

Parliament's special Budget part-session took place from 5 November to 7 November. After a day and a half of debate, in which Pieter Dankert insisted that unless the Community was prepared to 'take the knife to three-quarters of the money-hungry agricultural policy' it would have to 'throw non-obligatory spending out of the budget', the Budgets Committee's proposals to restore the cuts in non-obligatory spending and to 'budgetise' Community borrowing were carried without much difficulty. Its proposals on agricultural spending had a rougher passage. The Conservatives were enthusiastically in favour of the proposed cut in dairy spending, but they opposed the increase in the 'co-responsibility levy' on the grounds that it would penalise efficient farms and that it would increase milk production instead of curbing it. In spite of their opposition, however, the proposal was carried, as was the complementary proposal on dairy spending. Finally, Parliament passed the Dankert resolution of 5 November, including the menacing final paragraph spelling out its conditions for approving the Budget in the end.

The next move had to come from the Council. Under the treaties, a weighted majority was necessary to reject the changes which had now been approved by Parliament. In practice, this meant that the votes of two big countries and one small one would be enough to put them into effect. The Dutch, with their long record of support for the European Parliament and for direct elections, would hardly want to frustrate the elected Parliament's first big initiative. The Italians stood to gain from Parliament's decisions on regional and social spending, and had nothing to lose from its decisions on agricultural spending; they, too, could be expected to take Parliament's side. But the Dutch and Italians alone had too few votes to block a decision to throw Parliament's amendments out. As *The Economist* pointed out on 10 November, the decisive vote would be Britain's; and the British position was unclear. Even more than Italy's, Britain's interest was to support Parliament. She would make immediate, tangible gains from both the regional and the agricultural elements in the Dankert package. In the long run, she would gain even more from a successful assertion of the principle that farm spending should take up a smaller proportion of the Budget and that the farm ministers should no longer be able to count on Parliament's acquiescence in the consequences of their pricing decisions. On the other hand, the British Government's overriding priority was to persuade her partners to agree to a 'broad balance' between Britain's budgetary contributions and receipts. A Summit meeting was due in Dublin in December, when Britain's budgetary grievance would be one of the main items on the agenda. Britain's chief opponent at Dublin would be France. The French were also bitterly opposed to the changes which the European Parliament wanted to make in the Budget, partly because they were opposed on principle to such assertions of Parliament's powers and partly because they were opposed to the substance of the Dankert package. The Budget Council would have to decide its line on Parliament's amendments in late November, just before the Summit. If Britain joined Italy and the Netherlands in blocking a decision to reject the amendments, she might so alienate the French as to destroy any hope of an agreement at Dublin.

Attitudes in Whitehall were mixed. No doubt, some officials felt instinctively that Parliaments should never be encouraged to assert themselves against executives. More viewed the European Parliament's *démarche* as a diversion from the central issue. As Whitehall saw it, all the European Parliament had done was to jib at the consequences of the CAP: what mattered was to change it, and that could not be done by votes at Strasbourg. Despite this scepticism, however, the Government decided that Britain should cast her votes in the Council in favour of

Parliament's amendments, and run the risk of a further deterioration in relations with France. Then, at the last moment, the Germans intervened. On the eve of the Council meeting on 23 November, a message came through from Bonn, warning that if Britain joined in a blocking minority in the Council, and thus ensured the passage of Parliament's amendments, she would incur German hostility at Dublin as well as French. This turned the trick. A high-level meeting of ministers decided that the previous decision to support Parliament's amendments should be reversed, and that Britain should vote with the Council majority after all. In the end, only the Italians and the Dutch sided with Parliament. The Council accepted only trivial increases in regional and social spending and it threw out the agricultural modifications altogether. In a letter to *The Times,* Stanley Johnson, the Conservative MEP for the Isle of Wight and Hampshire East wrote indignantly: 'here was an occasion where, amazingly, Britain's larger interests happened to coincide with Europe's. And the British Government, for reasons of short-term political expediency, fluffed it!' The Council, commented *Agence Europe,* the Brussels news agency, had made a 'clear and intentional bid to humiliate the European Parliament. It is therefore the start of an institutional crisis'.

The crisis came to a head three weeks later. Parliament's next plenary session opened on 10 December. By now, its blood was up. In the next two days, complex and protracted negotiations took place between the Council and a parliamentary delegation, but to no avail. One of the MEPs involved commented later that he had been struck by the 'intellectually very poor quality' of the Council's arguments; another observer noticed that the ordinary members of the Groups – and particularly of the crucial Socialist, EPP and Conservative Groups – were even more intransigent than their representatives in the negotiations. The Council was equally intransigent. Where Parliament had demanded an extra 800 million units of account on regional and social spending, its maximum offer was 200 million. On the 'budgetisation' of Community borrowing, it was prepared only to examine the position. On the agricultural modifications it eventually accepted a text drawn up by Pieter Dankert, but it did so after the negotiations had ended and in a spirit which most members of the Budgets Committee considered too grudging to provide an adequate basis for compromise. On 13 December, Dankert accordingly reported to the plenary session that, in the view of the Budgets Committee, the conditions set out in its resolution of November had not been met, and that it therefore recommended total rejection of the 1980 Budget. Parliament voted accordingly by 288 votes to 64. Of the British members, only

Mrs Ewing voted against rejection. The Conservative and Labour members all voted with the majority, as did the three members from Northern Ireland.

What the vote meant for the Community would not be clear for some time. Some of its implications for British politics were more obvious. Whatever else the European Parliament did on 13 December, it voted to enhance its own role in Community decision-making. In voting with the majority, the British MEPs also voted to enhance its role. The Conservatives did so in support of a policy which their own Government at home had rejected. The Budget against which the European Parliament voted on 13 December was, after all, the product of the British Government's vote in the Council three weeks earlier. It is true that, by the time the Strasbourg Conservatives had to decide whether or not to vote for rejection, the Dublin Summit had come and gone. Mrs Thatcher's attempt to reduce Britain's budgetary contribution to an acceptable level had been rebuffed; and it could be argued that the line which the Strasbourg Conservatives had taken all along had been vindicated against Whitehall's. It is also true that the Strasbourg Conservatives had been among the most fervent advocates of a tough posture towards the Council, and that they would have lost credibility if they had flinched from rejection at the last moment. But that merely underlined the differences between the Strasbourg Conservatives and their party colleagues at home, and the extent to which the Strasbourg Conservatives were prepared to bring the differences into the open.

The Labour MEPs had no qualms about voting against the British Government. Indeed, they had an obvious political incentive to do so. Yet, in doing so, they had to flout some of the most cherished shibboleths of their own party. Immediately before the vote on 13 December, Barbara Castle took the floor to give an 'explanation of the vote' of the British Labour members. She did so, she declared

because, as I think is well known in this Assembly, we fought the election on a manifesto which pledged us to resist any extension of the powers of Parliament, any further encroachment on the rights and responsibilities of national governments, and if we believed that rejection of this budget would indicate an extension of the powers of this Parliament, we would not be voting for it. But in fact we believe that it is merely an effective use of the powers which Parliament already has – powers to fight for and carry out the political purposes for which we were elected to this Parliament in the first place.

Behind her explanation lay a more complex story. Immediately after the election, five of the newly-elected Labour MEPs had been classified as pro-Marketeers by the Labour Committee for Europe; and at the first plenary session in July, the gulf between pros and antis had still been wide. Gradually, the divisions narrowed, until one hardened pro could say, 'some of the antis are more pro than I am'. The difference that mattered was between 'strict constructionists' of the manifesto and those who interpreted it more loosely, and on that many antis were on the same side as the pros. Since the Group rarely took policy decisions, the difference in any case provoked few conflicts. But there was a sharp, if one-sided, conflict over the Budget. The Labour Group had been a loyal, but fairly inconspicuous, part of the Dankert coalition in the early stages of the argument, and had voted with the rest of the Socialist Group in favour of the amendments passed by Parliament in November. At a private meeting of the group before the final vote on rejection, however, Roland Boyes, MEP for Durham, argued strongly against rejection, on the grounds that it was inconsistent with the Labour manifesto. Barbara Castle took the line which she was later to take in the hemicycle, arguing that a vote for rejection was a vote to use Parliament's existing powers properly, not a vote to extend them. In the end, the group voted overwhelmingly for rejection. Mr Boyes then came into line with the majority. His colleagues could argue, with some justice, that they were voting for a more equitable distribution of Community resources and against the iniquities of the CAP, and that it would have been perverse for them to do otherwise. The fact remained that they were also voting against exclusive intergovernmental control of the single most important Community instrument, and that the official policy of the Labour Party was to prevent more power slipping from governmental to Community bodies.[4]

It would be wrong to suggest that either of the British Strasbourg groups had broken their links with their parent parties in Britain, or abandoned the attitudes which they had brought with them to Strasbourg when they were first elected. But there could be little doubt that their perspectives had altered. It seemed reasonable to suppose that they would alter still more in the four and a half years before the next election.

---

[4] The sequel was anti-climatic. The Parliament's massive vote for rejection in December 1979 assumed that a new Budget would be rapidly submitted. In the event the hassle over the British contribution to the EEC imposed a long delay. In July 1980 the Parliament adopted (with the Labour group almost in continued opposition) a new Budget that was only marginally different from the one rejected in December. It was conscious, however, that the next round – the debates about new Community 'own resources' – could not be long delayed.

CHAPTER ELEVEN
Questions

The European Community is a unique, precarious, yet remarkably durable experiment in international fusion. The attempt to integrate ten – probably soon to be twelve – diverse economic and political systems is fraught with difficulties. The difficulties may yet prove insuperable; the EEC may prove as ephemeral as the Achaian League. The early vision of ineluctable progress from a customs union to an economic union, and from an economic union to a political union, was destroyed by President de Gaulle's obstruction in the mid-1960s. The dream of monetary union by 1980, confidently proclaimed at the 1972 Paris Summit, was destroyed by the monetary turmoil of the following four years. More recently, the crisis over the Budget showed that the Community's future was still uncertain, and that its continued existence as anything more than a loose-knit free-trade area could still not be taken for granted. But durability is at least as salient a characteristic of the Community's history as precariousness. By the end of the 1970s, monetary union was still far away, but the European Monetary System had been established. The Treaty provisions on majority voting had not been implemented, but foreign policies were co-ordinated much more fully than in the early years. The prospect of enlargement to the South posed enormous problems for the future, but the fact that the applicant countries wanted to join was a sign of strength. Looked at from the inside, the Community often seemed divided and inchoate. Looked at from the outside – particularly from the Third World, but also from Eastern Europe and North America – it was a political as well as an economic force. No one could tell how it would develop: clearly, centrifugal pressures were at work in it as well as centripetal ones. But, on past form at least, the centripetal ones seemed likely to prove stronger, at any rate in the long run.

The first elections to the European Parliament took place against that background. They were themselves a product of these centripetal pressures – not least of the nominated Parliament's dogged insistence that the Treaty commitment to hold them should be honoured. Whether additional centripetal pressures would be generated as a result of their having been held was less certain. The nominated Parliament had generally allied itself with the Commission in pressing for further integration against the resistance of the Member States, but it did not follow that the elected Parliament would do the same. What did seem clear was that the arrival of an elected Parliament was bound to affect the other Community Institutions – and, for that matter, the institutions of its Member States – in a whole variety of ways, not all of which had been foreseen when the decision to hold the elections had been taken. From June 1979, 410 MEPs were in post, each of them with an independent popular mandate, and most of them without seats in any national Parliament. However different their views on particular Community policies, or even on integration in principle, all shared a common interest in ensuring that the opinions and interests of ordinary voters were given more weight in Community decision-making than hitherto, and that the activities of the Commission and Council of Ministers were more effectively scrutinised and controlled.

It is too soon to tell how successfully that common interest will be pursued. As Walter Bagehot wrote of an earlier extension of democracy,

A new Constitution does not produce its full effect as long as all its subjects were reared under an old Constitution; as long as its statesmen were trained by that old Constitution. It is not really tested till it comes to be worked by statesmen and among a people who are guided by a different experience.

Statesmen and people have to adapt more quickly in the twentieth century, but even so it will take more than the first five years to determine whether the elected European Parliament can use its existing powers to more effect than its predecessor did, or whether it can acquire new powers which its predecessor did not possess. Though it failed to see through the changes it wanted in the 1980 Budget, the episode shows that its appetite for the power was bigger than its predecesors. Future battles may end differently.

The coalition which voted to reject the Community Budget in December 1979, was a remarkably heterogeneous one – and in some respects a mutually incompatible one. Italian Communists voted with British Conservatives; determined opponents of the Common Agricultural Policy with moderate defenders. But although some of its members may not have been fully aware of the constitutional implications of their actions, all of them were voting to give the European Parliament a say in a highly sensitive area of Community decision-making, which had hitherto been the exclusive preserve of the Member States. They were doing so, moreover, in defiance of the clearly expressed wishes of most of the Member States concerned. It is true that they did not stay defiant very long. The fact remains that, on the first occasion when they had an opportunity to do so, the newly elected MEPs voted by a large majority to assert their collective rights at the expense of national ministers, accountable to national Parliaments. Though they climbed down in the end the factors which led them to assert themselves in this way have not disappeared and are unlikely to do so.

All this has a special significance for the themes examined in this book. There would have been a majority in favour of rejection even if the British members had all voted on the other side, but it would not have been a large enough majority to prevail. The British, in other words, were an indispensable element in the rejectionist coalition; without them, the Parliament's first big attempt to flex its muscles would have been a flop. In voting as they did, the British members were, of course, pursuing what they saw as a British interest, just as the French MEPs who voted against rejection were pursuing what they saw as a French interest. But the British were not only voting in defence of British interests: willy-nilly, they were also voting in defence of the European Parliament's rights. The Labour members were doing so in spite of having been elected on a manifesto which committed them to oppose any increase in the powers of the European Parliament, and, by implication at any rate, to interpret its existing powers as narrowly as possible. The Conservatives were doing so against the public position, even if not against the private wishes, of their own Government at Westminster.

It would be wrong to make too much of this. The British contingent at Strasbourg are not likely to vote solidly for all assertions of Parliament's rights, irrespective of the particular issues at stake. If, in some future battle between the Council and the Parliament, the interests of their constituents seem to point in the opposite direction from the way they pointed in December 1979, they will doubtless be found supporting the Council against their parliamentary colleagues. But the episode did at least show that the British members – including strongly anti-Market Labour members – would be prepared to assert Parliament's rights against the Council in some circumstances, even if the British Government were siding with the Council majority, and even if the rights which were being asserted had not been asserted in the past. More generally, it also showed that, after only six months,

Strasbourg perceptions could differ quite sharply from Westminster perceptions, that Strasbourg experiences could quickly modify pre-Strasbourg assumptions and that the Strasbourg Groups were determined to be masters in their own house. This, of course, was precisely what the opponents of direct elections had feared. Quite early on in the life of the elected Parliament, it looked as though these fears, at any rate, would be borne out. As we saw in Chapter 2, Strasbourg had a big impact even on the part-time members of the nominated Parliament. It would be surprising if it did not have a bigger impact on the full-time members of the elected one.

Whether the British members would have an equivalent impact on Strasbourg was less clear. Parliamentary reputations are rarely made overnight, and parliamentary skills take time to learn. Partly because of this, the first session of the elected Parliament, at any rate, was dominated by 'old hands', who had served before in the nominated Parliament: since the British contingent contained almost no 'old hands', its impact was likely to be weaker at the start than it would later become. Barbara Castle was the only British member to establish an early reputation as a Strasbourg force; only time could tell whether she would be followed by others, lacking her Westminster experience. Simple arithmetic suggested that the Conservatives were likely to make a bigger impact than in the nominated Parliament, and the Labour group a smaller one. But it was not at all clear how, in practice, either would bring its influence to bear. Both in the July 1979 vote to elect Madame Veil as President, and in the December 1979 vote on the Community Budget, sheer numbers gave the Conservatives a decisive influence on the outcome. In both, however, they followed a lead coming from elsewhere – in the election of Madame Veil, from the Christian Democrats and Liberals, and in the Budget vote, from the Socialist President and rapporteur of the Budgets Committee. It remained to be seen whether they, or their Labour counterparts, would take the lead on other issues in future.

The impact of the elected Parliament on British politics must depend, in part, on the evolution of a public mood which, in the past at any rate, has been extremely volatile. In the year after direct elections, the Community was more unpopular, and under heavier fire from all political parties, than at any time since Britain joined it. But this unpopularity was heavily linked to the British Government's battle with the other eight Member States over Britain's contribution to the Community Budget; it is doubtful if ideological opposition to the Community as such, though still strongly felt on the left wing of the Labour Party, was any more prevalent among the electorate at large than it had been in the 1975 Referendum. That ideological hostility would be unaffected by the outcome of the Budget dispute; so would grumbling about the imbalances of the Common Agricultural Policy or about unnecessary measures of harmonisation. The resolution of the Budget dispute was bound to affect popular attitudes. The fluctuations of British opinion on Community membership had not suddenly ended: those who told pollsters that they wanted Britain to withdraw might well think again, as they had done in the early months of 1975, when the Referendum forced them to face the alternative. Withdrawal would not cease to be a political issue – though it is worth remembering that Community membership has been the single most divisive issue in Labour politics since 1971, and that many Conservative activists are deeply committed pro-Europeans.

At an élite level, the impact of the British MEPs on domestic politics depends as much on the attitude of the Government in Whitehall as of the Parliament at Westminster. After the 1979–80 Budget crisis, some ministers belatedly recognised that Strasbourg could furnish allies in Britain's struggles in the Council of Ministers and the European Council. Even so, links between Westminster and Whitehall on the one hand, and Strasbourg on the other, remained tenuous and fragile. Only four MEPs were members of the House of Commons as well; their fellow Westminster MPs proved reluctant to accord Westminster facilities to the Strasbourg contingent, and paid little attention to its doings. Contacts between MEPs and ministers were civil, but they were not close. Partly because Westminster's attitude seemed patronising and distant, Strasbourg members showed a diminishing interest in establishing links with it. They had Euro-roles to play, and Euro-money with which to finance independent constituency bases, under their own control. There seemed a distinct possibility that they might withdraw into a private Euro-world of their own, cut off from the mainstream of British politics.

If that happened, Westminster would lose as much as Strasbourg. One of the main arguments for direct elections was that Community decision-making was not subject to adequate parliamentary scrutiny, and that only a full-time and democratically-elected Parliament could impose on the decision-makers the kind of scrutiny that was needed. Much Community decision-making can be scrutinised effectively only at the Community level, and, although the nominated Parliament did its best to discharge these responsibilities, its best could not possibly be enough. But although Community decision-making cannot be effectively scrutinised without a full-time Strasbourg Parliament, it cannot be scrutinised effectively by a full-time Strasbourg Parliament alone.

For the foreseeable future, the Community will be, at one and the same time, a supranational entity with supranational Institutions, and an association of sovereign states, reaching its decisions by the traditional processes of intergovernmental negotiation. Almost by definition, therefore, parliamentary scrutiny needs to be carried out at two levels if it is to be effective. Scrutiny at the Community level has to be complemented by scrutiny at the national level; and if this is to be done, there is an obvious need for close co-ordination between the two. Before direct elections, the House of Lords gave considerable thought to this; one of the most unfortunate aspects of the directly-elected Parliament's first session was that neither Westminster nor Strasbourg seemed to take the question seriously.

There was another unfortunate aspect as well. As we have shown in the last chapter, whatever might be true of the election campaign, the directly-elected Parliament has displayed considerable energy and vitality, and has grappled with one of the central issues of Community politics at least as vigorously as any national Parliament has done. Though the British members did not play leading roles in these battles, they did play important supporting roles, and they did so in a way that promised direct and tangible benefits to their electors. Yet for all the attention that the British media paid to them, they might as well have been on another planet. In the entire British press, only *The Economist* enabled its readers to follow the Budget story in anything approaching a full way. *The Times* gave it modest coverage, both through the columns of David Wood and through its reports of debates in the plenary sessions. For all practical purposes, the rest was silence.

This was not the fault of the media alone. The shuttling between Strasbourg, Luxembourg and Brussels imposes heavy costs on the European Parliament in publicity, as well as in money and efficiency. Inevitably, most European correspondents are based in Brussels, where most of the decisions are taken and where most of the Community's civil service is located. The Parliament cannot expect to be adequately reported until it is located in Brussels as well. Nor, for that matter, can it expect adequate reporting so long as many of its procedures remain opaque, tedious and confusing. The Budget crisis of 1979–80 proved that it has teeth, but it will need to use its teeth more often and more dramatically if it is to win a wider popularity and respect. It needs to stage more successful confrontations with the Commission and the Council of Ministers and to spotlight abuses through public hearings, with the press and television cameras present. The fact remains that no Parliament can do its job without the media, and that the British media have so far failed to live up to their responsibilities.

Watchdog achievements, however, will not in themselves suffice to generate public interest in the Community, or to give the MEPs impact on their electors. In the long run, policies will matter more. In all Community countries, it is the farmers, the main beneficiaries of the EEC, who bring most pressure on Brussels, and whose organisations follow what happens in Brussels most closely. That will remain the case for the foreseeable future: no conceivable 'reform' of the CAP, and no conceivable change in the Community Budget, will displace agriculture from its present position as the most important single Community policy and the biggest single consumer of Community funds. But if agricultural spending is brought under control – and if it is not brought under control it is hard to see how the Community can avoid a series of crises far more bruising than any which have occurred so far – it will, at any rate, be feasible to develop new policies in other fields, and to allocate more resources to regional, social and industrial expenditure. The European Parliament cannot, of course, determine whether or not agricultural spending is brought under control or what kind of new expenditures are made if it is brought under control. It can, however, continue to press for the kind of reallocation of resources for which it fought in the Budget battle; and it can move in with policy initiatives of its own in other areas as and when the opportunity offers. More than any other national contingent, the British members – from both parties – will have an incentive to take the lead in such developments.

In the last analysis, in short, the impact of the elected Parliament on British opinion and British politics will depend overwhelmingly on the conduct of the British MEPs themselves – on whether they have the flair and drive to dramatise the issues that matter to their constituents, on whether they have the tact and skill to persuade their parties that the job they are doing is worthwhile, on whether they have the organising ability to build up local power bases in their constituencies. In a sense which has not been true of any elected persons in British public life for many centuries, the future of the institution to which they belong, as well as their personal futures, is in their own hands.

An analysis of the results

John Curtice

The response of the British electorate to the European election was one of apathy. In Great Britain, only 32.1 per cent of the electorate felt it worthwhile to vote; this was lower than in any other country in the EEC and only two-fifths of the turnout in the general election the previous month. The turnout in the 1975 Referendum on Britain's membership of the Community (63.3%) was almost twice as large. Only in Northern Ireland (turnout 55.7%) did the election capture the public's interest; there participation was higher than in the 1975 Referendum.[1]

Despite the low turnout, the behaviour of the electorate in the European election still retains considerable interest, particularly if it is compared with previous Westminster elections. In some respects the European contest resembled a general election; the same electoral system was used and the familiar political parties contested the election on platforms which except for the Liberal Party made little reference to their continental allies. But in other respects it was different: the amount of campaigning, both in the national media and in the localities, was low, large and unfamilar constituencies were employed, and the political colour of the next Government was not at stake. The election thus provides some evidence on the importance of such factors in influencing the behaviour of the British electorate. In addition, the use of the first-past-the-post electoral system in this different context presented it with a new test of credibility; how far would it succeed in distributing the relatively small number of seats equitably between the political parties?

167

Table 1. Measures of change since May 1979.

	Seats included	Mean change	Overall change
Turnout	all (78)	−44.1	−44.1
Con. share of poll	75	+5.3	+5.7
Con. share of poll	60	+6.0	+6.4
Lab. share of poll	75	−4.1	−4.7
Lab. share of poll	60	−3.6	−4.3
Lib. share of poll	60	−2.1	−1.9
Total vote swing	75	+4.7	+5.2
Two-party swing	75	+5.5	+6.2

75: all seats excluding South of Scotland, Northumbria (split Labour vote in South Ayrshire and Blyth in May 1979) and Wales South (no Conservative candidate in Cardiff West in May).
60: those of the 75 in which the Liberals fought all the component Westminster constituencies in May 1979.
Mean change: the mean of the equivalent changes in each constituency.
Overall change: the change based on the total votes cast in the constituencies.

Table 1 presents some measures of the difference in the behaviour of the electorate between May and June. Because the Euro-constituencies were composed of sets of complete Westminster constituencies, such figures are easy to produce for each Euro-constituency. However, difficulties do arise in some constituencies because of changes in the pattern of candidature[2] – and these seats are omitted, where necessary, from the calculations in the pages that follow.

Even though the Conservatives benefited from a 6.3 per cent overall two-party swing[3] between October 1974 and May 1979 there was yet another large swing of almost exactly the same size – +6.2 per cent – between May and June. This was sufficient to give the Conservatives an overall majority of the votes cast in Great Britain – 50.6 per cent – a feat which has only once been achieved by a political party since 1918. In 1931 the Conservatives received 55.1 per cent and the Labour Party 31.1 per cent; never, since then, has Labour sunk so low as the 33.0 per cent received in the Euro-election.

On the other hand, there was relatively little net change in the strength of third parties. Overall, the share of the poll in Great Britain gathered by the two major parties rose from 82.6 per cent in May to 83.6 per cent in June. This limited increase was confined to England; in Scotland there was a considerable increase in the share of both the Liberals and the Nationalists, reducing the combined Conservative and Labour share from 73.0 per cent to 66.7 per cent.

The usefulness of these statistics might be considered to be negated by the large drop in participation. They might simply reflect differences in the propensity of the parties' supporters to abstain in the election rather than changes in the party preferences of the electorate. The Appendix therefore begins by examining the fall in turnout.

Turnout[4]

The coincidence of such a large swing to Conservative with such a low level of turnout led many commentators to suggest that a lower proportion of Labour voters had bothered to vote than of Conservatives. This hypothesis seemed highly plausible. Labour voters were generally more anti-Common Market than Conservatives.[5] They might therefore have been reluctant to participate in an election for an EEC institution which had been heralded by its supporters as a means of strengthening the Community; furthermore, Labour had not presented those opposed to the EEC with an explicitly anti-Common Market programme through which they could register their views. In addition, there is a widespread belief that when Labour are in office, they suffer from differential abstention in local government elections which have a similarly low level of turnout.[6]

The pattern of turnout in individual constituencies at first sight appears to lend weight to this argument. On average, the turnout in the Euro-seats that the Conservatives would have won on the May results (33.5%) was higher than in those that Labour would have won (29.8%). Spectacularly low polls were recorded in the Labour strongholds of London North East (20.4%) and Liverpool (23.7%). However, turnout is always lower in Labour-held seats than Conservative-held seats in Westminster elections. If it is to be shown from the individual constituency results that Labour suffered from differential abstention as compared with May, then it is necessary to examine the relationship between the *fall* in turnout and changes in party support rather than between the *level* of turnout and the level of party support. We have to examine two patterns. Firstly, did turnout fall more the greater the proportion of Labour voters in a seat? Secondly, does the pattern of constituency swing suggest that disproportionately more Labour voters than Conservative voters tended to abstain within a constituency?

The pattern of the fall in turnout does provide some apparent support for the thesis. The less middle class a seat was, (and thus generally the more Labour it was) the more turnout fell.[7] But there were other influences on turnout which to some degree counteracted this trend. As the table of regional results (Table 7, p. 138) indicates, turnout fell distinctly less in those regions which were both nearest (London, South East and South West) and furthest (Scotland) from continental Europe. Seventeen of the 21 smallest drops in turnout occurred in seats in these regions. While the South East and South West contained the most middle class and Conservative Euro-constituencies in the country, London and Scotland were among Labour's stronger areas.[8] Also, as Table 4 on p. 173 shows, while turnout fell least in the most rural (and generally more Conservative) seats, it fell just as little in the most urban (and more Labour) seats. Overall, therefore, the difference in fall in turnout between Conservative and Labour seats was not large; it fell by an average of 43.5 per cent in the former and 45.0 per cent in the latter. But this difference does enable us to explain why the mean constituency swing (+5.5%) was lower than the overall swing (+6.2%) as shown in Table 1.

That pattern, however, merely enables us to say that more Labour voters than Conservative voters abstained across constituencies. It does not necessarily follow that, in general, more Labour than Conservative voters abstained within a constituency, thus affecting the constituency swing and causing Labour to lose seats. Unfortunately, examination of this more important question using the evidence of the pattern of constituency swings is difficult as the statistics in Table 2 illustrate,

Table 2. Swing under certain hypothetical conditions of differential abstention.

2-party ratio at election A Con. : Lab.	2-party ratio at election B Con. : Lab.	Swing	Change in turnout
70:30	74.5:25.5	+4.5	−29.5
65:35	69.9:30.1	+4.9	−36.3
60:40	65.2:34.8	+5.2	−31.0
55:45	60.4:39.6	+5.4	−31.8
50:50	55.6:44.4	+5.6	−32.5
45:55	50.6:49.4	+5.6	−33.3
40:60	45.5:54.5	+5.5	−34.0
35:65	40.2:59.8	+5.2	−34.8
30:70	34.9:65.1	+4.9	−35.5

The ratios at election B are calculated by assuming that three-quarters of Conservative voters and three-fifths of Labour voters at election A participate at the subsequent election, and that no other movement occurs. The fall in turnout figures is based on the additional assumptions that there was a 100 per cent turnout at the previous election and that only Conservative and Labour Party candidates stand.

differential abstention does not produce a simple linear relationship between turnout and swing.

The table shows that if there were uniform differential abstention to the advantage of the Conservatives at an election, this would not produce the largest swings where turnout fell most. Swing is unaffected by an increase in abstention, irrespective of the two–party ratio, so long as equal proportions of both parties abstain. But the degree of disproportional abstention required to produce any given swing does vary with the two–party ratio; a greater disproportionality is required, the safer (whether Conservative or Labour) a seat. Consequently, if there were uniform differential abstention the highest swings would be found in the most marginal seats, where turnout fall would be near average.

It will be appreciated that the degree of variation in swing between the constituencies in our example is fairly small, and the pattern could easily be hidden from view if other factors were also influencing swing, especially if the difference in the proportion of Conservative and Labour abstainers were smaller than in the example. However, the degree of disproportional abstention required to produce on average +5.5 per cent swing is roughly of the order assumed in Table 2; if most of that swing were caused by differential abstention the pattern of that table should be discernible in the results. Even if the extent of the differential abstention varied from constituency to constituency, so long as that variation was randomly distributed, we should still expect the pattern to appear.[9]

Table 3. Swing between May and June 1979 by Labour share of the two-party vote in May 1979.

Lab. 2-party share (%)	Mean swing	(N)	Lab. 2-party share (%)	Mean swing	(N)
Less than 25	+0.5	(1)	50–55	+4.5	(11)
25–30	+5.4	(6)	55–60	+6.7	(7)
30–35	+6.3	(7)	60–65	+4.0	(4)
35–40	+6.6	(12)	65–70	+3.8	(4)
40–45	+6.6	(12)	More than 70	+6.7	(1)
45–50	+4.5	(10)	All seats	+5.5	(75)

Table 3 shows that the results of the election did not follow the pattern anticipated in our model of differential abstention in Table 2.[10] Neither does the pattern seem to have been hidden from view by the effect of systematic variation from the national norm by a particular group or groups of constituencies. It does not seem, therefore, that differential abstention explains the bulk of the variation in constituency swing.

It would be rash, however, to conclude that differential abstention within constituencies did not occur at all. One other piece of evidence is available. The turnout in the European election was made available by Returning Officers for most Westminster constituencies. In general, the Labour-held Westminster constituencies within a Euro-constituency suffered a larger fall in turnout than Conservative-held constituencies. This phenomenon alone would have produced some advantage to the Conservatives even if the proportions of Labour and Conservative voters who abstained in each Westminster constituency were equal.

There is strong evidence that more Conservative supporters than Labour ones voted in the European election; but the extent to which that benefited the Conservatives in terms of seats is uncertain. Turnout fell rather more in Labour constituencies than in Conservative ones – but that could have been caused by a greater propensity for both Conservative and Labour voters to participate in Conservative areas than in Labour ones. However, the turnout figures in each Westminster constituency suggest that it is likely that, in general, proportionately more Labour voters than Conservative voters did abstain within a Euro-constituency, thereby producing an advantage to the Conservatives – but the pattern of swing does not confirm the belief that differential abstention was responsible for all or most of the constituency swing.

Swing

One of the most marked features of the results in the 1979 Westminster election was the extent to which swing varied between seats.[11] This was even more true of the European election. The standard deviation of swing calculated for each Euro-constituency between May and June 1979 (2.9) was slightly higher than that between October 1974 and May 1979 (2.5), even though only one month separated the two elections.

But in contrast to May, there was little regional pattern to the swing in the European election. In particular, no marked division was evident between the north and the south of the country. There were, however, noticeably low swings in four geographically contiguous seats in Yorkshire – Leeds, Yorkshire South, Yorkshire South West and Yorkshire West (mean +1.7%) there were above average swings in the South East (+6.8%) and in five of the eight Scottish seats (+7.0%) (in Highlands and Islands and Scotland North East dramatic changes in the third party vote affected the results while in the South of Scotland there had been a split Labour candidature in May). The result in Scotland was particularly remarkable. The 8½ per cent fall in the Labour vote resulted in their conceding the position of leading party in Scotland to the Conservatives who won three more seats and 0.7 per cent more of the poll than Labour. The Conservatives have never secured more votes than Labour in Scotland in any Westminster election since 1959, and the result contrasts sharply with the third position they obtained as recently as October 1974.

Table 4. Result by degree of rurality.

	Change in share of poll			(N)	Change in turnout	Swing (N)
	Con.	Lab.	Lib.			
Very urban	+5.0	−2.4	−1.3	(16)	−43.2	+4.1(22)
Mainly urban	+3.8	−3.2	−0.4	(10)	−44.9	+5.4(15)
Mixed	+7.2	−4.8	−1.8	(17)	−45.5	+6.7(17)
Mainly rural	+6.7	−4.7	−3.0	(10)	−43.2	+6.9(11)
Predominantly rural	+7.3	−2.4	−6.3	(7)	−43.2	+5.4(10)

Definitions: Very urban, 0–1 per cent engaged in agriculture (1971 census); Mainly urban, 1–2 per cent; Mixed, 2–4 per cent; mainly rural, 4–8 per cent; Predominantly rural, over 8 per cent. As the census figures also include those employed in fishing, Humber is reclassified as Mixed.
    The changes in the share of the poll are based on 60 constituencies, the number of these constituencies in each category being given to the immediate right of those figures. Swing is calculated over 75 constituencies and the number of these in each category is given on the far right of the table. The change in turnout figure is calculated over 78 constituencies.

The remaining geographically definable variation in swing – the low movement in London and Birmingham – probably reflects the high degree of urbanisation of the seats in those cities rather than regional factors. In a number of recent Westminster elections Labour has performed better in urban constituencies than rural ones; Table 4 shows that this was also true of this election. Only in the most rural constituencies, in some of which a large fall in the Liberal vote appears to have particularly benefited Labour (see p. 175), did the pattern not fully hold.
    These factors, however, seem to exhaust the regional and socioeconomic correlates of swing. Indeed there are exceptions to many of the patterns that can be cited. Within the South East and Scotland there were examples of below average swing such as Thames Valley (+4.6%) and Strathclyde East (+3.1%). Amongst the more urban seats, unex-

pectedly high swings were recorded in Liverpool (+13.4%) (see p. 178) and London Central (+9.2%). *Prima facie,* it seems possible that local constituency factors influenced the swing from Labour to Conservative to a considerable degree.

There is evidence to suggest that some of the variation in swing between May and June 1979 was in compensation for an unusual movement between October 1974 and May 1979. The pattern of high swing in South Britain and low swing in North Britain that occurred in May was not reversed. But some of the deviations from the average for these areas in May do appear to have been followed by opposite deviations from the national average in June. The above average swing in Scotland and the below average swings in London and Birmingham may be such compensatory movements. Within London, the two seats that swung substantially to Conservative, London Central and London North West, had the lowest swings to Conservative in May, while London North East, which swung to Labour in June had had the highest. Lower than average swings in Essex South West (+3.2%) and Thames Valley (+4.4%) had been preceded by above average ones in May (+12.9% and +9.3% respectively). Overall, the standard deviation of swing calculated separately for South Britain and North Britain is slightly lower if calculated from October 1974 rather than May 1979.[12] Some, but not all, of the so far unexplained swing can, therefore, be interpreted as the adjustment of a constituency to wider norms of behaviour rather than a local deviation.

Liberal performance

The Liberal performance showed a remarkable degree of variation at this election. The change in the Liberal share of the poll between October 1974 and May 1979, aggregated to Euro-constituency level in 58 comparable constituencies, had a standard deviation of 1.5. Between May and June 1979 the standard deviation was 3.6. Change in preference for voting Liberal therefore varied dramatically from constituency to constituency. But, in contrast to swing, much of this variation appears to follow a general pattern.

Despite an average decline of 2.1 per cent in their share of the poll in the 60 comparable constituencies, the Liberals' share rose in 13 of them; but in only four cases was the increase above 2 per cent and they failed to win any seats. Their success among these seats was concentrated in the South. They performed above average in a geographically contiguous area consisting of most of the South East apart from the easternmost seat of Kent East, the northern and western corner of London and extending westwards as far as the Somerset and Wessex constituencies. This included three notable successes in Hertfordshire (+10.0%), Surrey (+9.9%) and Hampshire West (+4.4%). In addition, they continued their success of May in Liverpool, increasing their share of the poll by 2.2 per cent, a higher increase than between October 1974 and May 1979. This success was close to the one clear geographical cluster of comparable seats where they did badly; their share of the poll fell by an average of 4.1 per cent in the three Lancashire constituencies.

Although only one seat in the whole of Scotland and Wales is strictly comparable, the results in both countries are sufficiently clear to allow some generalisations to be made. The Liberals clearly did badly in Wales, where despite not having fought eight constituencies in May, their share of the poll dropped by 1.0 per cent; they conceded third place to Plaid Cymru in three of the four Welsh constituencies. In Scotland, while some of the 5.0 per cent increase in their share of the poll clearly came from Liberal supporters in the 23 Westminster constituencies where there had not been any opportunity to vote Liberal in May, the strength of their performance in the Highlands and Islands (+12.5%), Scotland North East (+15.2%) and the Lothians (+6.1%) was more than could be accounted for by the extra votes of those supporters. Only in the South of Scotland (−3.9%), which contains Roxburgh, Selkirk and Peebles where the Liberal Leader, David Steel, has established a substantial personal vote, was there clearly a considerable decline in their support.

That last result supports a more general pattern. Nearly all of the Liberals' largest declines came in seats in which they were relatively strong overall in May, and which contain two or three Westminster constituencies in which they have been in close contention with the Conservatives in recent elections, notably Cornwall and Plymouth (−12.3%), Lincolnshire (−8.4%), Devon (−7.1%), Wight and Hants. East (−6.2%) and Hereford and Worcestershire (−5.9%). Within these seats, some of the Liberal candidates for Westminster have established a substantial vote based partly on their personal popularity and partly on tactical support from third-placed Labour voters. In the absence of both the popular candidate and as strong a tactical impulse, much of the Liberals' support in these areas appears to have dissolved. Further, in three of the five above mentioned seat – Cornwall and Plymouth, Devon, and Hereford and Worcestershire – the Liberals' decline produced a clear advantage to Labour, the swing averaging 1.4 per cent in these predominantly rural seats.

Other parties

In general, the European election results were favourable to the other parties that contested the election. The Nationalists in both Scotland (+2.1% of the total Scottish poll) and Wales (+3.6% of the Welsh poll) succeeded in recovering some of the ground they had lost in May. The Welsh Nationalists' share of the poll (11.7%) slightly exceeded that in their best performance in any Westminster election (1970, 11.5%) and they also overtook the Liberals in Wales which they have only done once in a general election – again in 1970. As in the past, their success was concentrated in the most rural and Welsh-speaking part of Wales, Wales North (+6.6%). The Scottish Nationalists increased their share of the poll everywhere in Scotland (despite the extension of Liberal candidature) except in Scotland North East, where their support appears to have been particularly susceptible to the appeal of Lord Mackie's successful Liberal campaign. There was no clear regional pattern to their degree of advance; neither was it always related to the size of the increase in the Liberal vote. A somewhat above average increase in their share of the poll in the Highlands and Islands (+4.7%) enabled Winnie Ewing to overtake the Conservative and stay ahead of the advance of the Liberal, Russell Johnston (+12.5%) and so capture the seat.

In contrast to the May election, the number of independent candidates and those standing for parties without representation at Westminster was fairly small. Only 23 such candidates found it worthwhile to risk the £600 deposit, and neither the National Front nor the Communist Party fielded any candidates at all. While none of the 23 candidates succeeded in saving their deposit, a number did surprisingly well. The most interesting result was probably that of the Mebyon Kernow candidate in Cornwall and Plymouth (5.9%), whose performance confirmed the increased support for Cornish Nationalism that the May results had shown. If all his support came from voters registered in the five Cornish Westminster constituencies rather than the three Plymouth ones, it would mean that 8.8 per cent of those who voted in Cornwall supported the local nationalist cause.

The Ecology Party contested only three constituencies, but in all three they did better than any of their candidates in May (av. 3.7%), even though in one of the constituencies they fought, Cornwall and Plymouth, they faced competition from two other minor party candidates. In general, the assorted set of six candidates who stood on an anti-Common Market ticket did better than usual for British minor party candidates in Westminster elections (av. 3.0%). The best performance was that of the veteran right-wing activist, Air Vice-Marshall Bennett who received 6.1 per cent of the poll in the Cotswolds.

Impact of candidates

In the context of the European election it seems possible that some of the attributes of the individual candidates, rather than or as well as their party label influenced voting decisions and helped to produce some of the variation in behaviour between constituencies. Two attributes are of particular interest. Firstly, with a low-key campaign and unfamiliar candidates, the electorate might have shown a particular willingness to vote for better known candidates. Secondly, Labour candidates varied considerably in their attitude towards a central issue of the election – whether they generally adopted a pro- or anti-Common Market stance – and their position might have influenced the willingness of some of the electorate to vote for them.

Those candidates most likely to have had an established public reputation were current and past members of the House of Commons. Five such candidates did achieve unusually good results – Russell Johnston, MP (Liberal, Highlands and Islands, +12.5%), Lord Mackie (Liberal, Scotland North East, +15.2%), Christopher Mayhew (Liberal, Surrey, +9.9%), Barbara Castle (Labour, Greater Manchester North, swing −0.01%) and Winifred Ewing (SNP, Highlands and Islands, +4.7%). However, most of these candidates were campaigning under circumstances that, even in Westminster elections, are relatively favourable to the acquisition of personally based support – as third party candidates and/or in the far north and west of Scotland. Only Barbara Castle, probably the most widely known candidate and the only former Cabinet Minister standing, was not campaigning in such circumstances.

Among the largest group of MPs and former MPs, those standing as Conservatives, there is no discernible evidence of personal support. Five of the seven were either currently MPs or had been MPs until the election in May 1979, and were therefore likely to be relatively well known to the electorate. The average increase in the Conservative share of the poll for these five was 6.0 per cent, exactly the same as in all 60 comparable seats.

As a majority of Labour supporters were opposed to the Common Market (see n. 5), one might expect anti-Common Market Labour candidates to have been more successful than pro-Common Market candidates in pulling in the votes of Labour supporters. They might also have provided a means whereby anti-Common Market Conservative and Liberal supporters, faced with a pro-Common Market platform from their own party, could express their dislike. The principal authors of this book have classified the Labour candidates in the election as strongly or weakly pro- or anti-Common Market. The average swing against the anti-Common Market candidates, 5.0 per cent, was slightly lower than the national average. However, the anti–Common Market candidates were disproportionately located in urban seats, particularly in London and Birmingham, and the pro- or anti–Common Market stance of the Labour candidates in London, for example, does not distinguish between those who were relatively successful or unsuccessful. Further, there is little consistent pattern of advantage to anti–Common Market candidates nationally.

But the well-publicised views of two individual Labour candidates, situated at opposite ends of the political spectrum, do appear to have produced a particular reaction. The staunch left-wing and anti–Common Market candidate in Liverpool, Terence Harrison, suffered the highest swing against Labour in the whole country (11.3%), giving the Conservatives their most surprising success of the election. Meanwhile, in Cleveland, right-winger and director of the pro-EEC European Movement, Ernest Wistrich, sustained a 10.3 per cent swing against himself, while his anti–Common Market opponent won 3.2 per cent of the poll, the second best anti–Common Market performance in the election.

One other apparent candidate effect is of interest. Just one coloured candidate stood in the election, the Labour candidate for Hampshire West. He had the misfortune to suffer the second highest fall in the Labour vote in a comparable seat (−10.5%).

Northern Ireland

The election in Northern Ireland was held using the single transferable vote with the whole province forming one constituency electing three members. This resulted in its anticipated consequence – the election of two unionists and one Catholic – but there were electoral movements which were well worthy of note.

The result reinforced the evidence of the vote in the May election that the Official Unionist Party was losing its appeal for loyalist voters. The two OUP candidates together won only 21.9 per cent of first preference votes, compared with the 36.6 per cent of the total Northern Irish vote the party had gathered in 11 of the 12 Westminster constituencies in the province in May. Meanwhile, Ian Paisley, the Democratic Unionist Party candidate won 29.8 per cent of first preferences, easily more than the quota required for election. It is doubtful, however, that Mr Paisley's success can be interpreted solely as a move in favour of a more extreme form of loyalism, as distinct from a purely personal vote. Because Ian Paisley was elected at the first stage of the count a full profile of the second preferences of his supporters is available, as these were counted in order to distribute his surplus votes. Almost equal numbers of his supporters opted for the hard line Independent Unionist Westminster MP, James Kilfedder (44.9%) and for the two Official Unionist candidates (47.8%), John Taylor (32.7%) and Harry West (15.1%); only 3.0 per cent opted for other candidates and 4.1 per cent did not express any second preference. Thus nearly half of Mr Paisley's supporters expressed a second preference for an Official Unionist candidate, rather than take the option of supporting another relatively well-known extreme loyalist candidate.

For the then Leader of the Official Unionist Party, Harry West, the election was a particular disappointment. He trailed behind the party's other candidate, John Taylor, on first preferences, winning 10.0 per cent to his 11.9 per cent, and won fewer preferences, from other candidates' supporters than Mr Taylor did at each subsequent stage of the count. Consequently, he was eliminated at the last stage of the count, his votes ensuring that the second unionist seat went to John Taylor rather than James Kilfedder. Harry West resigned the leadership of his party following his defeat.

While there was substantial movement within the loyalist camp as compared with May, the overall unionist vote was little changed. But support for the principal Catholic party, the SDLP, increased (although it had fought only ten seats in May). Their candidate, John Hume, won 24.6 per cent of first preferences, only slightly less than was needed to be elected at the first stage. His increased support appears to have come particularly at the expense of the non-sectarian Alliance Party, whose leader, Oliver Napier, won only 6.8 per cent of first preferences, little more than half the party's support in the 12 Westminster constituencies in May. Unlike loyalists, Catholics did not display a drift towards extremism, although the most charismatic representative of republicanism at the election, Bernadette Devlin-McAliskey, the former MP for Mid-Ulster, won 5.9 per cent of first preference votes.

The turnout (55.7%) was 16 per cent higher than in any constituency in Great Britain. This difference has led some critics of the choice of the first-past-the-post electoral system for Great Britain to suggest that the electoral system must take at least some of the blame for the low turnout there. However, it is not clear that the higher Northern Ireland turnout can simply be explained by the electoral system. To the extent that in the long term joint membership of the Common Market by both the United Kingdom and the Republic of Ireland might have implications for one of the central issues in the province's politics – the future of the border – the election might be held to be of greater relevance to the concerns of the Northern Irish electorate. The election in Northern

Ireland also differed from that in Great Britain by the presence of so many well-known candidates, and as the analysis above has shown, the Northern Irish electorate's behaviour does appear to have been influenced by their assessment of the individual candidates. Within Great Britain itself, the highest turnout, in the Highlands and Islands, occurred in a constituency which was distinctive in having two well-known candidates of substantial local repute. However, because the choice of STV enabled the election in Northern Ireland to be fought on a province-wide basis, it did provide a unique opportunity for some of the province's leading politicians to be pitted directly against each other. Thus, indirectly the electoral system may have encouraged the Northern Ireland electorate's interest in the election; but it is uncertain if the use of a proportional representation system in Great Britain would have afforded a similar opportunity for the British electorate to be wooed by candidates of high standing from all the political parties.

The electoral system

The decision to use the familiar first-past-the-post electoral system for the European election in Great Britain was controversial well before the election was held and the turnout known. Two major fears were voiced by its critics. Firstly, because the system allocates seats so as to exaggerate the majority of the winning party in votes, if the election was held during a period of Government unpopularity, the opposition party could win a very large proportion of the total number of seats, thereby rendering the British delegation unbalanced and unrepresentative of public opinion. Secondly, it seemed likely that because their vote was fairly evenly spread across the country, the Liberals would be unlikely to win any seats at all; this could mean that the preference of between 10 and 20 per cent of those voting would be denied any representation at all.

Both these fears proved to be valid. Although they were the Government party, the Conservatives won slightly over 60 per cent of the vote cast for the two largest parties, which gave them 60 seats or over three-quarters of the total British delegation. The Liberals polled 13 per cent of the total vote, but failed to win any seats; the way the system worked against them was underlined by the success of the SNP in winning the Highlands and Islands while they polled less than 2 per cent of the national vote. But for the main parties two questions stand out. Was the exaggeration of the Conservative majority only what could have been reasonably expected from the electoral system? Given the existence of exaggeration, was the system otherwise equitable in its treatment of the two largest parties?

There are two ways in which we can approach these issues. Firstly, did the Conservatives win as many seats as would have been expected if the swing between May and June had been uniform? On the basis of the results in May, the Conservatives would have won 49 seats and Labour 29. If the mean constituency swing of +5.5 per cent had been uniform, 11 seats would have switched from Labour to Conservative; in fact, 12 did so. The Conservatives won four seats which required a swing greater than +5.5 per cent if they were to win them, while Labour won three that needed a lower swing than average for a Conservative victory. Much of this variation can be explained by the factors discussed above. Three of the four 'extra' seats which the Conservatives won were in Scotland where there was an above average swing, while two of the three seats which Labour 'saved' were in the most urban category of seats, where there was generally a low swing. Thus, on this basis, the Conservatives won one more seat than they might have been expected to.

Table 5. Operation of the electoral system.

		Result if leading party:		
(i) Division of 2-party vote	*(ii)* Cube law prediction	*(iii)* Con.	*(iv)* Lab.	*(v)* Mean of (iii) and (iv)
Leading party: Second party (%)	Leading party: Second party (Seats)	Con.:Lab. (Seats)	Lab.:Con. (Seats)	Leading party: Second party (Seats)
50:50	38.5:38.5	40:37	37:40	38.5:38.5
52:48	43:34	42:35	42:35	42:35
54:46	47.5:29.5	47:30	48:31	47.5:29.5
56:44	52:25	50:27	52:25	51:26
58:42	56:21	54:23	56:21	55:22
60:40	59:18	59:18	62:15	60.5:16.5
60.4:39.6★	60:17	60:17	62:15	61:16
62:38	62.5:14.5	62:15	65:14	63.5:13.5
64:36	65:12	66:11	69:8	67.5:9.5
66:34	68:9	69:8	71:6	70:7
68:32	70:7	70:7	73:4	71.5:5.5
70:30	71:6	71:6	75:2	73:4

★ Actual result.

The table is based on 77 seats throughout. It is assumed that the Highlands and Islands would be won by a third party at all given divisions by the two-party vote.

That approach, however, does not take into account the starting point from which the movement between May and June occurred. Table 5 offers a wider perspective on the electoral system that was used in the European election. Assuming a uniform swing from the result in June 1979, the table shows separately for the Conservative Party (col. (iii)) and the Labour Party (col. (iv)) the division of seats that would occur if that party was the leading party and the total Conservative and Labour vote was divided between them in the proportion stated in column (i). It also gives the proportion that both parties would be expected to win if the electoral system was conforming to the 'cube law' (col. (ii)). The law is a statement of the degree of exaggeration of the leading party's majority of votes into a majority of seats that can be expected from a first-past-the-post electoral system; if the two major parties divide their share of the poll between themselves in the proportion A:B, the law says that the seats that they win will be divided in the proportion $A^3:B^3$. The law has been found to have been a reasonable approximation to the way in which the Westminster electoral system allocated seats to the two major parties between 1950 and 1970, though it has been found to have been less applicable in recent elections.[13]

The Conservatives in fact won as many seats as would have been predicted by the cube law. Excluding the Highlands and Islands, they won 60.4 per cent of the two-party vote which the law would translate into 60 of the 77 seats won by the two leading parties – precisely the number the Conservatives achieved. However, Table 5 shows that the electoral system would not have conformed to the cube law if the support for the two leading parties had been divided differently. On the current distribution of party strengths amongst constituencies the system would treat the two major parties unequally at most divisions of the two-party vote, although the party that would be advantaged would vary. At equality of votes the Conservatives would win three more seats than Labour. But at divisions of the vote less close than 52:48, Labour would win more seats if they were the leading party than the Conservatives would if they were.

This complex pattern is to be explained by the varied impact of two separate sources of bias in the system. A bias to Labour partly arises because their vote was more concentrated than the Conservatives' was in those constituencies with a smaller number of voters. This occurred even though the Boundary Commission produced boundaries that treated the two largest parties equally; the average electorate in Conservative constituencies was 513,784 and in Labour ones was 515,468.[14] But the lower turnout in seats in which Labour were stronger undid their work; the average poll in Conservative seats was 171,808 and in

Labour ones 153,680.

That bias would benefit Labour whatever their share of the two-party vote; but it is hidden from view at very narrow divisions of the two-party vote because of a second source of bias. The Conservatives would win more seats than Labour at equality because they would secure more seats by small majorities; they would hold 15 seats by a majority of 6 per cent or less of the two-party vote, whereas Labour would hold 10. This produces a bias to the Conservatives if they win 50 per cent or more of the vote; but if they slip below 50 per cent of the two-party vote, then these seats quickly become vulnerable to Labour attack, and this second source of bias would then operate in Labour's favour.

The mean of the Conservative and Labour figures in column (v) of Table 5 provides us with an overall picture of the degree to which a majority of votes is exaggerated into a far greater majority in seats. This mean combines the effect of the underlying exaggeration of the system and (given that it favours both parties when they are in the lead) the impact of the second source of bias. A comparison of column (ii) and column (v) shows how the degree of exaggeration produced by the system varies according to the division of the two-party vote. At divisions of the vote up to 58:42 the system appears, on the current distribution of party strengths, to exaggerate the leading party's majority less than would be expected under the cube law; but at divisions greater than 58:42, the exaggeration is greater than would be anticipated.[15]

The electoral system used for the European elections was, therefore, one that more strongly exaggerated the lead of the largest party, the greater the difference in votes between it and its main competitor; it was particularly likely to produce a one-party predominance in the British delegation if there were an electoral landslide. But the predominance of one party in the delegation was not as great as it would have been, given the size of the Conservatives' victory. If Labour had won the election by the same amount, then, on the same distribution of party strengths as existed in June, they would actually have won two more seats than the Conservatives did.

The Regional List system

The House of Commons chose the first-past-the-post electoral system for the European election in preference to the Regional List system that had been devised by the Labour Government in 1977 and recommended to Parliament. Table 6 estimates how the seats would have been allo-

Table 6. Estimated distribution of Seats under Regional List system.

	Turnout (%)	Votes Con. (%)	Lab. (%)	Lib. (%)	Nat. (%)	Oth. (%)	Seats Total	Con.	Lab.	Lib.	Nat.	Oth.	Quota (%)
London	34.0	51.0	36.7	11.4	–	0.9	10	5	4	1	–	–	9.2
South East	35.9	57.3	20.0	16.6	–	0.9	14	9	3	2	–	–	6.4
South West	36.7	57.9	21.6	18.3	–	2.2	6	4	1	1	–	–	14.5
East Anglia	33.0	59.5	28.3	12.2	–	–	3	2	1	–	–	–	28.3
East Midlands	31.2	54.3	35.1	10.6	–	1.0	5	3	2	–	–	–	17.5
West Midlands	29.9	52.5	36.9	9.7	–	0.1	7	4	3	–	–	–	12.3
Yorks. & Humber	30.0	45.0	43.0	11.9	–	0.5	7	3	3	1	–	–	11.9
North West	30.4	50.1	38.4	11.1	–	0.7	9	5	3	1	–	–	10.0
North	30.5	43.3	45.8	10.2	–	0.6	5	2	3	–	–	–	15.3
Wales	34.4	36.6	41.5	9.6	11.7	–	4	2	2	–	–	–	18.3
Scotland	33.6	33.7	33.0	14.0	19.4	–	8	3	3	1	1	–	11.0
Total	32.1	50.6	33.0	13.1	2.6	0.7	78	42	28	7	1	–	–

The regions are those proposed in the original European Assembly Elections Bill 1977. They are the standard regions as defined by the Registrar General on the basis of the post-1974 local government boundaries, except that London is separated from the rest of the South East. The voting statistics have been derived by adding together the results of each Euro-constituency within each standard region. However, in all the regions except London, the Euro-constituency boundaries and, in some cases, the parliamentary constituency boundaries from which they were formed, do not correspond to the standard region boundary. In those cases, an estimate of the result in each of the constituent parliamentary constituencies that were wholly or mostly in a different standard region from the bulk of the Euro-constituency was obtained, generally by the use of the figure for turnout in each parliamentary constituency as declared by the Returning Officer, and assuming that the movement between May and June in each Euro-constituency was spread uniformly among the constituent parliamentary constituencies. This estimate was added to the total for the standard region in which the parliamentary constituency was located and subtracted from that in which the rest of the Euro-constituency was placed.

The seats are allocated by the D'Hondt or remaining average system. Each party receives seats in accordance with the number of times it is able fully to complete the quota. For further details see E. Lakeman and J. D. Lambert, *Voting in Democracies* (London 1955) pp. 87–91.

cated under those alternative proposals, assuming that the electorate voted exactly as they did in June 1979.

It is clear that the Regional List system would have produced a substantially different result. The Conservatives would have won 18 less seats than they did under the system that was actually used, while Labour would have won 11 more. The remaining seven seats would have been won by the Liberals giving them a noticeable presence in the British delegation. The SNP would have retained their one seat. Even so, the Conservatives' success in winning an overall majority of the votes would have been reflected in their gaining an overall majority of seats.

Although the Liberals would have won some representation in the British delegation if the Regional List system had been employed, they would still have suffered a disadvantage as compared with the larger parties. The Conservatives and Labour would have been treated equally, winning one representative for each 1.2 per cent of the total national poll that they received, whereas the Liberals would have gained one representative for each 1.9 per cent of the national poll (and the SNP, 2.1%). Such a result is characteristic of the remaining average system of allocating seats that it had been intended to use.

Conclusion

The European election results provide further evidence of the weak hold of the political parties upon their supporters. In the absence of some of the inducements to vote that normally exist in a general election – the opportunity to play a role in the choice of the next Government and the existence of a large number of campaigning pleas and promises from the parties – the electorate decided to stay at home. In addition, among those who voted there was a large swing to Conservative within the space of a month, a swing that does not seem accountable simply to differences in abstention. Local factors as opposed to the national message and situation may have played a greater role in people's choice between Conservative and Labour than they normally do in general elections. But, equally, the electorate did not feel enamoured of the other alternatives available to them; free from having to decide between two alternative sets of Governments, they still did not take the chance to express a preference for third or fourth parties.

Notes

[1] Northern Ireland, which used a different electoral system and where the election was dominated by parties competing only in the province, is dealt with separatley on pp. 178–180. The remainder of the text addresses itself solely to Great Britain.

[2] Two Westminster constituencies had split Labour candidatures in May 1979 and a further one was without a Conservative candidate; these distort the swing in three Euro-constituencies which are consequently omitted from all calculations of swing in the Appendix. The absence of Liberal candidates in 46 Westminster constituencies in May similarly affects the change in each party's share of the poll in 18 Euro-constituencies, including all of the seats in Scotland and three of the four in Wales. Calculations of this measure involving two or more seats only include the 60 strictly 'comparable' constituencies, but it is on occasion quoted for one or more parties in individual constituencies which are not strictly comparable, and in these cases it should be read with the necessary caution.

[3] Two-party swing is used throughout this Appendix. It is defined as the change in the Conservative share of the combined Conservative and Labour vote. It should be distinguished from total vote swing which is given for each constituency in the list of results on pp. 134–5, and for which summary statistics appear in Table 1. This is defined as the mean of the change in the Conservative and Labour share of the total poll, with a '+' indicating a swing to Conservative, '−' to Labour. On the differences between the two measures of swing see M. Steed, 'An Analysis of the Results' in D. Butler and A. King, *The British General Election of 1964* (London 1965) p. 337.

[4] The analysis in this section has greatly benefited from discussion with Michael Steed.

[5] An opinion poll conducted immediately after the election for ITN by Opinion Research Centre showed that 64 per cent of Labour supporters were against the Common Market, 25 per cent were in favour and 11 per cent didn't know. Among Conservative supporters, only 32 per cent were against the Common Market, 57 per cent were in favour and 11 per cent didn't know.

[6] See, for example, the analysis of the local government results in *The Economist*, 19 May 1979, p. 24.

[7] The Pearson correlation coefficient between the percentage non-manual in a Euro-constituency (1971 census) and the change in turnout was 0.48.

[8] The fall in turnout in the South East and South West was, however, lower than would be expected even after taking account of the percentage non-manual within those regions.

[9] The relationship between swing and turnout change as posited in Table 2 would, however, be liable to systematic disturbance under this assumption. Furthermore, that relationship would be affected by variation in the size of the third-party vote in the previous election. For these reasons the analysis concentrates on the evidence on the relationship between swing and the two-party ratio. Swing, in fact, does not show any clear unimodal or linear relationship with turnout change.

[10] Variations on this model have also been examined and found inadequate to explain the pattern that exists. In particular, we might assume that the propensity of Labour voters to abstain might be greater, the smaller their share of the two-party vote, either because they were subject to less social and political pressure to participate or because they felt it even less worthwhile if their candidate was bound to lose. The same might be said for Conservative voters. This assumption would result in a relationship closer to linearity than Table 2, with the highest swings occurring in Conservative-held seats, but with some tailing off of the size of the swing in the safest Conservative seats. Such a model could provide a better 'fit' to the pattern of swing in Table 3 than does that of Table 2, but would still be unable to explain the 2 per cent difference in swing between the 45–50 per cent and 40–45 per cent bands, or the 6.7 per cent swing in the 55–60 per cent band.

[11] See J. Curtice and M. Steed, 'An Analysis of the Voting' in D. Butler and D. Kavanagh. *The British General Election of 1979* (London 1980) p. 394 ff.

[12] The standard deviation of swing in those Euro-constituencies mostly or wholly in South Britain between May and June was 2.6, between October 1974 and June 1979, 2.4; the equivalent figures for North Britain are 3.5 and 3.4 respectively. North Britain is defined as the four northernmost (pre-1974) standard regions in Great Britain, South Britain as the remainder of the country. See Curtice and Steed, *op. cit.*

[13] For a full statement of the cube law see M. G. Kendall and A. Stuart, 'Cubic Proportion in Election Results', *British Journal of Sociology*, 1 (1950) p. 183 and G. Gudgin and P. J. Taylor, *Seats, Votes and the Spatial Organisation of Elections* (London 1978).

[14] Constituencies are here defined as Conservative and Labour on the basis of the vote in May 1979.

[15] It is indeed not surprising that the electoral system should produce a greater exaggeration at some of the possible divisions of the two-party vote; rather, it is surprising that it should not do so at all divisions. This is because the aggregation of Westminster constituencies into a smaller number of larger units will tend to reduce the variation in the distribution of party support among constituencies, the extent of which is one of the determinants of the degree of exaggeration a single member plurality electoral system will produce. Indeed, the Conservative share of the two-party vote had a standard deviation of 17.1 over all Westminster constituencies in May, while over the Euro-constituencies it was only 11.5 (rising to 12.1 in June). The cube law requires a standard deviation of 13.7; the European electoral system does not depart from the cube law any more than it does partly because the Westminster electoral system no longer conforms. The exaggeration is less than cubic at narrow divisions of the two-party vote because of another property of the distribution. The cube law will only operate consistently at all divisions of the two-party vote if the distribution of the Conservative share of that vote is approximately normal. The distribution in June departed from this by having a lower kurtosis (0.8 lower) than a normal distribution with the same standard deviation would have, i.e. there were less seats at the centre of the distribution than if the distribution had been normal. This reduces the degree of exaggeration produced by the electoral system at narrow divisions of the two-party vote.

Index